Green Consumption

Green Consumption
The Global Rise of Eco-Chic

Edited by
Bart Barendregt and Rivke Jaffe

B L O O M S B U R Y

LONDON • NEW DELHI • NEW YORK • SYDNEY

Bloomsbury Academic

An imprint of Bloomsbury Publishing Plc

50 Bedford Square
London
WC1B 3DP
UK

1385 Broadway
New York
NY 10018
USA

www.bloomsbury.com

Bloomsbury is a registered trade mark of Bloomsbury Publishing Plc

First published 2014

© Bart Barendregt and Rivke Jaffe, 2014

Bart Barendregt and Rivke Jaffe have asserted their rights under the Copyright, Designs and Patents Act, 1988, to be identified as Editors of this work.

British Library Cataloguing-in-Publication Data
A catalogue record for this book is available from the British Library.

ISBN: HB: 978-0-85785-501-5
PB: 978-0-85785-714-9
ePDF: 978-0-85785-798-9
ePub: 978-0-85785-795-8

Library of Congress Cataloging-in-Publication Data
A catalog record for this book is available from the Library of Congress.

Typeset by Apex CoVantage
Printed and bound in Great Britain

Contents

PART III: BODIES AND BEAUTY

List of Figures

Contributors

Bart Barendregt is an anthropologist who lectures at the Institute of Social and Cultural Studies, Leiden University, in the Netherlands. He is currently coordinating a four-year project funded by the Netherlands Organization for Scientific Research, which is hosted by the KITLV. This project, Articulation of Modernity (2010–2014), focuses on societal change through the prism of popular music, emphasizing the appeal of modernity rather than that of the nation-state, and thus offering a new way of studying Southeast Asia that foregrounds the movement of people, music, ideas, and technologies among the region's cosmopolitan centers. Bart has published and made films on Southeast Asian performing arts, new and mobile media, and (Islamic) pop music. He is now finishing his book on Islamist popular music in Southeast Asia.

Shyon Baumann is an associate professor of sociology at the University of Toronto. He specializes in the sociological study of the arts, media, and culture. His work primarily seeks to improve our understanding of the social processes leading to cultural evaluation and legitimation. In addition to advertising, his past work has examined the history of the American film industry and gourmet food discourse.

Raymond L. Bryant is a professor in geography at King's College London. His work includes *Nongovernmental Organizations in Environmental Struggles* (New Haven, CT: Yale University Press, 2005) and *Handbook of Political Ecology* (coedited with Soyeun Kim, Cheltenham: Edward Elgar, 2014).

Kate Cairns is a postdoctoral fellow in sociology at the University of Toronto. Her work brings an interdisciplinary approach to questions of power and subjectivity, drawing upon feminist theory, sociology of childhood, cultural studies, and critical geography. Kate's research spans the areas of gender, culture, and education and has appeared in venues such as *Gender & Society, Journal of Consumer Culture, Gender and Education, Ethnography and Education,* and *The Canadian Geographer.* She is currently coauthoring a book (with Josée Johnston) exploring questions of gender and inequality at the intersection of food consumption and social change.

Kim de Laat is a sociology doctoral candidate at the University of Toronto. Her research lies at the intersection of cultural sociology, organizational theory, communication, gender, and economic sociology. She is presently conducting research with professional songwriters in an effort to understand the unique effects of organizational change on women working in cultural industries. With Shyon Baumann, she recently published an article in *Poetics: Journal of Empirical Research on Culture, the Media, and the Arts,* titled "Socially Defunct: A Comparative Analysis of the Underrepresentation of Older Women in Advertising."

Marjo de Theije is an associate professor at the Department of Social and Cultural Anthropology at the VU University and a senior researcher at the Centre for Latin American Research and Documentation, both in Amsterdam. She has published on culture and religion in Brazil and Suriname and on the migration of Brazilians to Suriname. Recent publications include the coedited volume *Local Battles, Global Stakes: The Globalization of Local Conflicts and the Localization of Global Interests* (with Ton Salman, VU University Press, 2011). She currently directs a research project on conflict and cooperation around small-scale gold mining in five countries in the Amazon region (Bolivia, Brazil, Colombia, Peru, and Suriname), funded by WOTRO Science for Global Development, a division of the Netherlands Organisation for Scientific Research.

Robert J. Foster is a professor and the chair of anthropology and a professor of visual and cultural studies at the University of Rochester. He is the author of *Social Reproduction and History in Melanesia* (Cambridge University Press, 1995), *Materializing the Nation* (Indiana University Press, 2002), and *Coca-Globalization: Following Soft Drinks from New York to New Guinea* (Palgrave Macmillan, 2008). His research interests include globalization, corporations, gifts and commodities, material culture, commercial media, and museums.

Michael K. Goodman is a professor of environment and development in the Department of Geography and Environmental Science at the University of Reading and is broadly interested in the cultural politics of food, consumption, and sustainability. He is a coauthor on the recently published *Alternative Food Networks* (Routledge, 2012), has coedited (with Colin Sage) the forthcoming volume *Food Transgressions* (Ashgate) exploring the multiple and contentious boundary-crossings of food, and has coedited (with David Goodman and Michael Redclift) the volume *Consuming Space* (Ashgate, 2010). He edits the *Critical Food Studies* book series with Ashgate and, with David Goodman, coedits a second book series titled *Contemporary Food Politics* with Berg. Current work is focused on the powerful mediations of food, eating, and sustainability by celebrity chefs and other forms of contemporary food media cultures; both will figure heavily in a forthcoming special issue of the journal *Geoforum.*

Chris Hudson is a research leader in the Globalization and Culture Program in the Global Cities Research Institute and an associate professor of Asian media and culture in the School of Media and Communication at the Royal Melbourne Institute of Technology University. She has published widely on cultural politics in Singapore, including *Beyond the Singapore Girl: Discourses of Gender and Nation in Singapore* (NIAS Press, 2013), a study of the politics of fertility, narrative control, and resistance in Singapore. She is a coauthor of *Theatre and Performance in the Asia-Pacific: Regional Modernities in the Global Era* (Palgrave Macmillan, 2013). Funded by the Australian Research Council Discovery Project Scheme, this book examines the diverse theater and performance traditions in the Asia-Pacific region.

Rivke Jaffe is an associate professor at the Centre for Urban Studies at the University of Amsterdam. Her research focuses primarily on intersections of the urban and the political, with a specific interest in Caribbean cities. Her work in environmental anthropology has studied how environmentalism and the politics of difference articulate through Caribbean urban space. Her current research studies how private security companies and the state share control over urban spaces and populations, and the formulations of citizenship and sovereignty that result from this. Her publications include the edited volumes *The Caribbean City* (Ian Randle, 2008) and *Urban Pollution* (with Eveline Dürr, Berghahn, 2010) and articles in journals such as *American Ethnologist, Anthropological Quarterly, Ethnic and Racial Studies,* and *Social and Cultural Geography.*

Josée Johnston is an associate professor of sociology at the University of Toronto. Her major substantive interest is the sociological study of food, which is a lens for investigating questions relating to culture, politics, gender, and the environment. Josée Johnston coauthored (with Shyon Baumann) *Foodies: Democracy and Distinction in the Gourmet Foodscape* (Routledge, 2010) and is currently working with Kate Cairns on a book project on food femininities. She has published articles in venues including *American Journal of Sociology, Theory and Society, Signs: Journal of Women in Culture and Society,* and *Gender and Society.*

Anna-Riikka Kauppinen is a PhD candidate at the Department of Anthropology at the London School of Economics and Political Science. Her previous research focuses on beauty spectacles and everyday beauty practices in naturalizing ideologies of Africanness in Ghana, while also addressing the circulation and consumption of African American and Caribbean popular fashions in the capital Accra. Her current research, also on Ghana, explores tertiary-educated business youth, and will involve fieldwork in business schools affiliated to churches. While she continues inquiries into popular culture and Africanness, her future interest is to develop novel approaches to anthropological studies of capitalism from the perspective of the anthropology of religion.

Sabine Luning is a lecturer at the Institute of Cultural Anthropology and Development Sociology, Leiden University. Her earlier research dealt with the social dynamics of ritual practices in Burkina Faso, a topic at the crossroads of religious ideas, politics, and social identities. Her current research focuses on economic anthropology, in particular the booming business of gold mining in West Africa. She investigates interactions between (representatives of) multilateral organizations, the state, international mining companies, national entrepreneurs, artisanal miners, and local communities, as well as the moral discourses that accompany and shape these interactions. She is particularly interested in Canadian exploration companies operating in (West) Africa, and her current project consists of multisited fieldwork carried out in West Africa and Canada. In Canada, she investigates how overseas mining companies, in particular those targeting gold, are discussed in the public arena and at home.

Seth Murray is a teaching assistant professor of international studies at North Carolina State University and an associate member of the graduate faculty for the Department of Sociology and Anthropology. He has maintained an ongoing ethnographic research project in the Basque region since 1999 and also participates in a long-term interdisciplinary research project investigating the evolution of environmental risk/mitigation strategies among farmers in Burgundy, France, especially relating to water management.

Rachel Spronk is an assistant professor in the Department of Sociology and Anthropology at the University of Amsterdam. Her research focuses primarily on the intersections of the development of the middle classes in Africa and transformations in gender and sexuality. In her publications, she analyzes the complexities of gender, sexuality, and culture by focusing on public debates on the one hand, and personal relationships and self-perceptions on the other. She uses sexuality as a prism to study social transformations and how these generate new middle-class subjectivities. Her previous study concentrated on the lifestyles and relationships of the yuppies in Nairobi, Kenya. In her current research, she focuses on shifts in the practices and imagination of intimacy and how these relate to the notion of modern personhood, from an intergenerational perspective, in middle-class Ghana. She has published articles in various journals and her book titled *Ambiguous Pleasures: Sexuality and Middle-Class Self-Perceptions in Nairobi* (Berghahn) was published in 2012.

Meredith Welch-Devine is the associate director of the Center for Integrative Conservation Research at the University of Georgia and the director of Interdisciplinary and Innovative Initiatives for the University of Georgia Graduate School. Her research focuses on governance of the commons, the intersection of agriculture and conservation, and political ecology. In addition to her research in the Basque province of Soule, Welch-Devine works with the Coweeta Long Term Ecological Research project studying adaptive responses to exurbanization and environmental change, as well as the relationship between scientists and the public.

Richard Wilk is a provost's professor of anthropology at Indiana University, where he runs the Food Studies Program. He has also taught at the University of California, New Mexico State University, and University College London and has held visiting professorships at Gothenburg University, the University of Marseille, and the University of London. His research in Belize, the United States, and West Africa has been supported by three Fulbright fellowships, the National Science Foundation, and many other organizations. He has also worked as an applied anthropologist with UNICEF, USAID, Cultural Survival, and a variety of other development organizations. His initial research on farming and family organization was followed by work on consumer culture, globalization, television, beauty pageants, and food. Much of his recent work has turned toward the global history of food and sustainable consumption. His most recent books are *Time, Consumption, and Everyday Life* (with Elizabeth Shove and Frank Trentmann, 2009) and *Rice and Beans* (2012), coedited with Livia Barbosa, both published by Bloomsbury.

Sharon Zukin is a professor of sociology at Brooklyn College and the City University Graduate Center. She has written a trilogy of books about New York City: *Loft Living* (Rutgers University Press, 1989, new ed. 2014), *The Cultures of Cities* (Blackwell, 1995), and, most recently, *Naked City: The Death and Life of Authentic Urban Places* (Oxford University Press, 2010). Her book *Landscapes of Power: From Detroit to Disney World* (University of California Press, 1991) won the C. Wright Mills Award, and in *Point of Purchase* (Routledge, 2004), she examined shopping as the wellspring of public culture in the United States. Zukin has received the Robert and Helen Lynd Award for career achievement in urban sociology from the Section on Community and Urban Sociology of the American Sociological Association.

Foreword

Greenwashing is not just for corporations anymore—it has gone personal. Instead of feeling guilty about the huge gaps between wealthy and poor, the ways consumerism causes global warming, or how our daily pleasures cause rainforest destruction and despoil the sea, we can drink a few cups of fair-trade coffee and eat a rainforest crunch bar and instantly feel better. The consumer marketplace today offers us every kind of ethical, ecological, and healthy option we can imagine, from recycled toilet paper to household wind turbines.

The editors and authors of this book turn our attention toward the way goodness and moral values have been privatized in our post-Reagan-Thatcher neoliberal world. Green consumer goods promise the eternal lie of the huckster—that we can have our cake and eat it too, that we can change the world without sacrifice or any more effort than smarter shopping. Because our gold ear-studs have been ethically mined, we are absolved from thinking about why we feel we need to wear gold at all. We can take expensive vacations in exotic tropical lands, ignoring the poverty around us while we enjoy sustainable gourmet meals and a timeless beauty ritual enhanced by traditional bathing (chapter 10).

Through eco-chic consumption, all of the problems of the world are condensed into making the right shopping decisions. If the World Trade Organization is helping to bring sweatshop products into our local shop, it is up to us to go find some fair-traded alternative, certified by some impoverished nongovernmental organization and its idealistic unpaid interns. When illegal Spanish fishermen chase down the last bluefin tuna in the Mediterranean, we are supposed to find out where the tuna in our local sushi bar came from to make sure we are not partners in crime.

From a critical distance, the entire premise that justice and sustainability can be purchased in the marketplace is patently absurd. The proliferation of new consumer choices is just as likely to increase total consumption as it is to lead to actual cuts or measureable reductions. And without the intervention of trusted intermediaries, any system of certification is likely to be co-opted by producers and marketers, to the point where it just becomes another meaningless mark on the package. Products and brands that do establish some sort of trusted position among consumers are just increasing their brand value in a way that makes them vulnerable to takeovers and buyouts. This happened with iconic countercultural brands in the United States like Kashi (now Kellogg) and Ben & Jerry's ice cream, which is now a division of Unilever, though you would not know this from the company's website. In a marketplace now awash in green paint, candy bars have become granola bars from a fictional Nature Valley, which is actually the factory of megacorporation General Mills.

This is hardly the first time that frugality and morality have become fashionable in the marketplace. Nonslavery sugar was an early example of social marketing, followed by the Salvation Army's manufacture of matches made without the white phosphorus that poisoned match factory workers. At the higher end of the social scale, examples include Marie Antoinette's little farm at Versailles and Theodore Roosevelt's sojourn on a western ranch, where he toughened himself and regained his masculinity. Generations of the middle class have sent their children off to summer camps to live simply with nature and to colleges where they experience temporary poverty, hopefully relieved after graduation. Even ancient Babylonian city dwellers worried that opulence was spoiling their children, and by the time of the European Renaissance, a large fraction of the population was living in the enforced frugality of convents and monasteries. A hunger for authenticity, direct experience, and knowledge of origins and production has been deeply embedded in elite consumption for hundreds of years, for example in the connoisseurship of French wines and foods like truffles and caviar. Even the ancient Romans loved the simple life on their rural villas, at the same time that they sought the finest and rarest spices, clothing, cosmetics, and wines. Nostalgia for an imagined past or a perfect landscape has driven consumption and tinged it with a deep sense of morality for a long time, perhaps since the very first cities of the late bronze age.

What is different about eco-chic in the contemporary world is that the problems it tries to address are so much larger and more serious than the issues faced by previous generations. More people live in absolute poverty—without even the ability to feed themselves on subsistence farms—than ever before in human history. Consumers have never faced such a wide range of dangers from a witches' brew of toxic chemicals, resistant diseases, and engineered organisms. And we have rapidly burned through hundreds of millions of years of sequestered carbon in the form of fossil fuels, changing the composition of the planet's atmosphere in a gargantuan uncontrolled experiment in climate regulation.

Another difference between our own consumer culture, and that of our ancestors, is that now we know so much more about the way our consumption connects us to each other, to our own health, and to the health of the planet. For the first time, we can see, or even talk to, the people who grow our gourmet coffee, weave our artisanal rugs, and put beads in our cornrows on a holiday beach. This marvelous network of information leaves consumers more exposed to moral fault than ever before and makes the burden of moral behavior heavier and more perilous. Often the only choices seem to be tokenism—making changes that are more symbolic than substantive—or cynicism grounded in the experience of falling for new trends or solutions that turn out to be misguided, co-opted, or fraudulent.

This is why this volume of studies is so important. These chapters explore the territory in between cynicism and tokenism, showing us that by learning more about the way the consumer marketplace works we can think more productively about the kinds of strategies that can make a symbolic *and* material difference. While generally critical of the superficiality of eco-chic consumption, the authors recognize that green consumerism is just one of the ways that citizens try to change the marketplace. Rather than being an either/or choice, the passive activism of green (or greenish) consumption often articulates with other kinds of more overtly political activities, from changing local health codes to allow edible landscaping or backyard chickens, seeking further education on environmental issues, or joining an activist group. Green consumerism may play a key role as a kind of gateway drug for people who would otherwise be disengaged from any action at all. Changing your brand of toilet paper requires no more than a minimal commitment of time and money, but it might provoke some questions about the origins and effects of other consumer goods. Fear of bad publicity or consumer boycotts has also been a powerful force in getting the attention of manufacturers and service providers, eliciting many levels of response to issues of sustainability. But as the editors point out, there is a thin and often invisible line between green actions and greenwashing. Sometimes we can only tell in retrospect if actions by governments and corporations really do reach the intended goal of reducing waste, increasing efficiency, and promoting public health. At what point do thin coats of green paint add up to something more substantial and self-supporting?

The editors and authors of this volume have opened an important discussion about the complex practical and moral terrain of eco-chic and the more general marketing of sustainability and fair trade. They deserve a broad audience, particularly among those who are thinking about how much longer the planet is going to be able to support consumer culture in its present form.

Richard Wilk

The Paradoxes of Eco-Chic

Bart Barendregt and Rivke Jaffe

This book deals with what we call eco-chic: a combination of lifestyle politics, environmentalism, spirituality, beauty, and health, combined with a call to return to simple living. Eco-chic connects the fields of ethical, sustainable, and elite consumption, with the distinctions among these forms of consumption becoming blurred in practice. Where just a decade or two ago, green lifestyles and fair-trade purchases were perceived as the domain of activists or the open-toed-sandal-and-woolly-socks brigade, sustainable and ethical initiatives are now increasingly popular among affluent hipsters. The popularity of these forms of consumption should perhaps be located not so much in a newly emergent interest in saving the world, but rather be understood as indicating that eco-chic has become one of the many modern lifestyle choices that late capitalism has to offer. The question remains whether the effect of shifts in consumption choices is any less when these shifts are not informed by deep-felt ideological convictions.

Over the last few decades, achieving radical societal change toward sustainable development has come to appear less and less feasible. Displacing more revolutionary initiatives, green lifestyles and ethical consumption have emerged as attractive alternative propositions in moving toward environmentally friendly societies and combating global poverty. Where previously the environmental movement saw excess consumption as the global problem, green consumerism now places consumption at the heart of the solution. However, ethical and sustainable consumption—from organic and fair-trade food, fashion, and jewelry to eco-tourism and low-carbon forms of urban transport—are not just politically virtuous practices. These practices also represent forms of cultural and moral capital that are central to the creation and maintenance of class distinction. Eco-chic is increasingly a part of the identity kit of the upper classes, offering an attractive way to combine taste and style with care for personal wellness and the environment.

Specific cultural objects feature significantly in what has become a global upsurge of green consumption: local, natural, and artisanal goods are refashioned in terms of aesthetics and price to allow the gentrification of a back-to-basics, place-based nostalgia. Eco-chic consumption is evident in everyday consumer choices such as food, clothing, and transport options, as well as in luxury consumption such as spas and fair-mined gold jewelry. The classed nature of ethical and sustainable consumption is recognizable in leisure practices, such as green hobbies and eco-tourism, and in the adoption of clean technology in architecture or transport.

What we term *eco-chic* can be recognized in a wide range of sociogeographical loci as a set of practices and an ideological frame, but also as a widespread marketing strategy. The chapters in this volume discuss the emergence of eco-chic among the middle class, the newly rich, and the traditional elites. They present case studies in both the metropolitan areas and the rural landscapes of Europe and North America, as well as in postcolonial settings in Asia, Africa, Latin America, and the Caribbean. While many of the concepts underlying eco-chic consumption emerged primarily in the global North, these ideas have also been promoted, appropriated, and transformed in the less affluent South. Across the world, then, comparable consumption agendas connect often very different life-worlds.

African recycling experiences and Brazilian favela chic hit U.S. and European lifestyle blogs, which lend a sheen of trendiness and cool to cheap globalization practices that are often born out of poverty and a lack of alternatives. Simultaneously, what were previously deemed traditional and backward practices become popular among cosmopolitan elites across the world. Typical peasant dishes, prepared with organic, farm-to-table ingredients, are now consumed with relish in upscale restaurants by rich customers, who may pay tenfold the daily wages of the Javanese, Vietnamese, or Mexican farmers who have little choice but to eat such foods every day of the year. It is not our intention to resort to simple condemnations of such practices, which are after all the very drivers of today's global economy. Rather, we argue for careful scrutiny of the broad range of eco-chic practices: the anxieties and complex motivations that underlie their popularity, their differential effect on various actors and societies, and the diverse implications this form of consumption has for attempts to make the world we all live in more sustainable.

This edited volume connects research on consumption, identities, and globalization to debates on political consumerism. This introduction seeks to address three major questions, which the authors of the cases in this volume also engage with. Why is it now, at this particular moment in advanced capitalism, that eco-chic has become so popular in the formulation of new identities? To what extent do eco-chic's various forms and appearances rely on specific local contexts? And, finally, in what ways can eco-chic, with its apparent paradox of consumption and idealism, make a genuine contribution to solving the main problems of our time and thus contribute to debates on sustainable development?

A Global Green Culture: Why Now?

Asking why eco-chic has become such an important force at this moment in time points to the necessity of understanding green, sustainable, and ethical forms of consumption within their historical and geographical context. Ours is a time that is continuously accelerating, with many citizens and governments placing blind faith in digital technologies that maintain a 24/7 global economy, while e-commerce and e-governance are heavily promoted by various public and private actors. Some suggest that characterizations of our era as high paced and ever-accelerating are themselves marked by chronocentrism; perhaps the speed at which societal change is taking place is not all that different from the speed of change experienced in preceding eras (Eriksen 2001). Notwithstanding this contrary view, over the past few decades, the presumed acceleration of societies has given rise to a number of local countermovements.

In a context of fast-paced, high-tech global processes, including increased digitization and reproducibility, individuals and groups across the world feel moved to establish and safeguard slower, more traditional forms of living. These include the Whole Earth Catalogue, Analogue Living (which renounces information communication technology such as cell phones and the Internet),[1] and more recently the wellness revolution (see Pilzer 2002; Turner 2006). Other initiatives include the revalorization of secondhand clothing as vintage (Gibson and Stanes 2011) and the growth of organic, fair trade, and slow food certification schemes, which seek to minimize environmentally and socially exploitative production processes (Goodman et al. 2010; Guthman 2002; Petrini 2001). In trying to remedy societies seen as hurtling down the wrong path—and to counteract the accelerated pace and fragmented nature of postmodern life—these movements focus on nostalgic, neotraditional, and explicitly local solutions. What Lowenthal (1992) terms the "death of the future" seems to dictate a return to past possibilities, or at least a "slowing down" of the present. Many movements and activists argue that the technology that was meant to connect people and places actually disconnects them. Regaining control over one's own life, they claim, necessitates a turn to "slow speed" life (Honoré 2004; Parkins and Craig 2006). This might involve retro practices and outmoded technologies such as knitting, watching black-and-white television, or making cult books such as the *Cloudspotter's Guide* (Pretor-Pinney 2006) into a new bible (Barendregt 2012).

These are apolitical but apparently socially committed lifestyles that have attracted growing numbers of followers, whose adherence may be restricted to consumption rather than wholesale ideological conversion. A main feature shared by these lifestyle movements is that concern regarding the environment is no longer restricted to subcultural splinter groups. On the contrary, consuming the natural and the slow is instrumental in creating and maintaining class distinction. Eco-chic products are often crafted or marketed through processes of enchantment or by putting these products on spectacular visual display; they tend to target (consciously or unconsciously) aspirational consumers by making overt reference to aristocratic and celebrity lifestyles (cf. Mihaljevich 2007; Richey and Ponte 2011). Examples include the middle-class popularity of organic and fair-trade food and clothing, but also increasingly the reference to all things green and eco in public architecture, as Chris Hudson's contribution to this volume illustrates.

Early work on green economies was largely production-oriented and took an innovation and technology-centric approach, with limited consideration of how to persuade consumers of the desirability of green products (Spaargaren 2003). Similarly, much of the work that did focus on green consumption was monopolized by a few disciplines, in particular social psychologists and economists (to the extent that this could be termed "economics imperialism," see Fine 2002). This has changed in recent years as growing numbers of sociologists and geographers have sought to locate the origins and effects of ethical and sustainable consumption (e.g., Barnett et al. 2011; Bryant and Goodman 2004; Cloke et al. 2010; Lewis and Potter 2010; Shove 2005).

However, as green products and lifestyles are increasingly appropriated by new wealthy classes both in the global North and in many emerging economies (from the so-called Asian Tigers to the BRIC [Brazil, Russia, India, and China] countries and more recently the TIMP [Turkey, Indonesia, Mexico, and the Philippines] markets),[2] understanding the sheer cultural variety of eco-chic promises to be one of the next challenges for social scientists studying these forms of consumption.

Global Fantasies, Local Needs

In various sociogeographical spaces, one finds localism, environmentalism, and ethics tied—often paradoxically—to globalized identities, consumption, and elite lifestyles. A major paradox of eco-chic, then, is that ideas and movements that emphasize localism are subject to global circulation themselves, often with unforeseen consequences. Obviously, eco-chic commodities fulfill needs other than those related to sustainability or ethics alone. The specific cultural meanings and social functions of these commodities are always dependent on their historical and cultural context.

We propose a research agenda with a strong focus on the very stuff of eco-chic products, analyzing their materiality across cultural contexts, with attention to aesthetics in design and marketing. Our own research had focused on instances of eco-chic in Southeast Asia and the Caribbean, ranging from spa culture to the Rastafari-inspired "ital chic" (see part III of this volume). These studies show how similar tropicalist, often self-exoticizing representations may be used to invoke very different political projects, although the classed nature of these forms of consumption is very apparent.

There is no denying that much of what can be termed as eco-chic is designed by elite groups of producers who work from the privileged centers of the global economy. In architecture and urban design, for instance, so-called starchitects increasingly produce spectacular green plans that rebrand urban sustainability and biodiversity and more broadly shape popular understandings of nature in the city. Beyond consumption, a focus on the elite producers of eco-chic can shed light on what makes eco-chic chic, the kind of symbols their designs employ, and the extent to which these designs translate in different cultural contexts.

Eco-chic clearly has specific local dynamics that differ from one society to the other. The preference for vegetarian products over meat consumption may mean a conscious choice to abstain from animal products produced by a "cruel" industry in affluent European and North American societies, whereas high levels of meat consumption in China are more likely to signify newly gained class prestige. Where the use of green cosmetics may imply an awareness of harmful chemicals in the West, similar products may signify the longing for a long-lost feudal heritage in Indonesia or an engagement with Afro-cosmopolitan forms of modernity in Ghana (see chapters 8 and 10). Organic farming is not only a twenty-first-century Western trend, but also can be framed as based on ancient imperial yin-yang philosophies. Eco-chic consumption in these contexts may indicate a nostalgic longing for times when things were less complex, but also a desire to signal exclusive taste and prestige. As a form of cultural and moral capital, eco-chic is instrumental in achieving class distinction and self-aristocratization.

An important focus of this book is on eco-chic as an antidote to one-sided Western forms of modernization and globalization. While the best-known examples of eco-chic may have developed in Europe and North America, it is also evident in postcolonial settings such as Asia, Africa, and the Caribbean. It represents a combination of environmental awareness with a revalorization of local, often indigenous tastes and traditions that predate the global era, preferably harking back to precolonial times. Ironically, this reappraisal occurs through specifically global processes and phenomena, including global media, corporations, and advertising campaigns, while the eco-chic products and services are couched in a globally translatable aesthetics. Tropes of economic development and progress are replaced by sustainability and authenticity. In this fashion, indigenous qualities become modern and eco-chic provides an alternative to a unilateral Western definition of modernity.

By developing the concept of eco-chic, we seek to introduce a cultural turn to studies of green consumption. This cultural approach directs our attention to the specific aesthetics and material culture associated with eco-chic consumption. In this context, we want to understand what colors, which keywords, images, and fonts help to make products recognizable as eco-chic. Through which associations does off-white and pale-green packaging, decorated with Victorian fonts and hand-sketched illustrations and combined with terms such as "artisanal," "authentic," and "natural," evoke certain emotions and persuade consumers to pay exorbitant prices?

In addition, placing emphasis on the cultural meaning of green consumption involves closer attention to the cultural values of fairness and sustainability. This might entail more serious inquiry into the export of what might be seen as a specific Judeo-Christian subtext. Richard Wilk (2010), for instance, argues that people distinguish between good and evil types of consumption and seek to compensate one with the other in everyday acts of moral balancing, accounting cycles that frame a person's entire life in terms of good and bad deeds. But what about Green Daoism or Islamic environmentalism and other religious repertoires that feed into eco-chic?[3] Eco-chic can lead to the intensification of identities at specific scales (local, regional, and national), taking on a wide range of cultural forms—it is this variety of forms that we intend to interrogate in this volume.

The Politics of Eco-Chic Consumption

In addition to the global-local, modern-traditional puzzles presented by eco-chic, another paradox lies in its conservative politics in relation to sustainable development. As noted above, pursuing radical, eco-centric societal transformation to achieve sustainability—as many environmental movements did in the 1960s and 1970s—has more or less disappeared from the political agenda. The relative success of more reformist, light green environmentalism coincided with the hegemony of neoliberal ideologies that promoted the universal application of market logic. In this context, the popularity of so-called market environmentalism or green capitalism is unsurprising (Prudham 2009). Where previous incarnations of environmentalism saw ever-increasing consumption and ceaseless economic growth as a main source of environmental deterioration, these market-based approaches to sustainability see consumption and green growth as win-win solutions.

Green, sustainable, and ethical consumptions are all forms of political consumerism. Increasingly, consumer choices have become an important site of political action, a trend that has been received enthusiastically by many societal and academic observers. Spaargaren and Mol (2008) note, for instance, that green consumption overcomes the scalar divide between the local and national organization of formal democratic politics on the one hand, and the global nature of many economic practices on the other. Others argue that market-based conscious consumption can renew democracy and empower citizens (Micheletti 2003), offering a relatively easy-access mode for ordinary people to incorporate political and ethical considerations in routine, everyday activities (Barnett et al. 2005). However, various critics point to the neoliberal character of market-based politics and the contradictions between self-interest and collective good that this entails.

As the market has become progressively politicized, the figure of the consumer-citizen (or citizen-consumer) has become increasingly salient. As Johnston (2008: 232) points out, this hybrid concept "implies a social practice that can satisfy competing ideologies of consumerism (an ideal rooted in individual self-interest) and citizenship (an ideal rooted in collective responsibility to a social and ecological commons)." As a form of political action, consumer-citizenship can complement participation in formal democratic politics and other forms of political activism (Willis and Schor 2012). However, it may also diminish the power of the traditional political arena to effect social change. In addition, despite its implicit reference to collectivities, consumer-citizenship individualizes collective action, as individual consumers rather than social movements or political parties are the ideal agents of social change. Moreover, consumer-citizenship is more easily attained by those individuals who have sufficient means. Those with limited income and hence limited consumer power will necessarily have less political influence than their wealthier compatriots, in direct contrast with the equal political rights promised by many formal citizenship regimes.

Consumption as a form of politics has a long history. Various scholars have pointed to the connections between contemporary antisweatshop campaigns and fair-trade movements, and eighteenth- and nineteenth-century antislavery boycotts of Caribbean sugar or products from the U.S. plantation South (Micheletti 2003; Sheller 2011). In the twenty-first century, many of the largest global corporations act preemptively to prevent their brands from being targeted for, and tarnished by, consumer activism. As Sabine Luning and Marjo de Theije emphasize in chapter 4, the growing emphasis on corporate social responsibility (CSR)[4] has convinced many corporations that they need to be involved in an ongoing dialogue with consumers, nongovernmental organizations (NGOs), labor organizations, and other stakeholders. While in many ways laudable, this trend of partnering diminishes the possibility of radical change, giving priority to reformism and gradual achievement through stakeholder meetings or other more business-oriented events. In addition, CSR and other forms of voluntary corporate change are not only strategies to co-opt consumer activism, but they are often also intended to preempt state attempts at regulating industry. Corporate environmentalism tends to be strongest when win-win effects can be achieved. The availability of lucrative markets encourages the mainstreaming of sustainability and environmental awareness, witnessed for instance by the proliferation of major supermarkets' own brands of organic ranges. Greening business without the promise of new markets or cost-saving benefits is obviously much less attractive (Banerjee 2002). In such cases, greening can easily be displaced by greenwashing, discursive but largely meaningless gestures toward sustainability.

Beyond the benefits of green consumption to corporations, consumers may also have less than pure motives. A green disposition is no longer countercultural or subcultural; rather, natural and slow consumption has become instrumental in creating and maintaining class distinction. Many forms of eco-chic consumption make implicit or explicit reference to "simple living," suggesting a shift away from the opulence that is often associated with elite lifestyles and toward the celebration and romanticization of frugality. What does it mean when the wealthier classes move toward a simplicity that previously signaled a lack of income? Such practices may act to uphold class distinction even as they mask socioeconomic disparities.

Drawing on his work on food in Belize, Richard Wilk (2006: 123) uses the concept of the "style sandwich" to explain the imitation of lower-class consumption habits by the rich. Where the poor at the bottom eat or dress a certain way out of necessity, those at the top can copy this behavior out of nostalgia or as an exotic diversion, without fearing the stigma of poverty. Those in the middle, however, have not yet achieved a class position that is sufficiently removed from the poor, and securing a middle-class status involves avoiding poverty food and similar forms of consumption. This style sandwich is highly recognizable in eco-chic. The trend toward voluntary simplicity, and its celebration of going local, native, or traditional, is a signifier of class in that it only attracts those who have a choice. In addition, making low-status consumption practices suitable for elite appropriation generally involves processes of sanitization and distancing: upscaling previously marginalized products and practices often entails repackaging, repricing, and new spatial consumption contexts (see Finnis 2012).

In many cases, green, sustainable, and ethical consumption reinforces class divisions and other structural differences. As Barnett et al. (2005: 41) note, "both the material and socio-cultural resources required for engaging in self-consciously ethical consumption are differentially available" along the lines of class, gender, and ethnicity. Beyond money, knowing when, where, and how to consume what requires the right type of cultural sensibility—the cultural capital that is critical in reproducing class consumption as well as ethnonational belonging (Johnston and Baumann 2009; Wilk 2006). As Kate Cairns, Kim DeLaat, Josée Johnston, and Shyon Baumann point out in chapter 7, eco-chic consumption is also informed by highly gendered models of caring consumption. In addition, the more localist forms of eco-chic consumption may reproduce nationalist and geopolitical inequalities. While locavores who try to minimize their food miles can diminish their carbon footprint, their consumption practices may also affect negatively on the economic sustainability of producers in low-income regions, while overlooking local inequalities in production (DuPuis et al. 2006). The emphasis on eating and buying locally, as evident in the European politics of terroir or the farmer nationalism of Agro-Americans, can be understood as drawing on hegemonic geopolitical discourses that safeguard the status quo.

Global Value Chains, New Partnerships, and Persistent Exclusions

This book is organized into three parts, focusing on the global connections that underlie eco-chic; its spatialities and temporalities; and the centrality of practices and discourses regarding bodies and beauty in eco-chic consumption. In relation to the first focus, we are especially interested in the ways that eco-chic, as a cultural and historical phenomenon, travels from North to South. Given the predominant focus in studies of sustainable and ethical consumption on the global North, we need to know more about how such movements are appropriated and localized in often very novel contexts. At the same time, we urge scholars to look beyond such geopolitical categories and focus instead on the very connections between North and South, and the new forms of exploitation that now take place under the umbrella of eco-chic. While fair trade and eco-certification promise new opportunities to defetishize commodities (Guthman 2009), we need a thorough analysis of commodity chains to understand how such initiatives sometimes cause new instances of the global injustices they aim to mitigate. A wide range of literature has emerged over the past few decades on the topic of commodity chains, following Hopkins's and Wallerstein's initial development of the concept in 1977.[5] These authors introduced the term to describe the linkages between activities and agents involved in creating goods and services within the global economy. While the term *chain* may suggest "a logical and ordered system that we can follow link by link," actually unraveling the system is seldom an easy task (Stone et al. 2000: 21). However, focusing on commodity chains offers a means to go beyond the local level and in doing so helps to reveal the exploitation, unequal rewards, and hidden costs that may lie hidden elsewhere along the chain.

Referring to new developments in pro-poor and fair-trade tourism, Mowforth and Munt (2008) point to the tendency of large-scale tourism operators to diversify their operations by associating their products with the notion of sustainability, if always in ways that reflect their own interests.[6] These divergent interests are reflected in the proliferation of eco-labels and certification schemes. Eco-labeling is intended to indicate the measure of responsibility with which tour companies or hotels carry out their operations. Theoretically, labeling should enable both producers and consumers to identify service providers whose practices do not have negative social or ecological effects. However, today's bewildering array of labels and logos renders it virtually impossible to distinguish the relative merits of each scheme and may even influence the limited consumer demand for certified holidays (Mowforth and Munt 2008: 203).

Various authors have pointed to the pitfalls inherent in the practice of eco-labeling—popular from deluxe resorts to supermarkets—given the fact that the people responsible for awarding certifications are generally the same as those who run the businesses, resulting in little more than a green façade. Melo (2010), for example, points to the shakiness of some of the assumptions that characterize current eco-chic development models, emphasizing that producers and consumers are attracted to "fair trade" for widely divergent reasons. Whereas Ecuador's Ariba Cacao, for example, represents good taste and a genuine interest in traditional foods on the part of European and American consumers, it may prove to be an extremely risky enterprise for small Ecuadorian farmers who would be much better off growing newer cacao variants without all of the bureaucratic hassle.

As academics, we have a responsibility to point out the often long and untrustworthy commodity chains in which fair-trade goods are embedded and to call for strict national and international government policies to guarantee that such programs have a future. Notwithstanding a justified skepticism regarding the self-regulating behavior of green industries, there are a number of exciting new possibilities and actors on the near horizon. A relatively new focus in the global value chain, for example, is the consumer-citizen's manipulation of brands, as described by Robert Foster in his contribution to this volume. Foster argues that the importance of consumption in value creation—the marking and making of a product's difference and distinction—and of risk management in brand valuation present new possibilities for consumer-citizenship. On the one hand, the capacity of consumers' use of products to exceed the control of corporate brand owners potentially destabilizes the qualifications attached to a brand or product. On the other hand, the process of brand valuation itself introduces an element of uncertainty into the management of brands, one result of which has been the emergence of new ways of auditing the social and environmental responsibility of corporations. These conditions of value creation and calculation offer consumers and consumer groups modest resources for what Foster calls a "politics of products," which contests the ways in which corporate brand owners conduct business. To illustrate this phenomenon he draws from historical and ethnographic research on the Coca-Cola Company, especially on the company's recent initiatives in marketing its beverage products, some of which illustrate the concept of eco-chic surprisingly well. Foster's examples include the Campaign Against Killer Coke initiated in 2003 by U.S. activists responding to allegations of labor abuses at bottling plants in Colombia. Foster examines the company's response to this campaign, including partnerships with environmental NGOs, as forms of what former Coca-Cola CEO, Neville Isdell, calls "connected capitalism." Foster's chapter concludes with a sympathetic but critical assessment of the capacity of consumer-citizens to bring about economic and social justice.

Sabine Luning and Marjo de Theije's chapter focuses on another type of partnership, discussing ethical jewelry initiatives developed by NGOs such as Solidaridad and the Alliance for Responsible Mining. These initiatives promise to create supply chains that allow consumers to do good when they buy gold jewelry, creating positive connections with not only the recipient of their gift but also its producers. Gold has a longstanding reputation as a symbol of the social good, epitomizing social values such as trust, love, and loyalty—wedding rings and gold jewelry materialize such values. The morality that gold seems to embody makes it a perfect focus for ethical consumption. The crucial test, the authors suggest, is whether the circumstances of production and fabrication can be made as good as gold. Their chapter describes these efforts by focusing on representations of two players within the global value chain of Fairtrade and Fairmined gold: the celebrity designers involved in fair-mined initiatives and the producers who are often impoverished small-scale miners. Representations of the artisanal designer foreground the elitism of consumers, drawing on celebrity culture and banking on the association of the chic with the beautiful. Artisanal miners are represented in ways that suggest that small is beautiful, framing small-scale production as an almost intrinsically sustainable form of mining. Together these representations allow for a highlighting of the specific characteristics of good gold as a form of eco-chic ethical consumption.

The role of celebrity designers in fair-trade programs resonates with what Goodman and Barnes (2011) have described as "development celebrities" who are now at the front-lines of saving the world and saving us from ourselves. From fronting NGO poverty reduction campaigns to sitting in trees or driving hybrid Priuses, the rich and famous have turned sustainable consumption and development into a kind of eco-chic fashion statement for the rest of us. Goodman and Barnes emphasize the social, economic, and cultural inequalities at the heart of what they call the "celebrity-compassion-consumption complex" (see Richey and Ponte 2011). In this sense, eco-chic points to the gentrification of sustainability in terms of not only who can talk and teach us about it, but also who can partake in the growing cultural economies of salvation for the planet and the poor. In their contribution to this volume, Raymond Bryant and Mike Goodman address this phenomenon of social enclaving by illustrating how an alternative politics of consumption is often assumed to unite relatively affluent consumers and poor producers through the forging of bonds based on notions of fairness, ecological sustainability, and product quality. However, such spaces of intention are premised on the creation of borders that exclude people and knowledge, even as they seek to define new communities of the seemingly like-minded. The chapter assesses such exclusionary practices, drawing on examples from Costa Rica, Mexico, and Malaysia to highlight some of the possible ethical ambiguities and limits to sustainable consumption. In doing so, they and other contributors to this volume contribute to a growing critical literature on the meaning and utility of alternative market-driven solutions to contemporary social and environmental problems.

Spatialities and Temporalities

A second strong theme in this volume relates to the specific spatialities and temporalities that characterize eco-chic. As noted above, the local is a privileged form of spatiality in eco-chic discourse and practice. Specific geographies of authenticity take shape, with authentic places—such as untouched agricultural areas, unspoiled tourism destinations, or gritty urban areas—playing an important role in eco-chic forms of consumption

(Zukin 2009). This equation of specific places or regions with traditional, slow, and green products or activities is especially evident in relation to food consumption and agricultural production. An emphasis on traditional and quality agricultural products has become an important marketing tool in and beyond the European Union, offering rural areas a way of reinventing themselves in a perhaps counterintuitively modern and uniform way. The connections between agricultural product, producer, consumer, and place often rely on urban consumers' nostalgic ideas of rural places and their search for authentic or traditional products. Such discourses, however, are often supported by exclusionary nationalist policies and major agricultural lobbies, and may be informed by xenophobic anxieties.

In terms of temporality, a nostalgic gaze toward the allegedly slower, less complicated past combines with dreams of a future perfect. Among the former imperial powers, colonial nostalgia sometimes colors attempts to market eco-chic products, emphasizing the discovery of exotic difference and luxury by intrepid explorers. Surprisingly, sentimental representations of the colonial past can also be identified in elite consumption practices in former colonies, although visions of eco-modernity are also frequently articulated through references to the indigenous traditions of the precolonial era. What these different forms of nostalgia have in common is the celebration of a supposedly slower, greener preglobalization age.

Often, these forms of spatial and temporal orientation intersect. Ivonne Viscara Bordi (2006), for instance, shows how wealthier, urban Mexicans' craving for the authentic peasant taco represents nostalgic yearning both for a less urbanized society and a different, preglobalization era. These spatial and temporal themes come out in several of the contributions to this volume. In their contribution, Meredith Welch-Devine and Seth Murray analyze the politics of place that eco-chic often entails, scrutinizing the emergence and consequences of eco-chic ideologies and practices in the Basque region of southwestern France. Starting with the first Appellation d'Origine Controllée (AOC) designation of cheeses in 1980, the Basque region rapidly established itself as a place where small, family farmers adopted value-added modes of agricultural production, with quality rather than volume as an important strategy. This focus on quality products, which now extends beyond AOC-labeled products and involves nearly 40 percent of farmers in the Basque region, has become an important marketing tool, and is a way for rural areas to reinvent themselves by appealing to the eco-chic citizen. The authors present two parallel, yet distinct, modes of cheese production that suggest that the politics of production are juxtaposed with the historically situated politics of place and Basque identity. Their cases show that while the application of eco-chic ideologies may promote more sustainable and ethical patterns of consumption, and present powerful tools for rural development and advancement of political ideologies, the consequences of eco-chic practices may also blur the distinctions between rural producers and allow the co-optation of identity and place.

Chris Hudson takes a different approach to the relation between place-making and green consumption. Drawing on the case of Singapore's transformation into a regional model of development and a tourist/shopping mecca, she investigates the politics and the aesthetics involved in the regreening of the city-state's urban environment. Hudson points to the paradox of Singapore's obvious commitment to a sustainable environment and its equally strong dependency on consumption as the motor of the economy. Under Prime Minister Lee Kuan Yew, Singapore's natural environment became an intrinsic part of the developmental agenda, a form of aesthetic capital that was intended to contribute not only to ecological sustainability, but also to cultural and economic sustainability. This strong governmental focus on greenness not only served to turn Singapore into an important tourist and consumer destination, it was also intrinsic to Lee's project of transforming the former British colony into a member of the geopolitical elite of first-world countries.

The temporal contradiction of searching for slowness despite increasingly fast-paced urban lifestyles comes out in the chapter by Kate Cairns, Kim DeLaat, Josée Johnston, and Shyon Baumann. Drawing on interviews and focus groups with Canadian consumers, their chapter presents the lived experiences of consumers facing choices about ethical products in the marketplace. They outline some of the limits of outsourcing responsibility for eco-social change to individual consumers. The chapter argues that there is an idealized image of what an ethical consumer should be, and this image is seriously problematized by examining consumers' discussions about how these consumption choices are limited on a daily level. One of the key limitations the authors identify and discuss concerns the time constraints described by consumers when making difficult product decisions, an obligation that tends to fall on the shoulders of female consumers.

Body, Beauty, and the Global Mobility of Green Hedonism

Above, we made brief mention of the new breed of development celebrities and their role in making green consumption chic and fashionable. The third part of this book delves more deeply into the world of glitter and glamour, scrutinizing how these may contribute to the broader dissemination of things fair and sustainable. The fashion world— a sector not known for setting great store by societal responsibility—has seen a recent upsurge of interest in greener, ethical alternatives; in fact, the very term *eco-chic* first emerged in context of fashion. A number of recent publications have scrutinized the relationship between the fashion industry and environmental awareness, such as Sandy Black's *Eco-Chic: The Fashion Paradox* (2008). It was no accident that this book was launched during the 2008 London Fashion Week, a fashion spectacle that had just begun to include an eco-fashion rubric. The paradox of eco-fashion was also emphasized by Kate Fletcher (2008: 118), who describes the early 1990s trend of "environment friendly garments...dominated by natural looking colours and fibres [that] did not reflect real-world progress. Eco-chic was more a stylized reaction against simplistic perceptions of chemicals and industrial pollution than conversion to sustainability values."[7] Such contradictions were elided in the laudatory tone of glossy magazines such as *Vanity Fair,* which celebrated those designers producing eco-fashion for celebrities, boutiques, and the mass market in its April 2006 green issue. Sustainability had become the latest industry buzz (Winge 2008). Beyond fashion design, the fact that sustainable clothing is hot is also evident in the proliferation of vintage boutiques. In a typical eco-chic twist, terms and concepts such as *secondhand, recycled, preloved,* or *vintage* are co-opted by the same industry they originally critiqued and are used to persuade customers "that the fashion products they purchase are environmentally friendly and ethically sound" (Beard 2008: 450). Such contradictions and ambiguities are precisely what characterizes so much of contemporary eco-chic.

Mass mediation of the eco-chic concept has been instrumental in increasing its fashionability. A broad range of books, films, and magazines celebrate eco-chic products such as cosmetics and holidays. More than other products, however, fair, organic, and healthy food has proved a best-selling topic. U.S.-based documentaries such as *Food Inc., Fast Food Nation,* and *The Future of Food* not only criticize the commodification of food in modern society, but also contribute to the mainstreaming of health, wellness, and ethical consumption, raising awareness among audiences beyond metropolitan foodie or eco-fashionista subcultures (Lindenfeld 2003). Similarly, these documentaries have helped to trigger public debates that have forced major food corporations to reconsider their corporate social responsibility. Europe has a longer tradition of green cuisine, boosted by the recent "culinary edutainment" (Solier 2005) of celebrity entrepreneurs such as Jamie Oliver, who attempt to democratize eco-food. As Hollows and Jones (2010) note, such culinary entrepreneurs leverage their television exposure to secure various forms of political influence and place green consumption more centrally on the political agenda. Still very much understudied are the comparable culinary spectacles and celebrity entrepreneurs propagating a return to the diet of our ancestors on many of Asia's commercial channels.

The interest of mainstream media for things eco-chic have generated the "enduring public" (Foster 2008) necessary for sustaining green consumption, a public that includes not only elites with exceptional consumer power, but also those who aspire to partake in the twenty-first century's new aristocratic lifestyles. It is surprising to see how smoothly the vocabulary of green hedonism merges with local practices as it travels across geographical and socioeconomic borders; this is especially evident among the newly emergent middle classes of the global South. An important direction in studying green consumption as it goes global will be analyzing in more detail how an apparently global aesthetic is translated and appropriated and often turned into something entirely new and different as it reterritorializes in various local contexts. A focus on the cultural aspects of global green consumption may well illustrate the widely divergent reasons and ways in which societies and (sub)cultures adopt eco-chic practices; this becomes clear in the three chapters that make up the third and last part of this book.

Rivke Jaffe's chapter focuses on the Jamaican phenomenon of ital chic, a cross between ethical consumerism and the aesthetic repertoire of Rastafari. Symbols of a Rastafarian lifestyle, also known as *ital livity,* are today mobilized to market a variety of products and services, ranging from restaurants and hairstyles to candles, clothing, and cosmetics. Her chapter discusses the implications of this phenomenon for Jamaica in terms of postcolonial race, class, and cultural politics, as well as its relation to a wider politics of sustainable development. While ital chic's producers come from diverse backgrounds, its consumers tend to be mostly light-skinned, middle-class, or elite Jamaicans. There is, therefore, a risk that this mainstreaming of Rasta elements is not necessarily progressive. Jaffe explores the political stakes of ital chic and considers to what extent the capitalist logic and the classed strategies associated with ital chic may imply the commodification of resistance or even a pacification of the dread.

Dreadlocks also feature centrally in the chapter by Anna-Riikka Kaupinnen and Rachel Spronk, who show how natural hairstyles function as a site for negotiating different conceptions of modernity in Ghana, and reflect concerns with both postcolonial cultural authenticity and religious integrity. As in many postcolonial African societies, fashion and beauty have never been neutral in Ghana, always implying ethical and political choices beyond individual preferences. In recent years, as natural beauty products and natural hairstyles have hit Accra's upmarket salons, dreadlocks are associated less with outmoded traditions or religious fringe movements. A nonchemical, natural hairstyle and the green lifestyle associated with this have become not only a trend among Afro-cosmopolitan elites, but also instrumental in a reading of modernity that is very different from those adopting mainstream Western lifestyles and fashions. The chapters by Jaffe and by Kaupinnen and Spronk both illustrate how eco-chic may gain a very different momentum as it travels, becoming part of the construction of a larger Pan-African consciousness. Africans and Jamaicans of African descent now reassess long-standing, previously disreputable practices as eco-chic, and savvy entrepreneurs recognize that long-ignored traditions have commercial potential in the emergent green market. This points to yet another paradox of eco-chic once it goes global: the local, non-Western practices that were long deemed backward and incompatible with modernity are now redefined and revalorized through the vocabulary, ideas, and images of a lifestyle of health, beauty, and spirituality that are currently so fashionable in the same West with which these practices are contrasted.

Eco-chic has an intentional or inadvertent role in cementing a new sort of regional and often oppositional discourse, as is also illustrated in the final chapter, by Bart Barendregt. He points out how Western travelers, tourists, and scholars have long perceived the "Orient" as authentic, sensual, and mysterious. Even today, for many Westerners Asia represents all that is lost to modern (Western) man. Such Orientalist representations (and their appropriation in contemporary eco-chic in the form of vague notions of Eastern spirituality) primarily reflect Western audiences' longing for a sensual Other, expressed through a depiction of the East as a place of splendor, purity, and its inhabitants' closeness to nature. Recently, however, Southeast Asian middle and upper classes are now tapping into such stereotypes to retrieve authentic life experiences that, according to many, have been threatened by ongoing modernization, globalization, and, most dreaded, Westernization. Barendregt's chapter focuses on the most eye-catching manifestation of this "New Asian" lifestyle, the tropical spa. While not many can afford the lush and lavish spa resorts that capture the imagination most vividly, the lure of the tropical spa can also be brought home in the form of lifestyle magazines, spa recipes, cosmetics, and other derived consumables. As such, the current tropical spa craze and Asian-style eco-chic offer opportunities for constructing new, distinguished communities—communities that straddle the borders separating Asian countries, uniting those sufficiently moneyed to dedicate themselves to this brand of consumerism. This involves the construction of a possible postnational imagery in which the aspiration for a green upmarket lifestyle plays an increasingly important role.

These three examples draw our attention to the interplay and dynamics of green and elitist consumption beyond the global North. The question remains: what public discussions are engendered through these practices and through associated media such as spa magazines and foodie shows? What kind of audiences do the producers of these media have in mind, and more importantly, whose story is told here? As in Europe and North America, these practices and discourses give rise to public contestations not only over the meaning of healthy food, but also over who can claim to be the gatekeeping elites in all these processes.

Conclusion

The concerns we have outlined in this introduction are salient across the world. The most popular forms of green consumption are related to broadly shared anxieties concerning the social and economic changes associated with globalization. Eco-chic draws our attention to the unease many people feel regarding globalization's space–time compression, even as the forms of consumption discussed here rely on global economies and national mass media. The combination of ethical, sustainable, and elite consumption also forces us to consider the various ways in which politics and markets intersect. This politicization of the market—and the concomitant privatization of politics—is sometimes seen as providing a more effective answer to economic globalization than old politics. But what kind of new forms of participation are we looking at, and what is their potential for achieving ecological and social justice? How does green consumption relate to citizenship? The potential and pitfalls of consumer-citizenship have been outlined here and elsewhere. Ecological citizenship implies a different set of shared expectations about citizens' role in politics, and green consumption suggests a site where these two forms of citizenship might merge. With partnership and corporate social responsibility high on the agenda, new forms of active citizen participation are now among the possibilities. Despite the emphasis on the role of consumer-citizens as agents, it remains to be seen what the role of citizens, much less the state, will be in these processes, and how much of the future green agenda will be determined by multinational corporations or brands.

The chapters in this volume draw on various disciplines, making use of insights from anthropology, sociology, geography, and political science. What the different contributions share is a conviction that the study of eco-chic behavior should not restrict itself to the level of the individual: the most fruitful approach to green consumption is one that focuses on shared imaginaries, communal norms, and collective practices, as well as on civic responsibilities and the effect of consumption across space and time. Studying eco-chic should also include attention to our own responsibility in the concerns discussed throughout the book. How, for example, are we as academics complicit in creating notions of nature and of *terroir*? How do we negotiate the epistemic authority we may be granted when we prioritize what we feel needs to be sustained most urgently? How might we contribute more to the transparency of complex global value chains? In our critical assessment of the power structures that underlie certification, what better alternatives can we propose, and can and should we intervene in our own academic environments to promote the adoption of green consumption and regulation at our universities and research institutes? Can we be postcynical and as scholars link up to social movements that have put sustainability high on the agenda? While we hope that this book will shed critical light on the complexities of green consumption, moving toward a real commitment to ethical and sustainable academic practice will require us to develop a reflexive, publicly engaged stance that goes beyond these pages.

Part I
From Production to Consumption

–2–

Adversaries into Partners?
Brand Coca-Cola and the Politics
of Consumer-Citizenship

Robert J. Foster

Eco-Chic: Political Consumerism and the Paradoxes
of Corporate Partnerships

In her insightful book *Political Virtue and Shopping,* political scientist Michelle Micheletti (2003: 14) observes: "Economic globalization and concerns about global justice
have...shifted the venue of politics to the market sphere and change[d] the orientation
of action from pressure group politics and social movement agitation to targeting transnational corporations directly through purchasing choices and less conventional political
methods as culture jamming, hactivism, and guerilla media stunts." Micheletti accordingly cautions us not to dismiss the possibility that individual consumption practices
can function as a vehicle for political action and civic virtue. On the contrary, Micheletti
(2003: 15) argues: "Political consumerism carves out new arenas for political action by
its involvement in the market and the politics of private corporations....It considers individual citizens as main actors in politics by emphasizing the responsibility of each and
every citizen for our common well being."

　This chapter considers the possibilities of political consumerism or consumer-
citizenship directed against transnational corporations. The question mark in the title
indicates my ambivalence about the prospects of consumer-citizenship for effecting
progressive change—that is, for changing present conditions of social and economic
injustice through boycotts, buycotts, and other methods such as culture jamming that
appeal to individuals primarily as consumers, especially consumers of brand-name commodities.[1] My intention is neither to contrast so-called real politics to political consumerism nor to oppose citizen and consumer as distinct, irreconcilable identities. Nor is it to
expose consumer-citizenship as a corporate conspiracy to co-opt moral conscience and
social critique. Such a blunt analysis would fail to recognize the heterogeneous motivations, expressions, and consequences of commodity activism (see Mukherjee and Banet-
Weiser 2012). I am sympathetic to Micheletti's position, and I have previously adopted

it with respect to the politics of consumption surrounding soft drinks (Foster 2008a). But I have become less optimistic over the last several years, mainly as a result of observing how corporations such as The Coca-Cola Company (TCCC) have responded to agitation by concerned consumer-citizens.[2] I will discuss here some of the reasons for my declining optimism, highlighting in particular the paradoxical character of corporate partnerships made in the name of environmentally responsible consumption.

Selling eco-chic is now a minor part of the business of TCCC. For example, the company's website celebrates the possibility of "creating value through sustainable fashion" in its account of the Drink2Wear t-shirts launched in 2007.[3] These t-shirts, which sold for under $20 at the online Coca-Cola retail store, were made from a blend of recycled plastic bottles and cotton; they featured snappy slogans such as "Rehash Your Trash" meant "to promote recycling and eco-friendly food and clothing."

If you are understandably inclined to doubt the fashion credentials of these plastic t-shirts, then perhaps a more upscale example of eco-chic will persuade you to accept the company's claim. In 2010, TCCC announced the debut of a chair made from 111 recycled plastic bottles blended with glass fiber and offered in several colors (Figure 2.1).

Figure 2.1 Emeco 111 Navy Chair made from 111 recycled plastic Coca-Cola bottles. Image courtesy of Emeco.

The chair was modeled on the classic aluminum Emeco Navy Chair designed in 1944 for the U.S. Navy and manufactured in a way to make it three times harder than steel. Like many other instances of eco-chic, the Emeco 111 Navy Chair at $230 aligns tasteful and stylish consumer choices on the part of affluent shoppers with concern for the environment. This particular instance, however, is notable for its effort to co-brand the product. The chair is not only an Emeco chair, but also a Coca-Cola chair.

TCCC has engaged in other co-branding efforts that qualify as eco-chic. For example, in 2007 the company formed a partnership to produce a line of handbags made from misprinted or discontinued labels of Coca-Cola bottles. Kelli Sogar, then the company's merchandise manager, worldwide licensing and retail operations, commented: "We have made great strides in reducing our waste output from our bottling plants or label manufacturing facilities, and we are constantly seeking ways to reduce our environmental footprint. This partnership allows us to repurpose materials. Best of all, we are helping to create greater awareness on environmentally and socially responsible consumption."[4]

In this instance, fashion sensibility aligns with concern not only for the environment, but also for women struggling against the challenges of poverty. The co-branding links TCCC with Ecoist, a family-owned business that converts waste into raw materials for fashion accessories. Ecoist is committed to "investing in the lives of our workers, their families, and their communities." For example, the company's website claims that the Coca-Cola handbags are made by "a certified fair trade women's cooperative in Peru."[5] Ecoist itself, in turn, partners with Trees for the Future, and plants a tree "in places like Haiti, India and Uganda" for each handbag sold. According to the company's website: "By definition, an Ecoist is 'an individual that lives a modern, eco-minded lifestyle.' We hope to inspire people to become 'Ecoists' so we can all live in a healthier, better, and more peaceful planet."

How does fighting poverty and protecting the environment create value for companies like TCCC? Specifically, how are we to understand the sort of partnership into which TCCC has entered with Ecoist—partnerships with not only companies but also assorted nongovernmental organizations (NGOs) devoted to environmental and social causes in the developing world? What can we learn about eco-chic by asking about the partnership rather than the lifestyle politics implicated in the purchase of the handbags; by highlighting the corporation instead of the consumer, and business strategies instead of cultural trends? That is, what is the political economy of eco-chic as opposed to its psychology or anthropology?

Partnership is one of the key words in the discourse of corporate social responsibility (CSR) that has flourished since 1999. The term indicates a type of global governance that Christina Garsten and Kerstin Jacobsson (2007) call "post-political," in which consensual and voluntary forms of regulation take the place of involuntary regulation imposed by states on parties with conflicting interests (see Ferguson and Gupta 2002). The ideal of partnership epitomizes the post–UN Global Compact world in which political conflict around corporations is replaced by a set of transcendent moral codes of conduct, a world in which longstanding corporate adversaries—including NGOs and civil society organizations (CSOs)—are turned into allies.[6] Win-win solutions replace negotiated compromises and winner-take-all outcomes. As Cairns et al. emphasize in their contribution to this volume, it is precisely this perfect alignment between the interests of business and the greater good of society that eco-chic also promises.

What possibilities do these partnership strategies open up and shut down for the practice of political consumerism and consumer-citizenship? More generally, what are the prospects for economic democracy within the rubric of postpolitical governance? In addressing these questions, I will demonstrate how current understandings of brand value in the business world compel corporations to engage with consumers, including consumer-citizens. I will argue that brands—especially global brands associated with fast-moving consumer goods—can therefore provide a platform for civic action on a transnational scale. I draw on my work on one particular brand—Coca-Cola—to illustrate how corporations have developed new techniques for stabilizing this platform and for managing the actors who appear on it.

The shift in the venue of politics into the market sphere identified by Micheletti prompts a rethinking of what resistance to corporate power might look like (see Mukherjee and Banet-Weiser 2012). This rethinking in turn demands acknowledging a corollary shift in the venue of business into the sphere of NGOs and CSOs (as well as the continuation of corporate efforts to lobby public officials at all levels of government). I thus do not dismiss consumer-citizenship or political consumerism as inevitably oxymoronic, especially when the terms are understood broadly to include practices such as shareholder activism and coordinated public actions in the manner, for example, of civil rights protests against segregated buses and lunch counters. I suggest, however, that the corporate partnerships characteristic of postpolitical governance are themselves often oxymoronic inasmuch as they purportedly reconcile manifestly incompatible goals, such as protecting the environment and selling more bottled water. These alliances present difficult, new challenges to consumer-citizens wishing to harness the potential of markets for progressive social reform let alone radical change.

Political Consumerism in a Time of Brandization

Political consumerism has a long history, as the etymology of the word *boycott* attests.[7] There is, however, a new condition of possibility for political consumerism—for using market-based actions to achieve goals ordinarily imagined as civic matters. It is a condition associated with the increasing importance to corporations of intangible assets, that is, the increasing share of a corporation's market capitalization that is accounted for by intangible assets. By intangible assets, I mean, specifically, brands.

We are all familiar with how companies today routinely reduce costs by outsourcing commodity production to distant sites where cheap labor is available. The flipside of this global movement is perhaps less familiar. It is what Hugh Willmott (2010) gives the deliberately inelegant name of brandization: the monetization of brand value.

Willmott provocatively argues that in the current era of "financialization" corporations invest in branding not to extend the market or to increase market share or even to charge a higher premium price. Rather, the goal is to leverage the value of the brand for shareholders, for example, through royalties derived from its use by other corporations. Brands, therefore, become a source of revenue by attracting investors persuaded that brand-owning companies will grow at a faster pace than those companies without brands.[8] Investment increases share price, and thus market capitalization "against which cheaper lines of credit and the debt-financing of expansion or acquisition activity can be secured" (Willmott 2010: 524). Hence, the dividends and capital gains that accrue for investors as a result of increased share price represent surplus value created and extracted, in Willmott's words, "beyond the point of production." Given that CEOs have strong and multiple incentives to boost share price (incentives that include personal compensation packages tied to performance; see Bashkow forthcoming), brandization is an appealing managerial strategy.

Brandization, however, entails more than corporate ownership of strong brands; it requires the translation of brand strength into brand value by means of the market device of brand valuation—a device that puts an agreed upon monetary price on a brand (see Foster 2013 for a more extensive discussion). Without brand valuation, it is difficult to say how much of a corporation's market capitalization can be attributed to its brands (and to the work of the marketing department). A number of brand consultancy firms—most prominently, Interbrand—provide valuation services. The number-one global brand in terms of monetary price in the 2012 annual report released by Interbrand in conjunction with *BusinessWeek* magazine was Coca-Cola, valued at more than $77.8 billion and up 8 percent in value from the year before (Figure 2.2).

Interbrand 2012 Top Ten Global Brands by Value (in USD millions)

Coca-Cola	$77,839
Apple	$76,568
IBM	$75,532
Google	$69,726
Microsoft	$57,853
General Electric	$43,682
McDonald's	$40,062
Intel	$39,358
Samsung	$32,893
Sony	$30,280

Figure 2.2 Interbrand's 2012 Top Ten Global Brands.
Source: http://www.interbrand.com/en/best-global-brands/2012/Best-Global-Brands-2012-Brand-View .aspx, accessed February 2, 2013.

Brand valuation acknowledges, if only implicitly, that brands are contingent outcomes of relationships—ongoing, changing, not always predictable relationships. In this sense, a brand is like a reputation, an interactive social construction. And brand management and reputation management are closely connected corporate concerns. As Interbrand strategist Tom Zara (2009: 3) puts it: "Brand has become even more important in separating the winners from the losers in a marketplace where corporate reputations have been battered by scandals and bruised by recession." Furthermore, damage can now be done to brands more easily by agents outside the corporation—hacktivists and culture jammers empowered by an array of social media technologies. This observation is particularly apt in cases where the brand and the corporate entity are identical: McDonald's, Disney, and Coca-Cola—all companies in which brand value is estimated to comprise more than 50 percent of market capitalization (unlike, say, the case of Procter and Gamble or Pfizer, companies that own multiple brands with different identities).

Brand and reputation are thus similar economic objects with respect to the possibilities of political consumerism. They are both found at the limits of managerial control inasmuch as they involve a company's external relationships. These external relationships encompass a broad array of stakeholders. Interbrand identifies six fields of stakeholders—employees, customers, suppliers, the communities in which companies operate, the governments that influence operations, and the planet that all companies rely on for existence. The challenge of bringing all of these relationships under managerial control is daunting, to say the least!

Managing Relationships: Value Cocreation and Risk

There are two relationships in particular to which the idea of brandization calls attention: the crucial relationship between a brand owner and brand users (or consumers) and the relationship between brand owners and concerned citizens who are not necessarily consumers—more or less enduring publics that emerge around specific issues or events (see Foster 2008a). Both of these relationships are inherently unstable. Brandization requires turning both unruly consumers and unruly publics into willing partners.

There is far more at stake in the relationship between brand owners and consumers than what has been understood as customer loyalty. Corporations today readily concede that brands are often the creations of consumers as much as the products of brand managers, designers, and marketers. Consumers are regarded as "co-creators" (Prahalad and Ramaswamy 2004) or "prosumers" (Ritzer and Jurgenson 2010); they perform consumption work (see Miller 1988). That is, the strength or equity of a brand depends on the extent to which consumers use the brand as a medium or instrument of their own "affectively significant relationships" (Arvidsson 2009: 17), as a resource for the sort of self-realization that Marx associated with unalienated labor (see Miller 1987).

I have come to understand this use of brands as a form of consumption work that brand owners attempt not only to manage, but also to exploit as a source of surplus value (see Banet-Weiser and Lapsansky 2008; Foster 2008b, 2011). That is, brand owners derive rent from the purchases of consumers who pay to use a brand that, through a consumer's own particular postpurchase use, has become entangled in his or her life projects. The challenge confronting brand managers, then, is to make sure that the brand stays aligned with the consumer's autonomous interest in cocreating it. This challenge involves what Adam Arvidsson calls a risky "logistics of meaning and affect" (2009: 18), which if mishandled results in the consumer's withdrawal of his or her consumption work, thereby reducing the brand's social currency (its coolness) and thus its strength or equity.

Interbrand makes it clear that similar risk is distributed through all of a company's external relationships with stakeholders. For example, with regard to business-to-business relationships: "purchasers understand that they can be held accountable by the public for their suppliers' actions. So pressure that begins externally—in the net's 24-hour court of public opinion and among a press ready to feed the beast—winds up being passed along every link in the [supply] chain" (Zara 2009: 3).

In short, the rhetoric of Interbrand is a rhetoric that produces the risk and uncertainty that the firm's services promise to manage. Indeed, it is not implausible to argue that brand valuation is itself a new form of risk and uncertainty with which companies must deal. Michael Power's claim about "reputational risk" applies as well to "brand valuational risk": "Reputational risk is a pure 'man-made' risk because it is the product of evaluative institutions which explicitly manufacture a new kind of uncertainty with a high degree of calculative rationalization" (2007: 150). The response to reputational risk, according to Power, is to bring the outside in, that is, to internalize and therefore render manageable the risky external stakeholders whose values and interests must be addressed because they matter in the social construction of reputation—and of brands. As a result, companies create new market devices to make their "reputations easily readable and auditable by outsiders who are conceptualized as sources of vulnerability and fear" (Power 2007: 150).

I suggest that the partnerships of TCCC, including its partnership with Ecoist, should be understood in terms of the prevailing stakeholder model of brand value. That is, these partnerships are themselves market devices (or relationships for creating such devices as supply chain audits and carbon footprint measurements) developed to deal with the market device of brand valuation. Hence the recent report from the Economist Intelligence Unit, "Dangerous Liaisons: How Businesses Are Learning to Work with Their New Stakeholders" (2010). This report makes it clear that the number-one reason that corporations engage "non-traditional stakeholders," whether NGOs, charities and citizen groups, or sundry online communities, is to manage risk to reputation of both the firm and its brands.[9] Partnerships with activist NGOs, in particular, reduce a firm's exposure to attack or criticism. An article in the business journal *Strategy & Leadership* thus advises:

> One tactic that is consistently used to attack global companies is the allegation that they are "out of touch." Companies must pro-actively seek out dialogue, engagement and partnerships with stakeholders and organizations....Obviously in the case of substantive partnerships programs, companies will need to work with constructive, like-minded partners, but dialogue with difficult critics should not be completely avoided. (Deri 2003: 32)

I will return to the issue of partnerships. But note that the number-two reason that corporations engage with nontraditional stakeholders is brand building. The Economist Intelligence Unit (2010) report makes it clear that what is at stake in such engagements is the value of consumption work or cocreation. Companies regard their stakeholders—especially online communities—as resources for inspiring, designing, and launching new products: "The views of customers—gathered through chat rooms and social networking sites—are also sources of innovation, helping companies to learn more about what their customers want." The report approvingly cites the example of Dell's IdeaStorm, "a blog and website that allows customers to post their ideas and suggestions online, vote for the idea they consider most useful and join web-based forums to discuss their thoughts with other individual users of the site." The report makes no mention of who owns the ideas and suggestions posted or how the revenue that such ideas generate is distributed.

In sum, the main benefit that companies stand to gain from partnerships with external stakeholders is anticipation. On the one hand, corporate managers anticipate the shifts in use that otherwise threaten to misalign both brands and products with the personal projects of their users or consumers. On the other hand, corporate managers anticipate the criticisms that stakeholders such as activist NGOs might offer on sensitive issues such as environmental impact. The advice offered by *Strategy & Leadership,* a publication aimed at top executives and strategic planners, is unequivocal: "To the degree that a company plays a pro-active role in dialogue and debate with all relevant parties—both critics and allies—the more opportunity the company will have to shape the debate, set goals and define success, and possibly even find market-based solutions" (Deri 2003: 32).

Killer Coke: Brand on the Run?

Bringing the outside in, internalizing risky stakeholders is itself a risky business. The task often exceeds the capacities of corporate managers and sometimes succumbs to the law of unanticipated consequences. It is this excess and unpredictability that create possibilities for the exercise of political consumerism and, in turn, stimulate new corporate strategies for managing risk to brands and reputations.

I will support this claim with the example of one activist campaign directed against TCCC, the Killer Coke Campaign. Killer Coke illustrates the politics of a branded product network—a network that unlike, say, Fair Trade does not connect the consumers of a product with the producers of a product, but instead connects an assortment of people to each other through their various connections as stakeholders in a brand. As the name suggests, this campaign was launched in the spirit of confrontation, not cooperation; its tactics have been adversarial rather than partner-like. I will briefly outline the history of the campaign (see Foster 2008a for more detail), which reached a peak around 2006, and then describe the company's response.

Ray Rogers, a labor activist, directs Corporate Campaign, a labor-funded organization that in 2003 launched the Campaign to Stop Killer Coke.[10] Rogers was contacted by North American labor lawyers who had been earlier contacted by a union representing workers at bottling plants in Colombia. In Colombia during the 1990s, threats, kidnappings, and murders were carried out against trade unionists by right-wing paramilitaries while the government carried out a program of neoliberal economic reform. Trade unionists at Coca-Cola bottling plants were targeted, and in 1996 local union leader Isidro Gil was assassinated on the grounds of a bottling plant in the town of Carepa. Prior to the murder, workers reported observing managers conversing with known paramilitaries in the cafeteria of the plant (see Gill 2005).

In 2001, the labor lawyers filed a lawsuit in a U.S. federal court against TCCC and its Colombian bottlers, charging them with gross violations of human rights. The lawyers used an eighteenth-century statute, the Alien Tort Claims Act, to hold a U.S. company liable for its activities abroad. Rogers was recruited to pressure TCCC in other ways.

Rogers's strategy complemented the lawsuit by reassembling the Coca-Cola product network, that is, by transforming the company's relations with its various stakeholders. He began by attacking the company's most valuable asset, its brand, through the circulation (electronic and otherwise) of grisly images that subverted the company's familiar logos and friendly advertising. This sort of culture jamming was intended to get consumers to reevaluate the use value that they assign to a brand, and thus to refrain from participating in the consumption work and cocreation that provide the basis of the brand's exchange value.[11]

Rogers was less interested in orchestrating a general boycott of Coca-Cola products (which the trade union in Colombia had called for) than in cutting specific markets out of the company's product network. To this end, he was able to target the company's exclusive vending contracts with various organizations, including unions and, in particular, colleges and universities. This strategy brought students in the United States, Canada, and Europe into the campaign, in part through an alliance with United Students Against Sweatshops, the group that had spearheaded campus protests against sweatshop labor in the 1990s. About two dozen colleges and universities in the United States canceled their contracts with TCCC, focusing business and mainstream media attention on the campaign. By late 2005, the Killer Coke campaign had brought a coalition into being that loosely connected Colombian workers with North American and European students and some labor organizations. The Coca-Cola brand had become "the new Nike" (Blanding 2005). Campus-based protests were spreading across the United States, well beyond the capacity of Rogers to direct.

Although accusations against the company and its bottlers in Colombia prompted the campaign, Rogers's strategy also sought to make visible the extensive network of financial relations that in effect constituted the company and underwrote its eponymous global brand. He publicized how the board of directors of TCCC was interlocked with the boards of other companies, and he recruited new members to the campaign by linking Killer Coke with other causes. For example, by highlighting the company's sponsorship of the 2008 Beijing Olympics, Rogers reached out to groups mobilized against the mass killings in Darfur, because China is a major trading partner of Sudan.

Other NGOs with grievances against TCCC likewise became linked to the Killer Coke campaign, including the India Resource Center (IRC), which accused TCCC's bottling operations in India of depleting and contaminating sources of groundwater (Figure 2.3).

Figure 2.3   Cartoon by Latuff made for the India Resource Center. *Source:* http://archive.org/details/
CocaColaCrisisInIndia

The IRC was the effort of mainly one man, Amit Srivastava—an activist with a website
(Secklow 2005). Srivastava and Rogers would occasionally appear together on college
campuses to lecture about TCCC's operations in Colombia and India and to support
students lobbying their schools' administrators to terminate exclusive vending contracts
with the company's bottlers.

   My immediate point is that branded consumer products can provide a vehicle for creating large geographically dispersed publics. These publics consist of participants who
do not necessarily share a single perspective on a particular product—indeed, who are
probably not aware of each other's existence. Nevertheless, these publics demonstrate
the capacity of Internet activism to produce more than a like on a Facebook page. Indeed,
although fragile and ephemeral, these unruly publics can command the attention of corporations and, as in this particular case, elicit a corporate response.

TCCC Responds: Partners Not Adversaries, or Managing Ray Rogers

TCCC's response to the Killer Coke campaign and to other criticisms leveled at it (for
example, about adding to the problem of childhood obesity in the United States) took

definite shape with the appointment of Neville Isdell as CEO in June 2004. Isdell quickly declared his intention to make TCCC the "recognized leader in corporate social responsibility" (Ward 2006). One of the main instruments that emerged for doing so was partnership. In 2006, for example, Isdell finally responded to the demands of the Killer Coke campaign for an independent investigation of the accusations about labor violence in Colombia by inviting the International Labor Organization (ILO), a UN agency, to inspect operations in the country.

Similar moves were being made on other issues by Jeff Seabright, TCCC's head of environmental and water affairs. Seabright noted in 2006 that "Our brand has made us a target for critics to attract attention to their causes. But NGOs are starting to understand they can achieve more with us than against us because our brand and global presence makes us a powerful partner" (Ward 2006). Isdell, who retired from TCCC in 2008, continued to develop corporate partnership initiatives as chairman of the board of trustees of the International Business Leaders Forum (IBLF), a nonprofit organization that works with multinational companies on social responsibility. These partnerships between businesses and both governments and civil society organizations are the core of a "new model of social engagement" that Isdell calls "connected capitalism" (Bisoux 2010; Isdell with Beasley 2011).

The partnering initiatives championed by Isdell and undertaken by TCCC signaled a corporate approach to social activism consistent with the ideal of postpolitical governance—itself a reaction on the part of corporations to the street protests in Seattle in 1999. The game plan was foreshadowed by Richard Edelman of Edelman PR Worldwide in a 2001 report of a survey of opinion leader attitudes toward NGOs "commissioned in response to ["the"] first anniversary of the Seattle meeting" (Edelman 2001: 34). The survey found that NGOs were trusted nearly twice as much to "do what is right" compared with corporations. Edelman's recommendation followed accordingly: "If Seattle was a wake up call, then the survey's findings can be considered a smoke alarm, requiring decisive action. It is our recommendation that a company proactively manage relationships with NGOs to protect its global corporate reputation. No longer can corporations risk meeting minimal standards. Instead, corporate leaders must learn more about NGO concerns and begin dialogues with them to implement programs, strategies, and tactics designed to avert confrontational situations before they become major news stories" (Edelman 2001: 36).

Since 2007, TCCC and its subsidiaries have engaged in an aggressive bout of partnering with NGOs—big and small, local and global. Recently, for example, the company (along with the brewing company SABMiller) announced a partnership with Oxfam America to explore the links between international business and poverty reduction in Zambia and El Salvador.[12] But perhaps the most prominent of all the company's partnerships is its alliance with the World Wildlife Fund (WWF), an organization that the Edelman survey identified as having high levels of trust and credibility. This partnership, launched in 2007, focuses on water conservation and climate protection.[13] In addition to $20 million, the WWF receives the company's assistance in implementing conservation projects in seven selected river basins around the world. The company in turn receives WWF assistance in minimizing water and energy use throughout its supply chain.

The credibility that accrues to corporations through such partnerships ultimately depends upon the reputation of the NGO. This fact is candidly captured in some of the statements recorded in a report issued by the Partnering Initiative, a program sponsored by the IBLF, and SOS Kinderdorpen, the Dutch branch of the NGO SOS Children's Villages International (Bobenreith and Stibbe 2010: 10). The following comments were made in one-on-one interviews by Netherlands-based "representatives of multinational and national companies from a wide range of sectors" (Bobenreith and Stibbe 2010: 1):

- Our connection to a reputable, well-known organization is one of the key benefits for us.
- [The partnership] should enhance our brand.
- No risk assessment but need to be very well-established organizations with positive names,…we are engaged in children's issues so need to be confident that our partners have excellent reputations.
- Externally, we use the partnership to support our image in the market, which is maybe not the main reason, but we want to show that we are responsible.

As a result, not every NGO qualifies as a suitable partner. Anthropologist Dinah Rajak (2011) observed as much in one of the few ethnographic studies of how corporate–NGO partnerships are arranged. She notes that at high-profile CSR industry conventions: "The appearance of consensus between participants, and the allegiance to the shared goals of development through business, is produced by the exclusion of groups with alternative visions, conflicting agendas, or simply smaller budgets. Actors with fewer resources, who tell a different story to that of the common interests that the CSR movement tries to project, are thus marginalized from this hegemonic mainstream" (Rajak 2011: 13). So, for example, at the 2011 annual shareholder meeting of TCCC in Atlanta, CEO Muhtar Kent could respond to allegations of abusive labor practices by citing the support of third parties such as the ILO. Kent, according to my notes from the meeting, declared "We stand by what others say about us."

Corporations cannot, of course, entirely avoid engaging with NGOs that are not ideal partners. For example, it would be difficult to imagine a partnership between TCCC and Killer Coke. But company officials must engage with Ray Rogers at least once a year in the question-and-answer sessions at the annual shareholder meeting. In 2004, at the Hotel du Pont in Wilmington, Delaware, Rogers was forcibly removed from the meeting while then CEO Douglas Daft implored security staffers to be gentle and to "stand down, please, please" (Leith and Kempner 2004). The incident was widely reported by the media and attracted the criticism of the Rev. Jesse Jackson, who addressed the meeting about minority opportunities at TCCC.

At the 2011 meeting in Atlanta, home of the company's headquarters, CEO Muhtar Kent deployed a less physical strategy for managing Rogers. Rogers was the first person to be called upon from the podium by Kent in the question-and-answer portion of the meeting. Rogers began by offering praise and congratulations to the group of singing children whose anodyne performance opened the meeting. Kent thanked the instantly recognizable "Mr. Rogers" and with a wide grin further thanked him for his "interest in our company." Rogers then posed a question: "Mr. Chairman, do you and the board understand the consequences of lying to investors and withholding information on potential liabilities that could cost the company billions of dollars in fines, restitutions, and loss of brand value?"

Kent glared in icy silence. Finally, he spoke: "Continue, please, with your question. You have a minute to go." Kent insisted that Rogers finish his question. Rogers relented, adding "Alright, but I want some real answers!"

Rogers then launched into allegations of TCCC's attempts to put out of business thousands of mom-and-pop stores throughout Mexico and to avoid paying taxes to the Mexican government. In the middle of his statement, a chime rang, indicating that the two minutes allowed to each questioner had expired. Rogers continued, describing a preliminary investigation that had been conducted by the Mexican treasury department. He accused Kent of lying at the 2010 annual meeting about the legal case surrounding these allegations. The chime sounded again. "I'm summing up here," Rogers protested. He ended by mentioning other alleged instances of fraudulent activities on the part of TCCC in India, while Kent intervened to point out "We have given you enough time."

Kent then started to reply, claiming that the facts simply do not support the charges that Rogers makes year after year. He then offered to "take a few minutes" to talk about the company's initiatives to improve the lives of millions of people around the world, apparently referring to a prepared statement. Rogers rose to object, shouting from his seat in the auditorium that he wanted answers to his specific charges. Kent requested that Rogers sit down and listen: "Just like I listened to your question, you need to listen to my answer." The audience applauded. Kent then appeared to depart from his prepared statement to describe the company's positive relationship with Mexican government officials, noting that the president of Mexico had recently invited the company's board of directors to convene a meeting in Mexico. "We are one of the best social citizens in Mexico," Kent asserted. He concluded by reiterating his belief that all of Rogers's accusations were false and without merit. The audience again applauded.

Rogers continued to shout that Kent had not answered his questions, while Kent tried unsuccessfully to return to his prepared notes about workplace and human rights. At last, Kent pointed to Rogers, calling him "out of order" and warning him that if he did not sit down, then Kent would have to instruct security to "escort him out of this meeting." The exchange degenerated further. Rogers called Kent a liar. The audience booed. Kent proclaimed his pride in the work that the company does in Mexico and moved the meeting to the next item on the agenda.

There is much more to be said about this speech event—from how Rogers tried but was unable to set the frame of the interaction to how Kent in the end was forced to abandon a generic response about the company's do-good initiatives and instead say something in particular about the company's "social license" in Mexico. What struck me at the time, however, was how Rogers interrupted an event that was dedicated to celebrating brand Coca-Cola as a free-floating signifier by making visible the actual material conditions of producing and distributing cans and bottles of soft drinks. But only momentarily: Questioners are allowed just one opportunity to speak.

At the 2012 annual meeting of shareholders held again in Atlanta, headquarters of TCCC, Rogers once more confronted Kent. Rogers was called upon to ask the first question from the floor.[14] He repeated his demand that Kent acknowledge the company's wrongdoings in Mexico, and then asked about well-publicized charges of racial discrimination made by workers at two of the company's bottling facilities in New York City. The chime sounded three times during Rogers's statement.

Kent for his part stuck to a prepared statement, denying all allegations of fraudulent activities and criminal investigations in Mexico "full stop." He observed how year after year Rogers has made everything from "sensational claims" about Colombia to challenges about "the integrity of the ILO." He then named several admirers of the company's commitment to CSR: Secretary of State Hillary Clinton; Jacques Rogge, president of the International Olympic Committee; Carter Roberts, president and CEO of the World Wildlife Fund; President of Mexico Felipe Calderón; Melinda Gates, cochair and trustee of the Bill and Melinda Gates Foundation; and, finally, the rock star Bono. Kent brought the weight of TCCC's partnerships with both governments and NGOs (not to mention one activist celebrity) to bear upon the credibility of Ray Rogers and his campaign. The audience, full of local employees of TCCC, burst into sustained applause. What had once been an unscripted confrontation between two adversaries had devolved into a stage-managed annual rite of spring with little capacity for surprise.

The Prospects for Consumer Citizenship in a Time of Postpolitical Governance

What are we to make of these partnerships—alliances that function as reference points for marketing forms of green and ethical consumption to individual consumers and enhancing corporate reputations for social responsibility?

One response, which usually comes from the political left, would be to accuse the NGOs of selling out. Take, for example, the reaction of the noted scholar of food and nutrition Marion Nestle to the partnership between Oxfam America and TCCC. In a post to her blog Food Politics titled "The Latest Oxymoron: Oxfam Helps Coca-Cola Reduce Poverty," Nestle writes: "I keep arguing that partnerships and alliances with food corporations put agriculture, food, nutrition and public health advocacy groups in deep conflict of interest."[15] She complains that the Oxfam report said nothing about the nonnutritional value of sugary soft drinks and argues that the $3 million contribution from TCCC that Oxfam gets in this bargain comes at "the cost of serious questions about the credibility of its report and its independence."

Oxfam's director of private sector development responded to Nestle, claiming that his organization has a responsibility to engage with global corporations and that such engagement does not compromise the organization's independence. Nestle's reply was unequivocal: "The goal of Coca-Cola is to sell more Coca-Cola. The goal of Oxfam is to address world poverty. I'm having trouble understanding how these goals could be mutually compatible."[16] Or as Michele Simon, a blog poster sympathetic to Nestle's point of view puts it:

> The only way to truly hold corporations accountable is through a little system we call The Law. But Coca-Cola and SABMiller are happy [to] let Oxfam take the place of a legal system because they know it can't work. History tells us so. It's rather audacious for an NGO to think they can hold anyone accountable, let alone a multinational corporation the size of Coca-Cola. We don't expect NGOs to ensure criminals don't rob people. We have a legal system for that. Why should corporations be any different?[17]

Nestle's perspective implies that NGOs should not be assisting or legitimizing corporations that are in the last analysis bound to follow the imperatives of the market rather than the demands of public health. Taken further, as in Simon's blog post, this perspective implies that only state agencies ought to regulate corporations; corporate self-regulation or regulation by selected NGOs is if not utopian then at least antidemocratic. CSR is at best a distraction (see Reich 2008) and at worst an excuse for paradoxical partnerships of the sort that allowed McDonald's and PepsiCo along with several public health NGOs to help write UK government policy on crises such as obesity and diet-related disease (Lawrence 2010).

Simon's position has merit even if it "overestimates the integrity of the political process" inasmuch as it highlights the "fundamental corporate interest in maximizing public distrust of government" (Bashkow forthcoming). But it also obscures the extent to which people rely on the market—on corporate assets—to pursue what must be regarded as a political aim, namely, the creation of a space for productive self-realization. How could it be otherwise in a mass-consumer society (see Miller 1987, 1988)? As I have argued, brand management stimulates the production of social relations (in the form of brand communities, for example) and offers consumers the material means and symbolic media for self-fashioning. From this perspective, partnerships appear even more sinister. Partnerships brandize NGOs; that is, partnerships treat NGOs as brands (as assets built partly out of consumption work) and then subsume these brands under the corporate brand, consequently increasing the value of the corporate brand and generating revenue for shareholders. NGOs—to which Edelman (2001) referred as "the new super brands"—do not merely legitimize corporations; they function as a source of surplus value for corporations.

But perhaps this claim, in turn, obscures the extent to which the interface between market life and civic life might provide a space for new political possibilities—for bringing the ethical standards of community life to bear upon neoliberal market values. Arvidsson (2009), for example, entertains the possibility of evaluating corporate actions in terms of their contribution to "affectively positive relations" among various stakeholders. Indeed, it is precisely such public evaluations, circulated rapidly through evolving social media, about which Interbrand warns and advises its clients and which already factor into the calculation of brand value. Arvidsson imagines a similar but open-access, negotiated, and user-led ethical rating system that could monitor and discipline corporations much as Moody's or Standard and Poor's financial strength ratings do now:

> As you sweep your phone over a sweater in the store, you might get immediate ratings of its environmental sustainability, the extent to which its production process has respected worker rights or unfolded according to particular religious concerns, generated by people positioned all along its global production chain. The emergence of such global public spheres following the "global assembly lines" that most brands now employ will significantly shift the power balance back from capital over to consumers, workers and other stakeholders. It will be very difficult for brands to claim the moral high-ground...without this being reflected in reality, if every such claim can be rated by virtually everybody concerned in ways that are easily accessible and immediately visible. (2009: 25–26)

The upshot of such an ethical reality check would of course not be a revolution, but perhaps progressive reform toward greater social responsibility.[18]

The promise of complete transparency and commodity defetishization offered here is utopian. It would require only a modest leap of faith, however, to accept Arvidsson's claim that definition of a new value standard might nudge "capitalism in a more ethical, 'blended value' direction: a sort of global New Deal organized around sustainability and corporate social responsibility" (2009: 27). Even so, the metaphor identifies the problem; after all, the New Deal was initiated and supervised by the U.S. government. And it is precisely such oversight that partnerships like that between TCCC and the WWF serve to preempt, at least in the view of an Interbrand report on the benefits of corporate citizenship published in the wake of the U.S. presidential elections and the financial crisis of 2008:

> There is tremendous potential upside to initiating positive social responsibility programs. With a return to increased government regulation a real possibility, and the public's awareness of corporations' environmental impact peaking, sustainability measures will help cut business costs and demonstrating willingness to self-police may forestall more aggressive regulation. (Zara 2009: 3)

The limits of such voluntary sustainability measures are demonstrated by the ironic story of the bottle-to-bottle recycling plant that TCCC opened in 2009 in Spartanburg, South Carolina. After investing about $60 million in the much-hyped facility, the company has considered selling its 49 percent stake in the joint-venture recycling business. Why? Not enough recycled, bottle-grade PET (polyethylene terephthalate) to meet the company's goals. (In fact, there was about half as much recycled content in the company's plastic PET bottles in 2011 than the previous five years). There are several reasons for this short supply, but both the *Wall Street Journal* (Esterl 2011) and *Plastics Today* (Goldsberry 2011) point to one major cause: the success of the soft drink industry and its resourceful lobbyists to prevent the enactment of container deposit laws in most of the United States. The company decided to source its recycled bottles *only* from states without such container deposit laws. But these bottles—often recycled at curbsides along with newspapers and other plastics or just thrown away in the trash—were too dirty to be used without the major cost of cleaning and a major change in the technology for processing the bottles. The company's very success at forestalling government regulation has contributed to its inability to self-police.

Conclusion: Discursive Paralysis

Like the Coca-Cola recycling plant, the corporate–NGO partnerships that sometimes underwrite eco-chic bring together incongruous elements. Consider, for example, this improbably sounding partnership. In 2007, Conservation International and Fiji Water announced a partnership aimed at making the designer bottled water company "carbon negative." Already chic, Fiji Water was to be made eco-friendly.

What does it take to make such a counterintuitive alliance seem plausible? I suggest that an answer can be found in the response of Glenn Prickett, a Conservation International senior vice president, when asked if green groups should endorse bottled water: "That nation is going to find something to ship out of Fiji. It could be logs or an industrial product. We'd much rather see it be a clean product that is produced with renewable energy." Prickett similarly claimed: "Maybe it would be morally preferable to carry a bottle I filled at the tap, but bottled water is a consumer reality. So rather than operate in a moralistic framework, we'll use the economy as it exists to make a difference" (Deutsch 2007).

There is an assumption of inevitability in these comments and a resigned assertion that clean bottled water is at least better than some dirty industrial product. Such is the discourse of harm reduction, a discourse that includes what Benson and Kirsch (2010a) have called "corporate oxymorons" (see also Benson and Kirsch 2010b). Corporate oxymorons are a prominent feature of CSR talk. Clean coal. Safe cigarettes. Sustainable mining. The first term deflects attention from the harmful implications of the second, "suggesting that some degree of corporate harm is ordinary, acceptable, and perhaps even necessary" (Benson and Kirsch 2010a: 48). To make sense of corporate oxymorons, one must entertain two contradictory beliefs; and in so doing, one becomes vulnerable to the sort of resignation exemplified in Conservation International's position as well as to the cynicism that the organization's partnership with Fiji Water predictably elicited.

Like corporate oxymorons, eco-chic partnerships produce discursive paralysis: the inability to formulate and articulate an alternative version of things. The effect is similar to that which Michael Schudson (1984) famously associated with advertising, namely, capitalist realism. Advertising does not work by persuading us to buy things that we do not want. On the contrary, advertisements promote a sort of ironic detachment by not obliging us to believe their statements literally. Instead, advertising works by making natural a hedonistic, self-centered view of the world, one in which "people are encouraged to think of themselves and their private worlds" instead of public or collective values (Schudson 1984: 221).

Eco-chic likewise promotes a particular view of the world, one in which public or collective values are invoked, but to be pursued only through small voluntary changes in individual consumption practices. It is a world in which the win-win solutions epitomized by corporate–NGO partnerships do the social work formerly done by states acting in the name of citizens. Indeed, states and citizen groups do not inhabit this world.

The threat of eco-chic, then, is not so much that anyone actually believes in it but, rather, that its proliferation, like that of advertising, will crowd out alternatives, other ways of seeing the world and imagining the future. This process is exactly what Rajak witnessed at the CSR conventions in which she was a participant-observer: "Compelling visions of global partnership in the service of local development have proved a particularly powerful tool for recruiting support from non-corporate actors, while marginalizing dissenters from the arenas in which these cosmopolitan alliances are forged" (2011: 16). These dissenters are then characterized as irrational because they eschew constructive dialogue, as when Neville Isdell (2007), promoting his vision of connected capitalism in the *Wall Street Journal,* observed: "a small minority of activists will always prefer confrontation, with its attendant publicity, to the search for mutually beneficial common ground." The arenas in which critics like Ray Rogers can engage corporate officers are becoming fewer, although the Occupy Wall Street actions in 2011 perhaps demonstrated that new arenas can be made.

The challenge for both academics and citizens wishing to harness the potential of political consumerism, therefore, requires not only reforming capitalism "in a more ethical, 'blended value' direction," as Arvidsson (2009: 27) suggests. Greater accountability on the part of corporations and individuals is surely welcome, but more ethical consumption and CSR are not enough. The challenge is also to imagine how to push in other directions, to find political as well as economic alternatives that depart from the logic of capitalist markets and that promise a form of social justice resembling something other than a handbag made out of discarded Coca-Cola labels.

Acknowledgments

I thank Rivke Jaffe and Bart Barendregt for inviting me to participate in the European Science Foundation research conference on eco-chic and for their helpful comments on this chapter. I also thank Emeco for permission to use the image of the 111 Navy Chair. Material support for research drawn on in this paper has been provided by the National Endowment for the Humanities and the University of Rochester.

–3–

Peopling the Practices of Sustainable Consumption: Eco-Chic and the Limits to the Spaces of Intention

Raymond L. Bryant and Michael K. Goodman

Sustainable consumption—as one of the defining forms and processes of eco-chic and green consumption—is gaining favor in the Global North as consumers increasingly vote with their shopping carts. For example, the fusing of citizenship, politics, and consumption has helped to generate a UK market for ethical goods worth nearly $72 billion in 2011, despite the continuing recession (*The Guardian* 2012). Yet, debate has been sparked here. For some (Barnett et al. 2005), this is encouraging: consumers are acting politically without having to think too deeply about their effects on people or the planet and as a part of other political repertoires like protesting and boycotting. Yet, consumers of commodities like fair-trade coffee or organic tomatoes are located in situations distinguished by their enviable ability to govern themselves (Goodman et al. 2010) at the same time their eco-chic purchases are working to "save" poor Others and the planet. Care-full shopping choices are thus made, albeit only thanks to the toil of producers and networks of transnational regulatory regimes. Consuming these goods—so the argument goes—not only allows the purchaser to engage with specific movements associated with these items, but, when atomized buying is aggregated, the magic of a broader consumer politics is also realized through market-mediated change. Others disagree, pointing out that the politics of choice are not only historically and geographically contingent, but also unequal and unpredictably voluntary (Bryant and Goodman 2004; Guthman 2007). Either way, there has been little work engaged in either "peopling" or exploring the practices of sustainable consumption and the growing networks of eco-chic.

This chapter is an attempt to begin to rectify this absence and to do so in a particular way. Here, using three cases, we wish to explore the tension-filled practices of the production of eco-chic goods as well as the consumption of some of these goods in the expanding middle classes of parts of the Global South; in telling us something important about the embedded materialities, power relations, and distinction-laden aspects of eco-chic and sustainable consumption, we hope not only to build on related and parallel work (e.g., Freidberg 2003; Mutersbaugh 2002; Sirieix et al. 2011; Wilson 2010), but also to do so through novel theoretical and conceptual means. In this, we use the idea of the *spaces of intention* that stitch together the sites of production and consumption in eco-chic, sustainable consumption as they work to connect relatively affluent consumers to poor(er), marginal producers. Directing us to fully contextualize the production and consumption networks of eco-chic in both time and space—thus, really asking for a shift from eco-chic to eco-social-chic—these spaces of intention are thus linked into more relationally related *networks of intention* that work to produce novel geographies of hope, care, and responsibility. Here, these networks of the spaces of intention can be specific to particular commodities or classes of items, such as fair trade, organic, and the like, or, at a more macrolevel, they can be combined into the wider landscapes of eco-chic and sustainable consumption that circulate as consumer-led cultural politics of capitalism designed to make better worlds.

Yet, our specific interest in this chapter lies in understanding what these spaces may mean and how they operate—in short, how they are *peopled* and *practiced*—in an exceedingly unequal, market-driven world. For us, a key aspect of the spaces of intention is that these spaces assume a drawing of borders that exclude people and knowledge even as they define new networks and communities of the like-minded. Yet exclusionary practices may lead to paradox inasmuch as communities are based on unclear intentions. This chapter assesses selected exclusionary practices—with reference to the production spaces of Costa Rica and Mexico and the consumption spaces of Malaysia—to highlight some ethical ambiguities and limits to sustainable consumption, market-led sustainability, and, more broadly, eco-chic. We hope to contribute to a critical literature that debates the meaning and utility of alternative market-driven solutions to contemporary problems—a literature that does not simply view these spaces of intention as arenas of economic, political, and affective opportunity but ones embedded with tensions and relations of power, class, contingencies, and histories.

The chapter is organized as follows. First it outlines what we see as the spaces of intention in the complicated and ambiguous arenas where the material and discursive connections between and among eco-chic consumers and producers are constructed and made real. Here we suggest that the drawing of borders and boundaries in these spaces— necessary in demarcating spaces and creating eco-chic markets—leads to exclusionary practices as much as novel networks of the spaces of intention. The chapter then considers the productionist exclusionary practices from research done in Costa Rica and Mexico and consumerist exclusionary practices from Malaysia. The conclusion then assesses the overall utility and prospects for and eco-chic consumer- and market-driven reformist politics or progress and livelihood betterment.

The Production of the Spaces (and Networks) of Intention in Eco-Chic

The sustainable consumption sector is predicated on the production of spaces of intentions that give it meaning and purpose. These spaces combine discourses and material practices, while linking together far-flung people and places to produce distinctive, if changeable, and always multiple, ways of seeing and doing.

A variety of elements go into the making of spaces of intentions. First, this process involves epistemic collusions—a coming together of people and groups around a basic set of ethically based knowledge claims that seek to establish the facts in a given domain. These include such things as the need to reduce the human impact on the environment via less harmful organic agriculture, the quest to tackle rural poverty through fairer trade, or (in historical times) the imperative to eliminate slavery. The word *collusions* is important here. Unlike the epistemic communities described by Haas (1991), which tend to suggest a more settled and predictable pattern of interaction, we privilege the perpetual contingency and ambiguity of the epistemological foundations of spaces of intentions. And yet, the great achievement of these epistemic collusions is that they enable an analytical and problem-solving set of practices to occur in the first place.

Second, spaces of intentions encompass reflexivity-in-action on the part of the diverse participants involved in the sector—be they producers, consumers, retailers, and so on. The degree of reflexivity naturally varies from person to person and group to group but helps to inform positionality in the process. The latter is not, however, purely or simply about crude function (e.g., I am a consumer, you are a producer), but also includes self-awareness of the special roles that the different actors play therein—producing quality goods or paying premium prices, for instance. Still, the conclusions that actors derive from the reflexive act can also vary dramatically, notably combining what James Scott (1990) has called in a different context public and hidden transcripts—discourses that are publicly admissible or not in light of their anticipated reception. At the same time, multifaceted and multi-actor reflexivity can be held in check by the general commitment to action. Because something must be urgently done (about this or that problem), there is a tendency to ring-fence the potential for paralyzing anarchy that might follow from a proliferation of reflexive acts among participants. Nonetheless, tensions persist here.

Third, spaces of intentions require affective ordering as distant strangers develop selective and prioritized affective bonds. This is often centered on a normative sense of injustice that is directly experienced or otherwise witnessed in social and/or socioecological relations. Emotions play a big role here (Held 2006; Pile 2010). Thus, caring at a distance is anchored by such things as empathy, joy, and anger in complicated emotional geographies (McEwan and Goodman 2010; Smith 2000). These geographies help in turn to overcome or at least contextualize differences among participants involved in building spaces of intentions. Affective bonds thus help to stitch together spaces of intentions that link people and groups who have often never met—and will probably never do so. At the same time, volatility in the emotions and commitments of participants (who after all live in a wider world marked by conflicting needs) suggests once again that ambiguity remains at the heart of the production of these spaces.

Fourth, there are space-making activities that involve the crafting of new forms of spatial understanding to overcome existing spatial barriers to effective action. On the one hand, there is the peopling of space through the identification of specific, special individuals involved in production and consumption through product advertising, regulatory boundaries, and the like. This activity directly challenges spatial anomie in the market through the personification of space. On the other hand, there is the creation of place in space—through the identification of specific, special locations involved in production and consumption. This activity challenges spatial distanciation by increasing awareness among participants of how seemingly empty space is in fact populated by unique places throughout the alternative sector (Barnett et al. 2005). Through peopling and place-making activities, spaces of intentions thus take on a personality of their own—in a manner of speaking, they become warm and enlivened.

Finally, and perhaps most contentiously, spaces of intention necessitate the production of borders. Without some sense of what (people, processes, things, knowledge, etc.) is inside rather than outside a given space, it becomes all but impossible to even speak of a specific space. Most work on borders has focused on their deployment around the "imagined communities" (Anderson 1991) and "containers" (Taylor 1994) that are called the "nation-state" (Flint and Taylor 2007). Beyond debates over the geopolitical nature and role of borders in relation to (inter)state action, work has probed how borders help to define both collective and personal identity (Newman and Paasi 1998). Yet such identification is complex, contradictory, and contingent—especially in light of processes of neoliberalization and globalization that render borders simultaneously less and more important.[1] In a world of "overlapping" sovereignties and territorialities, the meanings that attach to borders change even as their utility as a means of delimiting and regulating "inside" from "outside" is debated (Storey 2001; Walker 1990). Still, the production of borders inevitably and centrally revolves around specifying what is excluded as well as what is included in a particular space. In any given time and place, therefore, certain opportunities are opened up for some people even as selected opportunities are closed down for other people.

The various elements that go into the creation of spaces of intentions all seek in various ways to fix social understanding and identity in relation to interconnected meanings of space and intention—the better to channel the energy of participants into achieving alternative sector ends (eliminating poverty, cleaning up agriculture, etc.). Yet this is in many respects a Sisyphean task—a point that becomes clear when considering the inescapably dynamic and differentiated nature of these spaces and their connected networks.

Spaces of intentions differ in important ways from each other depending on the nature of the alternative sector to which they are attached. Indeed, there is a continuum of these spaces ranging from the diffuse at the one end to the concentrated at the other end—with relative density notably contingent on the complexity of the issues involved. On the whole, more concentrated spaces of intentions seem to be easier ones in which to achieve progress toward goals than more diffuse spaces are. Thus, in the nineteenth century, the antislavery movement encompassed a boycott campaign of slave produce (sugar, cotton) exported from the Caribbean and the United States (Sheller 2001) that represents a good example of concentrated spaces. Here both the immediate target (undermine income that slave owners derived from slave produce) and the ultimate end (abolish slavery) were fairly tightly defined and hence relatively straightforward to act on. In contrast, the fair-trade campaign is an example of diffuse spaces of intentions precisely because the chosen tool (fair trade) is rather modest in comparison to the sheer complexity of the desired outcome (ending poverty through trade), and insofar as fair trade is only one part of the overall trading relations and economic commitments of poor participants. Worse, poverty itself has deep noneconomic (as well as economic) roots—implicating a series of political and cultural processes that fair trade has little hope of changing in and of itself. In this regard, fighting poverty (via fair-trade spaces of intentions) is somewhat akin to the battle against climate change (diffuse and relatively intractable), just as the historical example of combating slavery is reminiscent of the struggle over ozone depletion (concentrated and relatively manageable). From this perspective, the problem for many contemporary spaces of intentions (fair trade, organic agriculture) may well thus be precisely that they are diffuse in character—and hence can be more difficult to resolve than their concentrated counterparts.

A good measure of the dynamism associated with spaces of intentions relates to the different ways in which people enact their roles therein. One particular source of tension relates to the individualistic as opposed to collective tendencies in a given alternative sector. Thus, a notable feature in many such spaces is the prominent role of collectives and social movements in their operation. These include producer cooperatives (e.g., fair-trade coffee), as well as nongovernmental organizations (NGOs) and social movements (e.g., Oxfam) that find collective action most efficacious in achieving ends for reasons that might include economic efficiency or political security or even have an ideological basis. Yet, this needs to be set against the strong individualistic streak typically found in many of these spaces as they pursue social change in part through the market. Especially among consumers (but also often among producers), individualism is the leitmotif of action—even when such action is informed by the potentially unifying elements of space making noted above (e.g., reflexivity-in-action, epistemic collusion, affective ordering). These divergent tendencies need not work against each other, but there is always the possibility that they might—leading to a general dissipation of people's energy when they do so.

Because spaces of intentions typically involve unequal relations of power, they are also often characterized by cooperation and conflict. That conflict among participants in these spaces is the norm should hardly surprise. For one thing, all of the elements noted above that go into the creation of spaces of intentions are potential minefields, where both the subjective interpretations of actors and the (sometimes) unintended consequences of their actions are common. For another thing, the sheer number of people and groups involved (especially in diffuse sorts of spaces) represents a potential logistical nightmare, even when such things as fair prices (for producers), quality standards (for buyers), and fair premiums (paid by consumers) are sorted out.

Indeed, the unequal power relations that are embedded into all spaces of intentions point more generally to a potential dark side to this sector. First, there is the way in which individuals or groups that lead in defining these spaces embed their own interests and concerns at the heart of the process—interests and concerns that may not be shared by all others involved. The material and discursive construction of these spaces is never neutral as it reflects the political, economic, and cultural beliefs of those who construct them. Moreover, the construction process may have unintended consequences that are ethically dubious. For example, the codes of conduct and labeling schemes that are an important part of the sector may provide a sense of security and sanctioned knowledge for some, even while enhancing the insecurity of others left marginalized under this system. The path of good intentions can be littered with unintended victims of eco-chic.

A second issue relates to the ways in which the malleable nature of these spaces of intentions can lead to their appropriation by individuals or groups who may use them in ways not intended (or desired) by those involved in their initial construction. Here, the ambiguous quality of human intentions comes to the fore—something that was first hinted at in our earlier discussion of epistemic collusion among participants. Such intentions are multifaceted. For instance, scholars note how those seen acting on behalf of others may be simultaneously pursuing their own self-interest—the two are not mutually exclusive (Bryant 2005). People's intentions can also be duplicitous—either intentions are not what they seem or declared intentions mask nondeclared intentions. This pattern of behavior combining public and hidden transcripts may reflect wider changes in human conduct in an era of liquid modernity in which flexible personal and group identity formation is the norm (Baumann 2000).

A final issue is how spaces of intentions fare when opponents hit back. There is already the dilution effect—a process whereby mainstream firms clamber on the alternative bandwagon in a process that all but drains that alternative of meaning. Other techniques may be deployed to take advantage of the fissiparous tendencies of alternative sectors and their associated spaces of intentions. For instance, there is a standard strategy of seeking to drive a wedge between (often) Southern-based producers and (still frequently) Northern-based consumers, taking advantage wherever possible of residual mutual ignorance in the sector that is related to space distanciation.

The discussion so far has defined what spaces of intentions are, as well as some of the key dynamics and tensions that inform them, in relation to sustainable consumption and eco-chic more broadly. We next turn to a comparative empirical exploration of contemporary spaces that underpin the sustainable consumption sector. In doing so, we seek to assess both how these spaces of intentions work in general and how contention is often at the heart of their operation in particular. While not the only aspect under investigation, this is notably achieved by focusing on the role that exclusion plays in their working, beginning with those spaces of intentions linked to the places of production of eco-chic goods in Costa Rica and Mexico.

Practicing Eco-Chic: Ironies, Power, and Exclusions in the Places of Sustainable Consumption Production

Much is often made in the alternative sustainable consumption sector of the need to render as transparent as possible processes of production and consumption typically hidden in conventional market activity. Indeed, this transparency provides the basis—informational and imaginary (see Goodman 2004)—that lets consumers articulate their ethical-ness in the relatively comfy confines of the postindustrial North. Yet how do these spaces of intention—and here we refer to fair trade—operate? What is left out of these narratives and who or what is left out of the material networks that form the basis for the articulation of ethical subjects and spaces? Much work on sustainable and ethical consumption is only really engaged in telling one side of the story—that is, the happy and consumerist angle. Indeed, ethical consumption might well be

> a *political* phenomenon … [and] one that deploys the register of "ethics" and "responsibility" in pursuit of some classically political objectives: collective mobilisation, lobbying, and claims-making. … [I]n these campaigns consumption is emphatically not understood simply in terms of a "neoliberal" problematic of markets, exchange and choice. Rather, it is understood in terms that link material modes of consumption to the transformation of broader systems and social relations of production, distribution and trade. (Clarke et al. 2007: 246; emphasis in original)

And yet, it is exactly the problematic of markets, exchange, and choice—that is, the realities of doing ethical business at multiple scales—that mold spaces of intention in ambiguous and politicized ways, especially in relation to sites of production. Thus, we suggest the need for more detailed research in this regard—involving a more rounded peopling of alternative networks—to yield insights on the ethical tensions and limits to caring at a distance.

Bounding Quality and People in Costa Rican Fair-Trade Cacao

One key factor that renders our understanding of spaces of intention more complex is the exclusionary practices of knowledge and taste that underpin them yet which sit uncomfortably with lofty network aims. Take product quality—an issue that has long been an overriding concern in the alternative market. This is certainly clear in fair trade (Bacon 2005; Renard 2005)—dogged as it is by a reputation for goods that taste horrible, look poor, and appear unfashionably hippie. As with sustainability standards in general, the exigencies of good taste have livelihood consequences even for producers in socially just markets. Thus, the creation of spaces of intention is party to processes of neoliberal disciplining and associated exclusion—according to quality and taste—that reflect a reliance on market-based approaches. As such, these spaces are bounded entities—not open-ended meeting points for action-at-a-distance (Barnett et al. 2005: 29). The example of fair trade and organic cacao networks in Costa Rica considered here underscores the ethical ambiguities and limits to spaces of intention as aspirations about product quality entail that some marginal producers end up excluded.

Indeed, in a cruel irony, demand for top quality in fair trade and other alternative networks has had the unintended effect of sometimes leaving the poorest and most marginal producers on the outside of these networks (Lyon and Moberg 2010; Moberg 2005). This is a variation on the barriers-to-entry theme that Guthman (2007) in particular has noted in work on organic foods, farming, and labeling.

This quality problem is neatly exemplified in what happened during a recruiting mission run by the Asociación de Pequeños Productores de Talamanca (APPTA) in the

Talamanca region of Costa Rica several years ago, which is located near the northern Panamanian boarder and the Bri Bri Indigenous reserve. This cooperative sought to build up its exports of organic bananas and cacao by inducting new member-farmers. With this aim in mind, the mission interviewed candidates in the mountains near San Clemente above the lowland banana plantations run by Chiquita. As one of us recoded in his field notes:

> After one or two successful stops at some individual farms (where new members were enrolled), we came to the settlement of one particular family which was studded with sweeping views of the Caribbean, two sets of cacao-drying racks, a small amount of land and the basic wooden-slatted buildings in which they lived. After the usual greetings, [one of the members of APPTA] shoved his hand into a bag of cacao that had come from the surrounding farm, while the other went off with the farmer to have a look at his production facilities. As the farmer left, [the APPTA member who stayed behind] turned to me with a rather bleak look and, after popping a bit of dried cacao into his mouth for a quick taste, shook his head. Curious, I asked him what the matter was; his reply was simple: 'Poor quality and taste'. The implication was that this very poor farmer would continue to be left to his own devices until the quality of his cacao improved, at which time there might be room for him in the cooperative. Interestingly, the next and final farmer visited by the recruiting mission that day—up the mountain trail a bit further—received more of a favourable reaction for both his cacao and bananas and so would become a member of the cooperative then and there.

In short, the natural capital (soil quality, drainage, etc.) that largely determines the quality of goods in alternative networks such as this one in Costa Rica is unequally distributed among poor farmers who are themselves socially and economically differentiated. Such inequality then helps to determine, in turn, the boundaries of inclusion and exclusion that define spaces of intention. There is a symmetry involved here: just as inequalities of wealth help determine who consumes eco-chic commodities, so too inequalities of wealth help decide who will produce goods of sufficient quality to enter alternative networks.

Such exclusionary practices are the norm. Thus, the head of a key fair-trade certification agency in the North remarked that "this was indeed the way things worked" in a market-based approach (personal communication 2003). Indeed, in recognition of the importance of quality goods to the mainstreaming of fair trade, the Fairtrade Labelling Organisations International (FLO)—international housekeeper of fair-trade standards and certification located in Bonn, Germany—has belatedly introduced a program designed to boost production quality in marginal cooperatives.

There is, too, the question of the uneven playing field that producer cooperatives encounter as they struggle to make their mark in fair trade. Thus, the cooperatives involved in this market (particularly those in the coffee and chocolate industries) are not created equal. Many of the most successful cooperatives such as CONACADO in the Dominican Republic and Kuapa Kokoo in Ghana—both leaders in organic cacao production and export—have had substantial organizational support through early NGO involvement from GTZ and Twin Trading, respectively. This is to detract neither from their success nor from their immense efforts to make themselves commercially viable. It is also not to deny the invaluable support that these organizations provide to the livelihoods and welfare of members.

Rather, this is to recognize four characteristics of the yet further bounded nature of fair trade that amount to a powerful set of exclusionary practices:[2] (1) the fundamental importance of early technical and economic support from international NGOs that assists producer cooperatives to enter the market, often at the expense of other unassisted cooperatives; (2) the competitive state of the market means that new cooperatives find themselves at a strong disadvantage as late entrants to a field in which better-established cooperatives dominate; (3) a de facto barrier to entry that requires each cooperative to pay a $3,500 fee to FLO before it can be registered as a fair-trade supplier—a fee that falls hardest on the poorest cooperatives; and (4) the fact that cooperatives must show evidence of a buyer for their products before they can be put on FLO's list of cooperatives—another administrative measure that sifts out the least well connected and/or business savvy. Thus, fierce competition as well as new pricing structures and access requirements erect entry barriers to these spaces of intention that cast doubt on the perception of these spaces as an unmitigated ethical good.

Evidence drawn from Costa Rica thus suggests a strong need *not* to take the claims—or indeed theorizations—made in the sustainable consumption sector at face value. Our point is not to dismiss either the material importance or ethical significance of this sector. Rather, it is to argue that critical analysis must explore the actual practices associated with these spaces of intention by peopling them. Indeed, at a time when the harsh fluorescence of the capitalist market illuminates and seemingly molds behavior around the world to an unparalleled degree, such analysis is essential. Clearly, the possibilities of an ethics of care through consumption at-a-distance might be tempered by the bounded-ness evident in not only the standards and certification regimes that govern these products, but also the penchant of neoliberal influenced policies to use the invisible hand of the market against the most vulnerable. This is not trivial: Gibson-Graham's (2006) "diverse" or "proliferative economies"—of which fair trade and organic production might be central in Southern contexts—work for some poor individuals and groups but not for others. This is no accident, because there are particular historical and economic reasons for inclusion and exclusion, which may or may not (be seen to) be "fair." The "spaces of hope" (Lawson 2005) opened up by novel ethical/sustainable geographies of care need to meet the tastes and preferences of those gatekeepers who mediate entry into new consumer markets for these spaces even to operate at all.

Excluding the Powerful in Mexico

That spaces of intention are seen to represent new ways of doing things based on market-based alternative practices. Yet, as noted, work on sustainable consumption has begun to underscore the pitfalls of this approach to reforming global capitalism. One problem relates to the ambiguities and contradictions that occur as an effort is made to embed new spaces of intention in producing regions where the desperately poor are numerous and existing ways of doing things based on powerful and highly inequitable local political economies are entrenched. Here, we take the example of a traditional product for which there appears to be an emerging global market—*chicle* or natural chewing gum—and explore how efforts to link it to new sustainable production and trading arrangements on behalf of poor producers living in the high forests of the Yucatan Peninsula in Mexico met with resistance from those who would be thereby excluded from this sector.

The creation of a space of intention around natural chewing gum reflected a complex history ripe with political, economic, and cultural meaning. The mass production of chewing gum was, until the 1950s, dominated by chicle, a latex-like substance extracted from the resin of the *chicozapote* tree, found mainly in the tropical forests of Mexico and Guatemala (Redclift 2004). Thereafter, chewing gum was produced synthetically—largely from hydrocarbons, derived from a form of vinyl. Its history as a natural forest product appeared then to be over even as the ranks of forest producers began to dissipate. However, natural chicle is now making a comeback. Indeed, it is attractive to Northern consumers wishing to combine a taste for gum with ethical support for fair trade and organic products.

Natural, chicle-based gum is thus now available on the Web, where the customer is told (in the case of the company Glee Gum) that it is an "all natural chewing gum made from sustainably harvested rainforest chicle." Such gum also comes with Co-op America's Business Seal of Approval, which "helps consumers identify and support socially responsible companies that have been screened and approved by Co-op America." This seal of approval is designed to show customers that there is a firm commitment on the part of businesses, such as Glee Gum, to uphold the highest production standards.[3] The benefits of such commendation include listing in Co-op America's Green Business Pages, "the national honor roll of socially responsible companies." Companies are screened to establish their green credentials, following which, if they are approved, they can advertise using the Co-op America logo.

A similar product, Jungle Gum, is advertised on the Raintree website's online store whose products, it is there claimed, are "extensively documented, thoroughly researched and unconditionally guaranteed."[4] The consumer is invited into a veritable Aladdin's cave of ethical, sustainably sourced products, all of which come from tropical rainforests (Fedick 2003). Material is presented on both sites about the history of the *chicleros* (or chicle tappers), who built empires for corporations such as Wrigley's and Thomas Adams in the early twentieth century—firms that grew fantastically wealthy by establishing chewing gum as an iconic, global product. However, the recent development of commercial chicle has a darker history than that presented on such websites, oriented as they are to sales to Northern consumers. This history supports our wider analysis of the ethical ambiguities and limits of sustainable consumption—and its (at times) quite tenuous links to a spatial politics of intention for producers.

The commercialization of Mexican chicle became a key function of diverse federations of chicle cooperatives, the first of which was founded in Quintana Roo in 1937. These federations were strict hierarchies linked closely to the Mexican State; indeed, no sale could be made without authorization from the federation president. It was not until 1978 that the presidents of chicle cooperatives and federations were elected democratically. However, even this step did not end state intervention. Thus, the entire national production of chicle was sold through one export company—the Impulsadora y Exportadora Nacional (IMPEXNAL)—a branch of the Banco Nacional de Comercio Exterior (National Foreign Trade Bank). This monopoly was created through a government law, which exempted IMPEXNAL from paying export taxes. For the producers, it was thus impossible to influence the prices that they were paid. As such, most revenue (and profit) was retained by IMPEXNAL.

The declining importance of chicle in the latter half of the twentieth century (when synthetic gums were dominant) led the federal government to lose interest in this sector, providing thereby an opening for producers to seek a better deal for themselves. A case in point is the Union of Chicle Cooperatives that has sought to deal directly with manufacturers of chewing gum. Yet this goal has been difficult to attain as powerful interests fight exclusion from these sustainable consumption networks.

Thus, former managers of IMPEXNAL directed foreign buyers to a new company, Mexitrade, set up in the wake of the unraveling of IMPEXNAL. This new firm was also closely linked to the state. Not surprisingly, buyers were initially reluctant to buy from the Union, especially because former IMPEXNAL managers had strongly advised them to buy from Mexitrade. Such state-linked economic practice is common in Mexico (Banister 2007)

The Union initially then had no choice but to sell to Mexitrade and accept their prices. Thus, although production of chicle varied markedly above and below an average of 395 tons per annum in the mid-1990s, the price that the Union received from Mexitrade changed little. Indeed, between 1999 and 2002, the price remained the same, irrespective of international demand during that period. Frustrated by this situation, the Union of Chicle Cooperatives looked to bypass Mexitrade. There was some success here in 1998 when the Union completed direct negotiations with Wild Things (an organic chewing gum manufacturer from the United States), as well as with Mitsuba (an intermediary that sells chicle to Japanese manufacturers). Mexitrade's control over chicle began to slip.

However, powerful state-linked interests behind Mexitrade did not take kindly to this effort to thereby exclude them. The fight back began almost immediately. This involved a campaign against the Union based on a counterexclusionary practice: an enhanced bureaucratic burden for producers working through the Union and strong financial incentives for individuals who defected from the Union scheme through illegal smuggling of chicle.

Opponents of the Union took advantage of the thick layers of bureaucratic red tape that were still involved in any effort to export goods—and, above all, their strong connections to those in government who controlled this process—to stymie Union deals. Indeed, there are an array of regulations and export licenses that have to be dealt with before legal shipping of chicle can proceed. These include an authorization of forest exploitation, a shipment authorization from the federal government, authorization from the state government, authorization to transport dried resin to storage houses, and even federal government requirements concerning reshipment of merchandise previously stored. In addition, there must be a report of transaction each time any part of a previously authorized quantity of chewing gum is shipped (all chicle is not usually transported at once).

To complicate things further, these procedures cannot be tackled directly by the Union or individual cooperatives. Instead, they are undertaken indirectly through the *comisario ejidal* (administrative authority of communal lands) that manages land on behalf of local communities. This arrangement reflects legislation on forest management that specifies that all *chicleros* in cooperatives must also be members of an *ejido*.[5] The chicozapote trees, from which chicle is tapped, are mainly located in *ejidal* forests, which are communally owned and managed by this ejidal authority. In keeping with these regulations, therefore, forest inspectors must go to the ejido to verify information contained in a report each time a document is handed in to this authority.

These bureaucratic procedures are difficult to meet at the best of times. However, when powerful groups linked to Mexitrade worked behind the scenes to drag out the process even further, then the capacity of the Union to make contracts and export chicle was diminished. During 2002–2003, for example, the Union could not meet new export orders received in relation to the Korean market. When Union managers explained the convoluted procedures they had to follow to win official approval for exports to their Korean counterparts, the latter thought it impossible that a government could act so plainly against the interests of its own exporters and hence accused the Union of commercial misconduct. The matter was eventually resolved. Yet this experience forced the Union to change marketing strategy. Given the administrative measures that it needed to fulfill, Union managers calculated that they could not accept orders for chicle beyond 900 tons a year—even though they could produce 2,000 tons per year.

High transaction costs associated with these measures only exacerbated Union woes. These costs include funds for a technical study of forest resources, stamp duty, fees for forest exploitation, and the transport permit fee. Then there are the regular operational costs of the cooperatives, which include contributions to member retirement funds as well as to the hospitalization and sickness fund through which chicleros access health services. Such costs are yet another burden that enhances the cost of Union chicle—leaving them vulnerable to attack.

The counterexclusionary campaign has thus encompassed illegal smuggling of chicle (known as *coyotaje*) in a move designed to undermine the Union's legal export program. This is a grave matter. Indeed, Union representatives (former chicleros) who liaise with the rank and file identify coyotaje as the biggest single threat to the Union. At the heart of this process are *coyotes*—individuals who tempt chicleros with a price superior to that offered by cooperatives. Coyotes can do so because they do not pay the routine costs that cooperatives incur and also smuggle chicle to Chetumal, on the border with Belize.

The smugglers found a ready ally in the disgruntled groups linked to Mexitrade. The latter would buy chicle from coyotes in Chetumal through intermediaries such as the PFSCA (Forest Products of Southeast Mexico and Central America). The PFSCA is mainly dedicated to the commercialization of hardwoods, but dabbles too with nontraditional forest products). This move reflected worsening relations between Mexitrade and the Union, especially after a fraught 1998–1999 season. Following the Asian crisis of the late 1990s, the purchase of natural gum from Asia dried up—a major blow because Asia was the largest market for Mexican chicle. Mexitrade, which had just bought chicle from the Union, but then found could not sell it in Asia, refused to pay for that order. The Union took Mexitrade to court over the matter and in response the latter refused to buy from the former, opting to work with PFSCA instead. Both coyotes and Mexitrade benefited from this illegal trade even as the original exclusionary practices of the Union backfired.

Yet the Union too has fought back. Thus, it slowly rebuilt its export links. It courted former business partners seeking to respond to their shifting requirements while working to improve delivery reliability. It also addressed the demand of firms (especially in Japan) for better quality via new processing techniques. Contracts followed with firms in Japan, Indonesia, Korea, and Italy. Meanwhile, efforts by the Union and affiliated cooperatives to woo back individual producers from the smugglers are paying off. Indeed, no chicleros have been forced to sell to coyotes recently (even if the threat of smuggling persists).

The effort by the Union of Chicle Cooperatives and its allies to control the production and export of chicle is small scale. Yet this effort is revealing in that it illustrates once again the important, if complex, role of boundaries in creating spaces of intention for sustainable consumption. In this case, the exclusion of powerful groups linked to the production and export business in Mexico achieved mixed results, in part due to the counterexclusionary measures pursued by those excluded by the Union. While it seems that the Union has been able to outcompete its opponents, at least for now, this situation could well change in the future as market conditions change and/or local opponents devise new ways to tap into the hopeful spaces that the Union seeks to embed in Mexico's traditionally unequal political economy. Inclusion—and exclusion—as with much else in these spaces of intention, is always a contingent phenomenon.

Excluding the Common Consumer in Malaysia

The creation of spaces of intention in which like-minded producers and consumers come together in the context of sustainable consumption suggests a unity of purpose that may not exist in practice. While producers are in the business of maximizing livelihoods, the role of consumers is far from clear—especially as alternative consumption practices appear in non-Northern countries. Critical work documents the sometimes ambiguous personal reasoning that informs the consumption choices of individuals in the North (e.g., Seyfang 2005). We pursue this critique further here by considering the possible relationship between the erection of barriers around spaces of intention and the slippery nature of middle-class consumer intention. We do so with a Malaysian example—a prospering Southern country where alternative consumption is only now beginning to make its mark.

In rapidly developing Malaysia (as in a number of other countries in the South), a prospering middle class is beginning to translate interlinked concerns about environmental degradation, healthy living, and general social well-being into a set of alternative practices linked to sustainable consumption (Hobson 2004). An entire industry is gearing up to cater to these concerns, drawing a new group of consumers into the alternative fold. Yet it is not clear that the intentions of this group are a mirror image of liberal intentions (however complex and ambiguous) often espoused in North America. The social and environmental circumstances under which Southern consumers (as in Malaysia) resort to sustainable consumption usually differ from conditions that existed when such consumption was pioneered in the North.

The rise of alternative sustainable consumption in Malaysia as a middle-class phenomenon is recent and still limited when compared (for instance) with neighboring Singapore.[6] Most of that growth has occurred since 2000. Typically, it is a practice that is most noticeable in urban areas, especially in the two biggest cities—Kuala Lumpur and George Town—located on the more developed and populous west coast of peninsular Malaysia. In George Town (a city of 400,000 inhabitants located on Penang Island), there were thus some half-dozen small organic shops in operation with most of them having opened their doors only several years ago. These were pioneering outfits—local supermarkets had yet to tap into the organic trend as has happened in the more mature markets of the North. Further, the decor and products were entirely pitched toward a middle-class clientele in one of Asia's most livable cities.

In the case of the Green Organics Mart, for example, the focus was on organic consumption as a source of healthy living with an array of expensive foodstuffs (e.g., coffee, tea, bread, juice, fresh fruit and vegetables) and health care products (including supplements) on offer. Products were sourced mainly from Kuala Lumpur with many originating in the United States and Australia. There was, too, an assortment of reading materials on personal well-being on hand for the discerning customer. Its location in a North American–style shopping complex in a relatively affluent area completed this picture of a middle-class refuge.

Organic shops such as Green Organics Mart form part of a wider pattern of middle-class concern emerging over wasteful and unhealthy consumption. Thus, to take another key activity in the sustainable consumption sector, recycling centers supported by local government and residents' associations have become more common in Malaysia since the turn of the millennium. Here, again, middle-class consumers are at the forefront, as people become more environmentally aware (for one survey, see Haron et al. 2005). Thus, for example, office manager Teoh Hooi Lee was reported in one local newspaper as driving over to her local recycling center (in Petaling Jaya in Selangor State) "with her 4-wheel drive full of recyclable materials"—as she proudly put it: "It's been a routine for me every end of the month, bringing recyclable materials to the centre. I wash everything first, and sort everything out, although they don't ask us to" (Koay 2005: 2). Such fastidious behavior on the part of Malaysia's new model citizenry stands in sharp contrast to a still all-too-widespread throwaway culture in the country. Thus, for example, when recycling bins were first introduced in George Town's Botanical Gardens, visitors simply used them as general rubbish receptacles. To the despair of activists, this sort of practice is common, earning the city the title *Pulau Pinang Darul Sampah* [Penang, Land of Rubbish]—a shocking indictment for a city famed for its beautiful beaches and known as the "Pearl" [*Mutiara*] of Malaysia (Loh 2005). Here, alternative shopping is tantamount to a detox politics that cleanses the nation's environmental behavior through the example of personal cleansing.

Meanwhile, the Malaysian government is showing interest in alternative sustainable consumption. Speaking at the Fourth Malaysian Exhibition on Organic and Natural Products held in Kuala Lumpur, one Department of Agriculture official noted that organic farming was still in its infancy in the country with but 900 hectares planted. Hence, it needed to import organic food to satisfy growing demand. To meet this demand, and to enable the country to even become a net exporter of organic food, the government set out ambitious growth targets for the sector (Ramli 2005). Concurrently, the government is pushing the message that ethical traders get more customers through advertisements in national newspapers that promote a new ethical outlook.

These sorts of private and public practices—still small in scale but growing—bespeak a broader shift in Malaysian society that is conditioning how social identity and activism takes place. Two things stand out. First, alternative sustainable consumption there suggests the advent of market-driven detox politics that seeks to cleanse the consumer of actions that are harmful to the environment and that is somewhat reminiscent of countries in the North (and the United States and United Kingdom notably). There is a parallel emphasis too, now, in Malaysia on human-induced environmental crises at the local and global scales fed by extensive media coverage that seems to associate public anxiety with environmental problems, a possible complement to alternative consumption everywhere. During one of the hottest summers on record (2005), for instance, the newspapers were full of articles on global warming and related environmental catastrophes (such as the widespread haze caused by fires in nearby Indonesia) as well as the way in which Malaysia's growing ecological footprint was adding to the problem (e.g., Ooi 2005). The message was clear: Malaysians needed to "do something" as they had become, in the words of one fisherman, *mahluk perosak* [destructive creatures] who behaved "without any thought to the consequences" (cited in Sabaratnam 2005: 3).

Yet uptake of this kind of intentional politics also fits well with Malaysian history. Thus, the country has been governed since the interethnic riots (pitting Malays against Chinese) of 1969 by a Malay-led political coalition that has sought to regulate political, economic, and cultural practices to ensure peaceful and harmonious relations. Notable here is the New Economic Policy (NEP) that promoted the advancement of the more numerous, but traditionally poorer, Malays in relation to the less numerous but richer Chinese. To some extent, the NEP enabled the emergence of a sizable Malay middle class, ensuring thereby relative political stability as the country pursued its own distinctive brand of Asian capitalism (Talib 2001).

The country did experience once more a confrontational style of politics in the 1980s and 1990s as the environmental implications of state-sanctioned accelerated development (itself linked to the NEP) became apparent. Notably involving activists working for NGOs such as Sahabat Alam Malaysia (SAM) and the Consumers Association of Penang (CAP), a social movement directly challenged the environmental record of the government of Prime Minister Mahathir Mohamad (Hong 1987). This challenge covered everything from rapid deforestation (and associated oppression of indigenous people) to polluting industrial development. The result, in a country where the political economy is predicated on accelerated development, was a severe crackdown: activists were imprisoned or gagged while surveillance of unpatriotic "foreign-linked" NGOs intensified (Eccleston 1996). Clearly, activism that confronted the (unsustainable) economic activities of Malaysia's political and economic elites was unwelcome (Doolittle 2005; Jomo et al. 2004). Such activism did not disappear but was more circumspect in its challenge to official practices. Social space was thereby created for nonconfrontational politics more to the liking of Malaysia's leaders as well as its affluent consumers.

An awakening interest in alternative sustainable consumption also fits with the desire of Malaysia's increasingly powerful middle class to stand out from the crowd. Here, the wish for "distinction" (Bourdieu 1984) is compelling. Indeed, it is perhaps even more acute in a rapidly developing society such as Malaysia than in the more economically developed North, if only because of greater proximity for many citizens (including many nouveau riche) to a recent poverty-stricken past. We must tread carefully here— consumption can mean different things to different people and is often conditioned by wider religious and cultural debates (Chua 2001). In contemporary Malaysia, for example, a complex and multifaceted debate is under way over the role of Western consumption practices and influence in a modern Islamic state.

Shopping in an expensive organic shop (modeled on outlets in the North) seems in many respects akin to shopping in the globally connected mainstream sector (e.g., Gap, Armani). It might suggest a strong desire to imbibe globally powerful signifiers (associated with a healthy and affluent lifestyle) that help, in turn, to separate globally connected middle-class consumers from their less-privileged brethren. For this kind of alternative consumer, even the retail setting needs to be perfectly controlled—consider, for instance, the reaction of stay-at-home and work-at-home mother Doris Chua, a thirty-something event director and Kuala Lumpur resident, to the opening of an organic shop in her area:

> I am an organic food advocate and have been rather blessed to have access to many organic shops around my area. One of my favourite is JustLife which often captivates me with their freestyle graphics, creative food labels and marketing concepts. Most importantly, I like to buy fresh vegetables and fruits from the shops as they are carefully selected and freshness is guaranteed. JustLife has recently opened its flagship store in Ikano Power Centre, Kuala Lumpur with a sit down café serving organic food. There is a wider selection of fruits and vegetables in the long storage place which resembles very much like the ones you see in supermarkets. I am very impressed by their interiors and décor, which is nicely designed— kudos to the design team at JustLife. The root vegetables are placed in wooden baskets like the ones in the market...a nice touch to getting close to nature.[7]

This passage of one devotee is interesting on several grounds. First, there is an emphasis on presentation and style, as Doris is "captivated" by the concept and layout of JustLife—thereby underlining that this shop is about much more than simply being a purveyor of fine organic food. Thus, she compliments the "creative" and "nicely designed" shop—a retail space packed with intentions. The "just life" is also a "stylish" life fit for twenty-first-century middle-class Malaysian consumers. Second, there is a nod to a more traditional way of shopping—the wet (or farmer's) market. These markets, once ubiquitous in the country, have long been the meeting place of producers and consumers of sometimes quite different ethnic and class backgrounds. However in modern Malaysia, there is seemingly less room for such mixing in the marketplace, as the prospering middle classes retreat to clean and modern supermarkets as well as to specialty upmarket organic shops. In the latter, selective admiration for a rapidly receding past nonetheless becomes a symbolic part of the decor as wooden baskets "like the ones in the market" hold root vegetables. Doris carefully notes this "nice touch" and goes on to suggest it brings the shopper "closer to nature"—or, more precisely, the producers who are seemingly nature's stand-in within this narrative.

In the process, though, alternative consumption is turned inside out: where once it might have been seen to be a marker of political distinction, it has seemingly now become just another marker of social and economic distinction for status-hungry middle-class consumers. Here, then, spaces of intention acquire new meaning. As sustainable consumption practices and rituals derived notably from the North are often mimicked, new borders are created that reflect and demarcate the shifting new realities of social inequality and class in Malaysia. In the process, exclusion is not an accident—it is probably partly intentional. In an ironic twist on what was noted earlier about poor marginal producers, here the espousal of environmental causes through consumption is itself a prime means by which to boost one's standing in society.

Conclusion

This chapter has explored some of the ethical ambiguities and limits to the burgeoning sustainable consumption sector of eco-chic. Our focus was on the understudied, yet crucial, issue of border making—something that is inevitably involved in the creation of the distinctive spaces of intention that define this sector. Such border making is ongoing, as new aims, people, and knowledge come to the fore often challenging prior ways of seeing and doing. There is much that is positive here. A politics of sustainable consumption would seem to imply a politics of border marking so that battle lines can be clearly drawn across the marketplace. How else would consumers know how to make ethical choices? Yet we also saw a darker side: creating bordered spaces of intention inevitably raises the issue of which people and knowledge are included and excluded.

Certainly, exclusionary practices associated with the creation of spaces of intention form part of a broader politics and geography of care. Thus, and as our Mexican example illustrated, the quest by producer cooperatives to boost their role in the space of intention surrounding chicle involved them in crafting a new production-cum-export regime. However, this entailed a fierce battle with powerful groups and thereby excluded those who were primary beneficiaries of the prior regime. Indeed, they even mounted a counterexclusionary campaign designed to frustrate this instance of hopeful border marking. This campaign is ongoing and is a sobering reminder of the weapons of the strong that can stymie change in the alternative sustainable consumption sector.

Exclusionary practices sometimes also end up excluding some of the poorest and most marginal producers from that sector. Here, exclusion reflects the unintended yet hardly neutral consequence of the quest for quality by consumers. To take our example of Costa Rican cacao production, quality requires that production there take place on land with good natural capital (e.g., organically rich well drained soils)—yet, such land is typically beyond the reach of the poorest farmers. Here, then, quality serves as a means by which the poorest producers are excluded—just as poorer consumers at the other end of the network also tend to be weeded out as quality products fetch premium prices beyond their ability to pay.

Indeed, as the Malaysian example revealed, the question of borders delimiting spaces of intention concerning alternative sustainable consumption can simultaneously raise the issue of class distinction. This is especially so among the nouveau riche who hunger for cultural and economic markers to place themselves in a rapidly changing world. In this sense, quality and ethically good behavior come to signify not so much a politics of contestation against the status quo, as a self-conscious consumption politics that might promote the self in a hip or fashionable manner while being supportive of that status quo.

We are clearly skeptical about the merits and utility of some aspects of eco-chic and the market-driven politics that it reflects and reinforces. True, there are areas of hope—for instance, inasmuch as elites who have long preyed on poor producers are excluded from new spaces of intention (as is partly the case in the Mexican example). Further, some unintended exclusions—as with the poorest producers who cannot produce quality goods—are changing over time as others in the network (such as Northern NGOs) seek to redress injustice through assistance to such individuals.

Yet all of the ethical ambiguities and limits surrounding the sustainable consumption sector cannot be eliminated so readily. Insofar as some issues reflect structural problems with the entire approach and philosophy of the sector, such tinkering (however commendable individual outcomes might be) will fail. This raises in turn a series of issues about the direction and *raison d'etre* of this alternative to the status quo.

The first issue is the precarious and contingent nature of the ability to exclude people and knowledge from the spaces of intention that surround the sustainable consumption sector. Because that sector is embedded in the wider capitalist system, there is always the strong possibility that those who are intentionally excluded (such as greedy elites and brokers who enjoy excess profits) will simply resort to mainstream economic channels to undercut that sector. Certification schemes are designed to prevent this process. Yet, much depends on the nature of the product and its transparency in the network since some products are more readily monitored than others in the journey from producer to consumer. The more complex the journey in terms of such things as product transformation and/or the number of intermediary actors involved, the more likely it may be that good intentions to help poorer producers are frustrated along the way.

There is also the problem of the voluntary nature of consumer intentions that underpin sustainable consumption. This sector is embedded in a wider economy that is premised on—and disciplines consumers in the art of ephemeral consumption choices. While the alternative sector may not seek to encourage ephemeral consumer decision making, there is a steep gradient here, given the discursive and material power of capitalism. There are no guarantees that alternative consumers might not switch products in search of new experiences—especially where they desire a distinctive identity. Yet the livelihoods of producers are not ephemeral—leaving them vulnerable to the whims of consumers who may be caring but not careful in their choices.

Third, alternative sustainable consumption is vulnerable to subversion by elites attracted to a sector that is sexy—a fashionable marker of status rather than a political statement of protest. Such motivation makes a mockery of the underlying ethos of the sector even as it ensures that it never fulfills its (theoretically) challenging initial premise. Yet how does one exclude elites who are inauthentic consumers? Indeed, what does *authentic consumer* mean? This is probably an impossible endeavor, yet it matters precisely because, ultimately, the future of sustainable consumption is based on affinity of purpose (and not simply outcome). To see it otherwise is to reduce the sector to a plaything of those who wish no alteration to the status quo.

Finally, the ethical ambiguity of this sector is deepened when its role as a means to sustain a status quo based on great inequalities of wealth is considered. To what extent does the sustainable consumption sector serve a key function today in disciplining people to work within a system that is always likely to be based on inequality? A bit like the Keynesian welfare state of old (albeit without the more systematic redistribution of wealth and universal welfare support that were hallmarks of that system), this sector persuades (some) people that capitalism is not bad after all—it is worthy and capable of reform. Can an alternative politics thus ever be truly alternative? Indeed, it may simply divert energy from more radical initiatives.

Thus, hope residing in spaces of intention linked to sustainable consumption and eco-chic may be somewhat misplaced. If people's intentions are often ambiguous, then a politics based on the consumption choices of winners in the global economy that does not simultaneously address structural inequalities that sustain the privileged position of these consumers seems doomed from the start. As such, those desiring a hopeful politics based on alternative market-based exchange need to look beyond the bottom of a (fairly traded coffee) cup or the green consumer emporium that trades on elite food and fashion.

–4–

Global Gold Connections:
Ethical Consumption and the Beauty
of Bonding Artisans

Sabine Luning and Marjo de Theije

Good Gold

On May 7, 2012, the Dutch launch of fair-trade and fair-mined (FT/FM) gold took place during an event organized by the nongovernmental organization (NGO) Solidaridad at a trendy location on the waterfront of Amsterdam North. The afternoon's host was Jort Kelder, the former editor of *Quote*[1] and an iconic figure in terms of elite lifestyles. He interviewed a range of guests who represented the production side of the supply chain, including representatives of a Peruvian cooperative of small-scale miners; the celebrity jewelry designer Bibi van der Velden; representatives of the NGOs involved in setting up the supply chains and the certification; and Dutch television celebrity Katja Römer-Schuurman, who had the honor of receiving the first bracelet made from FT/FM gold in the Netherlands. Both the general ambiance and the guests made it clear that the consumer side of the supply chain was chic. Kelder—a celebrity who has branded himself as a wealth watcher—explained to the audience which consumers the FT/FM gold campaign was targeting: those wealthy enough to buy designer jewelry at a price topped up by a 10 or 15 percent premium. His ironic style of interviewing—"in a minute we can forget about all this and enjoy what really matters: the drinks"—underscored that ethical consumption can go hand in hand with lavish lifestyles.

Fair trade necessarily involves representations of global connections. It involves informing a specific audience of consumers about labor conditions and ecosystems in distant places where the products they buy are mined, grown, and manufactured. Fair trade consists of forms of global interactions in which distance-crossing is central. It has been argued that fair trade differs from other forms of trade precisely in the construction of a distance-crossing moral economy (Goodman 2010: 115). It consists of attempts to organize global supply chains in such a way that by doing good at home, lives can be improved elsewhere. These global connections are mediated by certification organizations, NGOs, and so on, and they are mediatized through, for instance, news reports, information on websites, and celebrities who are involved as product ambassadors.

As the launch of this eco-chic good gold initiative indicates, the role of celebrities deserves attention. Jort Kelder and Katja Römer-Schuurman are just two Dutch examples of the many celebrities involved in branding fair-trade products. The actress Helen Mirren and musicians Bono and Chris Martin of Coldplay all play prominent roles as ambassadors of fair-trade organizations (FTOs) and products. These instances represent a broader trend in which celebrities increasingly bring their personal political convictions into the public realm (Goodman 2010: 106). Katja Römer-Schuurman, who received the first good gold design at the launch, is a good Dutch example of such a do-good celebrity. She hosted a television program called *Return to Sender*, linked to the eponymous foundation she runs. The program would feature Römer-Schuurman visiting those sites where our consumer goods originate. Her persona fitted perfectly with the goals and styling of an upmarket, eco-chic product such as ethical jewelry. She not only embodies a sense of caring and a mode of media attention for the situation in those places where consumer goods originate, but also represents the lifestyles of the rich and famous that potential consumers of good gold jewelry are expected to identify with. Fans are invited to identify with this celebrity's ethical concerns and to reflect critically on their own consumption practices. As such, celebrities like Katja Römer-Schuurman serve as a mirror for consumers.

In this chapter, we analyze yet another relationship in which a celebrity acts as a mirror. At the launch, a small documentary was shown of celebrity jewelry designer Bibi van der Velden's visit to a good gold project in Colombia. In the analysis presented here, we discuss how the mediatization of this event emphasizes the bond between the celebrity jeweler and the Colombian producers: they celebrate their shared work as artisan producers. We go on to analyze the practices of promoting so-called good gold, particularly in the Netherlands. We center on those strategies that aim to draw attention to current practices of gold mining and the improvements that FT/FM initiatives hope to establish. We address three questions: (1) How do good gold initiatives fit in a wider trend of eco-chic consumption and ethical capitalism? (2) How does the idea of good gold epitomize the social good? (3) How are the local mining sites and artisans involved in the supply chain represented in the promotion of this form of ethical consumption?

Ethical Consumption and Corporate Social Responsibility

Eco-chic is a specific form of ethical consumption, endorsed by social movements trying to improve practices of production from within the capitalist system. Until the late 1980s, social movements tended to target governments with requests to regulate companies more stringently. The shift toward neoliberalism, in which the state's role as central agent in the economy became increasingly devalued, has also been marked by changes in social movement strategies. Rather than asking states to regulate multinational companies, the campaigns of large social movements such as Greenpeace began to target these companies directly.

Dinah Rajak (2011) shows how this shift is particularly evident in lobbying efforts targeting large mining companies. The outrage over major scandals involving Rio Tinto in Papua New Guinea, Shell in Nigeria, and Talisman in Sudan compelled transnational corporations (TNCs) to clean up their act. As Rajak (2011: 8) notes,

> Since then, the TNCs seemed to have managed to cast off the image of pariah of capitalism and have emerged as the leaders of the Corporate Social Responsibility (CSR) cause. In response to consumer vigilantism and non-governmental (NGO) "brandjacking,"[2] corporations emerged extending the hand of CSR to their former combatants. The rise of CSR has established TNCs as more the solution to the challenges of global poverty and under-development, than the cause.

Big business, then, has come to present itself as the path to development in places where states have failed due to corruption. CSR is propagated as improver of the world and as savior of the disenfranchised. Or, as John Comaroff and Jean Comaroff (2000: 292) put it: "capitalism as gospel of salvation."

Redefinitions of value are central to this shift. A company's value is now seen as also incorporating communal and sustainable aspects. CSR foregrounds a moral economy of care and benevolence, in apparent contrast with a market discipline characterized by impersonal autonomy. CSR blurs the distinction between market and gift. The gift, associated with communal, lasting bonds, has often been portrayed as the antithesis of the market, which is characterized as determined by short-term transactions between anonymous buyers and sellers (Mauss 1923). To understand CSR, Rajak (2011) argues, we should move beyond such dichotomies. Morals of responsibility, generosity, and community—and the social bonds of affection and coercion that these create—are intertwined with business interests. To understand CSR initiatives, it is important to acknowledge that the market works through moral practice.

This analysis of big business CSR is relevant for our understanding of good gold initiatives. First of all, it shows a shift in combat style. Rather than dismissing the system of capitalism categorically, most social movements look for niches within capitalism where improvements of economic practices are seen as feasible. Within these niches, they may opt for partnerships with corporations, as Robert Foster details in his chapter in this volume. This trend is evident in the fair-trade movement from which good gold emerged. In the 1970s and 1980s, FTOs began to establish alternative distribution chains, with the aim of circumventing the pressures imposed by profit-driven transnationalism and the imperatives of capitalism (Dolan 2010). Fair-trade initiatives developed during this period, such as the Wereldwinkel,[3] tried to provide cooperatives of producers with alternatives to capitalist market mechanisms. According to Fridell (2006: 12–13), fair-trade initiatives are all increasingly explicitly involved in attempts to work from within the belly of the beast, trying to exploit global capitalism to their own shaped advantage. This trend covers a variety of strategies, ranging from making the chains between producers, traders, and consumers tangible to monitoring more general flows of goods through labeling and certification. The first strategy involves the alternative distribution chains of FTOs, and depends on an approach known as the "integrated supply chain route," while the second strategy, known as the "product certification route," works through mainstream distribution channels for certified products (FLO),[4] provisioning supermarkets and other retailers. Both strategies reflect and reproduce neoliberal logic and trends within international capitalist markets.

Since the early days of fair trade, the valorization of fair products has been subject to changes. Marketers have clearly discovered the fair-trade niche, incorporating it in wider strategies to expand the ways in which value can be added to consumer goods. Two aspects of such value-adding attempts are particularly relevant for our purposes: first, the trend of marketing fair-trade products while promising explicitly to not compromise on good taste; and second, marketing efforts that add value by supplying knowledge about a product's origin. These trends are especially evident in the marketing of coffee, as William Roseberry has shown in his study of the rise of yuppie coffee. He demonstrates how marketers developed new ways of outcompeting one another: rather than continuing to merely cut on price, they began to promote coffee in terms of quality, value, and image (Roseberry 1996: 765). These forms of branding capitalize on how consumers can be made to feel about themselves. Starbucks's slogan "What good can a cup of coffee do?" is exemplary in the context of ethical consumption, assuring the consumer that being good to oneself can coincide with doing good elsewhere (in the world of producers). Connecting feeling good and doing good has proved to be an extremely effective marketing strategy. Starbucks is also a good example of how information on the supply chain and on products' origins is used to add value in contemporary branding practices. Starbucks coffee shops often display information on the value chain of the coffee they serve, decorating the shops with colorful images portraying the successive steps of processing coffee. Representations of the labor and expertise necessary to create and improve the consumer product, then, have become an important asset in branding practices.

Scaling Solidaridad

The Good Gold campaign in Amsterdam was organized by Solidaridad, a well-known Dutch NGO. Solidaridad's history parallels the development of fair-trade movements outlined above. However, rather than entirely replacing older organizational formats with more neoliberal ones, Solidaridad has opted to combine the different approaches to fair trade. The organization models this diversification strategy in what they call "the pyramid of change" (see Figure 4.1). At the top of the pyramid, we find adapted forms of fair trade dating back to the 1970s and 1980s, while the lower levels feature initiatives in which Solidaridad has teamed up with major corporate players. The fair-trade certification organization Max Havelaar is situated at the top; certification schemes associated with the CSR initiatives of TNCs such as Unilever and Nestlé are located in the middle; at the bottom we find roundtables and codes of conduct involving entire industrial sectors. The pyramid stresses a historical movement from the narrow top to the broader basis of the pyramid: critical consumers triggered the initial interest in fair trade, followed by TNCs forced to pay attention to sustainability, both at the level of CSR strategies within specific companies and broader sector-wide initiatives.

The pyramid's top-to-bottom axis shows that, over time, the scale of initiatives has changed. Indeed, the issue of scale—which is often associated with quality—is

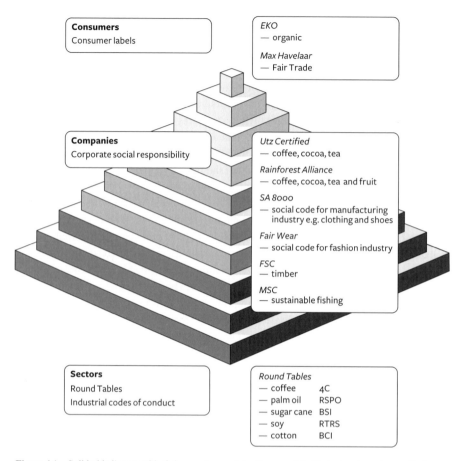

Consumers
Consumer labels

EKO
— organic

Max Havelaar
— Fair Trade

Companies
Corporate social responsibility

Utz Certified
— coffee, cocoa, tea

Rainforest Alliance
— coffee, cocoa, tea and fruit

SA 8000
— social code for manufacturing
industry e.g. clothing and shoes

Fair Wear
— social code for fashion industry

FSC
— timber

MSC
— sustainable fishing

Sectors
Round Tables
Industrial codes of conduct

Round Tables
— coffee   4C
— palm oil   RSPO
— sugar cane   BSI
— soy   RTRS
— cotton   BCI

Figure 4.1   Solidaridad's pyramid of change. *Source:* http://www.solidaridadnetwork.org/pyramid-change

emphasized to justify Solidaridad's diversified participation in fair-trade initiatives. Max Havelaar, situated at the top, is the outcome of Solidaridad's impressive track record in linking up with cooperatives of producers. These relationships have centered primarily on food products such as coffee, tea, and bananas—commodities that have supply chains that are relatively easy to trace and control. The initial consumers of these fair-trade products were motivated by a strong political engagement,[5] and their primary concern was not so much the taste of the product as ensuring fair conditions of production. In terms of numbers, however, these committed consumers remained rather marginal (Roozen and Van der Hoff 2001). In 1988, the labeling organization Max Havelaar was set up to improve certified cooperatives access to markets and to increase the market share of fair-trade products. Solidaridad's current director, Nico Roozen, was one of the main protagonists involved in establishing this product certification and labeling organization. Nonetheless, given its strict criteria and the fixed premium, Max Havelaar cannot enroll more than a limited group of producers nor cater to more than a relatively small group of consumers. Due to this restrictive approach, these initiatives are situated at the top of the pyramid.

Max Havelaar was the first label for fair trade globally and has been a trendsetter in the certification of direct supply chains. It marked the beginning of a proliferation of certification and labeling practices and currently involves major multinationals producing and selling consumer goods. This proliferation was embraced by Solidaridad; its diversification strategy results from efforts to scale up their effect by partnering with major retailers and firms and by collaborating in mainstream certification programs aimed at broader groups of consumers. CSR initiatives and sector-wide agreements criteria feature less strict criteria, but the volume of production and numbers of consumers are much larger. The model of the pyramid of change gives an excellent view of the current range of initiatives in which ethics and capitalism appear to be intertwined. Companies and consumers operating at different scales proclaim adherence to ethical principles of fairness that transgress the dichotomy of gift and market.

Aspects of scale also play a role in how Solidaridad positions itself in fair-trade initiatives in the gold sector. Indeed, the website informs us that 80 percent of gold mining worldwide takes place at an industrial scale. These forms of mining have large disadvantages: they are monopolized by multinationals that take the revenues out of the country; the use of cyanide poses major environmental problems; and the postmining phase often leaves the local population empty-handed in a scarred landscape. Only 20 percent of gold mining is classified as small-scale, but even within that category there are large differences: many small-scale miners, in particular in Latin America, use excavators to work alluvial sites or blast into hard rock underground mines with dynamite.[6]

Solidaridad teams up with actors in the gold-mining sector, including both small-scale and large-scale miners in its efforts. It is currently attempting to increase the scale of its program activities in collaboration with the Council for Responsible Jewellery (CRJ). The CRJ is an international-standards-setting organization that connects over 420 member companies across the jewelry supply chain, including major mining companies, refiners, jewelry manufacturers, and retailers. In addition, Solidaridad is involved in setting up programs with midscale industrial mines that are owned by local companies and jewelers with international brands.

Until recently, Solidaridad's *gold program* has mainly targeted small-scale miners, which was occasioned by two motivations. First, revenues of small-scale mining are allocated to local populations so that support at that level can directly help poverty alleviation. Second, Solidaridad is able to collaborate with existing initiatives by organized small-scale miners, in particular the Oro Verde project in Colombia. Oro Verde, literally Green Gold, is a special initiative that unites gold miners who live up to strict standards regarding working conditions, child labor, women's rights, cleaner technology, health and safety, management of chemicals, and responsibility to the environment.[7] The Alliance for Responsible Mining (ARM) is now promoting the introduction of these standards in a broader range of mining communities worldwide.[8] Groups of miners can obtain training and help that will allow them to become certified following adherence to FT/FM standards.

The gold program centers on a certification program that functions like a tax, earmarked for specific purposes. This initiative covers a particular niche in what Robert Foster (2008: 173–74) calls "cause marketing." Consumers pay a premium price for a product guaranteed to have been produced under environmentally safe and fair labor conditions, or for which its producers have been paid a fair price. According to a staff member of Solidaridad, the campaign slogan "on our way to good gold" was chosen to express the journey toward better practices. It allows Solidaridad to communicate the story of the risks associated with gold mining, outlining the work that Solidaridad and its partners are doing to improve conditions, and helping consumers understand how they can contribute to positive change. Consumers can choose to buy good gold, either in the form of FT/FM-certified gold or through the CRJ-certified supply chains that will soon be available. In addition, the program's information also urges consumers to support Solidaridad's work more broadly.

Even though the name *good gold* aims to emphasize the goodness of its cause, the choice of this brand name appeared to be contested. At the launch in Amsterdam, a Max Havelaar board member expressed her regrets that the certified gold had not been launched as Max Havelaar Gold. This well-known brand name would provide the initiative with better exposure. In the somewhat cynical view of this informant, Solidaridad appeared to have been more interested in branding its own organization, rather than the product as such. A number of jewelers also voiced their reservations regarding the good gold label. No matter how successful the campaign might become, this jewelry will always remain a small niche displayed and sold in jewelry shops. Selling a selection of one's jewelry as good gold risks triggering the question whether the other jewelry is made from bad gold. In terms of jewelers' overall marketing strategies, the name *good gold* risked being counterproductive; employing cause marketing might cast doubts over the rest of the jewelry market.

Branding Fair Gold: Consumption Work

In his work on the Coca-Cola Company, Robert Foster analyzes practices of branding in terms of value creation, identifying different sources of value (2008: 28–31). An important notion of value relates to Marx's theory of labor value, which posits that the value of a product is equal to the amount of labor put into the product. Capitalist hegemony manages to obscure this: goods appear to be valued and priced in relation to each other, concealing the efforts of laborers. The physical coercion of laborers and the exact locations of production plants do not feature within the frames of representing value creation; commodities appear to have value without having to take into account the tangible circumstances of production. Marx referred to this obscuring of labor, the rendering invisible and anonymous of sweat and oppression, as fetishism. In contrast, "the second source of value creation involves a reattachment of this alienated product to another personality, the consumer. It is this reattachment that is achieved through branding" (Foster 2008: 28). Whereas the work of producers is often hidden, value creation through the linking of products to the personality of the consumers is prolific and explicit. Foster calls this "consumption work" and sees this as the center stage for branding activities. In contrast to Daniel Miller (1995), who identifies a free, creative, and political potential in the agency of consumers, Foster is pessimistic; consumers may experience their personal identification with products as free choice, but this may be a parroting of what marketers want consumers to feel and believe (Foster 2008: 29).

Robert Foster's emphasis on the two sides of value creation—production and consumption—provides an excellent point of departure to analyze fair-trade initiatives. The marketing of fair trade is an interesting variant in that it is characterized by (1) defetishization, as fair trade foregrounds rather than obscures production practices; (2) consumption work, as the value of consumer purchases is explicitly attached to the consumers' identity; (3) and a mutual reinforcement of aspect 1 (defetishization) and 2 (consumption work).

The defetishization is evident. Fair trade's main claim is that it makes the connections between a product's source and its consumers transparent. The social movement's explicit aim has been to improve the social and environmental circumstances of production. This involves making a distinction between improved practices (which qualify for certification) from ordinary production practices. The No Dirty Gold campaign slogan—"the more you know the less gold glows"[9]—exemplifies fair-trade initiatives: the circumstances are unfair unless consumers do something about it and to make the right choices consumers need to know. This agenda is based on the idea of consumer power (Miller 1995).

To analyze the shape of defetishization, we have to take into account aspects of consumption work. How are gold and good gold jewelry attached to consumers? This issue immediately foregrounds the fact that gold—in the form of jewelry—displays the classic features of a fetish. That is, gold has qualities that the potential owner may wish to obtain. In his classic work on the history of the gold industry, Timothy Green analyzes the slogans used in branding gold jewelry, in particular by South African mining companies (Green 1981: 241–42). In advertisements for gold jewelry, the idea is circulated that "gold is irresistible, like you" *(L'or est irresistible…comme toi)*: the appeal of gold will enhance the owner's attractiveness. Gold as a "piece of happiness" *(Gold, ein stück Glück)* affects the state of those associated with it. Advertisers also capitalize on the idea that gold is an eternal material—it cannot be destroyed—and build on a long tradition in which gold is associated with timelessness. Green (1981: 242) quotes the Greek poet Pindar stating that "gold is the child of Zeus—neither moth nor rust devoureth it." Gold's beauty, malleability, and indestructibility have bestowed it with an aura of superiority and nobility. Indeed, advertisements suggest that these qualities that gold possesses can be transposed to its owners, making it a lover's gift par excellence. Gold epitomizes the social good: a gift to express bonding, eternal love. In these associations we see a specific form of attaching gold to the consumer and his or her social life-world. Indeed, buying gold affects and expresses aspects of consumers' identities, but it appears to do so because of some inherent agency that gold possesses as a material. Indeed, on the website of the World Gold Council wedding rings are advertised with texts like "Gold makes it a marriage."

Andrew Walsh, writing on gemstones, links the specific value of such gifts to the debate on fetishism. Sapphires are attributed with anthropomorphic qualities that purportedly affect wearers: "friendly entities or benevolent energies expressing themselves through… stones" (2010: 109). Blue sapphire, for instance, is presented as possessing the inherent quality of enhancing insight. With gold as with gemstones, it is the recipient rather than buyer of the gift on whom such qualities rub off. Like gold, gems are also gifts between lovers; giving someone a sapphire—"the gem of fidelity"—entails "a pledge of trust, honesty, purity, and loyalty." Gemstones are seen as possessing the capacity to create or foster social relations: affective powers inherent to fetishes. Accordingly, Walsh (2010: 112) argues that rather than seeing gemstones as fetishized commodities, it is better to see them as "commodified fetishes."

These aspects are crucial for our analysis of the promotion of FT/FM jewelry. Ethical jewelry raises questions about how the beauty of this bonding on the consumer side of the value chain is affected by—and should, in turn, affect—social relations on the production side. The FT/FM promotional campaigns clearly take a critique of commodity fetishism as their point of departure. They stress repeatedly that our perception of this jewelry as beautiful relies on an omission of the dramatic and damaging circumstances characteristic of normal mining: exploitative labor situations, pollution, and permanent damage to the natural environment. The headline of an article on Solidaridad's Good Gold campaign in the Dutch newspaper *Trouw* (October 23, 2010) is telling: "When you put a golden ring on your beloved's finger, you'd prefer not to think about cyanide and mercury."[10] In the words of sustainability consultant Alice Doyle: "we want to educate the consumer as well as inspire. Jewellery is beautiful but you have to question just how beautiful it really is, by asking where it came from."[11] The fetish agency with which gold and gems are attributed in the context of consumption work is predicated on the fetishism on the production side, these messages seem to suggest. However, as we start thinking about the dirty circumstances that characterize mining activities, the gift's purity becomes tainted. The campaigns draw on this contrast between dirt and purity, between purity and danger, very explicitly (Douglas 1966). In this regard, the slogan "No Dirty Gold" works effectively, as it refers to both ecological disturbance and unfair social work conditions. Eco-chic jewelers' ethical jewelry campaigns categorically represent gold mining as a dirty business, principally due to its polluting effects on water resources and its scarring effects on the landscape. Gold mining is portrayed as intrinsically dirty, unless drastic measures are taken to prevent social and ecological disasters.

This baseline sketch provides the basis for claims about how FT/FM gold and ethical jewelry may improve the world. The implicit promise is that the premium the consumer pays will allow improvements that make the world of producing gold as beautiful as the wedding bonds symbolized and consolidated by golden rings. The headline "Real beauty: purity and fairness unveiled" of one article on good gold says it all. For gold to be able to do its fetish work for consumers, its source has to be purified: the social circumstances of gold mining need to be brought to the same elevated level as the quality of gold jewelry itself. In addition, the ecological effects need to be as clean and pure as gold.

As an article promoting a bridal jewelry collection suggests, ethical jewelry can "limit the damage and social injustice that can lie in the wake of something as beautiful and pure as a wedding band.... We applaud this marriage of ethics and aesthetics.... Brides to be can transform lives and celebrate their wedding day with a marriage band created responsibly."[12] The purchase of ethical jewelry improves the lives of producers, so that the wedding bonds' beauty and purity remain untainted.

In short, once the connection between production and consumption is acknowledged the task at hand is one of purification: the source must be cleansed of its dirt, to prevent gold's glow from becoming tarnished. Once this has been established the reverse effect is possible as well, with the source's shine reflecting on the jewelry. CRED[13] jewelry advertises their fair-trade products as follows: "This sense of beauty comes straight from the source; the stories behind them that perhaps even match the beauty of the collection itself. Handmade by CRED the entire Penelope Collection is made from Oro Verde Fair Trade 18ct White Gold."[14] The relationship between the source of production and the consumer destination must be mutually reinforcing, amplifying their purity and beauty. This characteristic makes ethical jewelry a specific form of eco-chic, in which the consumer product has the characteristics of commodified fetishes. The fetishization of these commodities can only be attained by either denying the facts of the production process or—as in the case of good gold—by suggesting that these facts can become characterized by the love and beauty associated with attaching gold to consumers.

Branding Fair Production: Sites and Artisans

Bibi van der Velden, a jewelry designer who has the status of ambassador of the Good Gold campaign, was at the heart of the Amsterdam launch. During the event, she explained that goldsmiths make products that are all about emotion, and that this explains why moral qualifications such as good gold are appealing. They are in line with the emotional association consumers have with the product in the first place. Along with other jeweler designers, van der Velden has been attempting to place more attention on this type of ethical jewelry. In addition to wedding rings, more figurative and artistic designs and jewelry are now emerging. Currently, a line is being developed to market ethical gold to younger consumers. Developing a market that encompasses a diverse range of consumers is clearly one of the campaign's aims. Van der Velden designed a bracelet that symbolizes the value of this project, and bracelets made with Oro Verde gold were given publically to several TV celebrities in November 2010. A brass version of the same bracelet was then offered for sale at a price of $20, for consumers who wished to express their adherence to the good cause of good gold. In 18 months of campaigning, some 15,000 bracelets were sold.[15] The presentation of improved mining practices to this eco-chic audience is closely associated with the feel-good emotions and moralities that are part and parcel of the consumption work surrounding gold.

We have seen that the good gold project consists of attempts to collaborate with small-scale miners who can become FT/FM certified. In the presentation at the launch, but also in online information, particular forms of small-scale mining are foregrounded as emblematic for a small, beautiful way of mining. The Oro Verde project in Colombia involves mining operations that are highly suitable for such purposes. We have seen that the FT/FM premium is 10 to 15 percent; for certified miners to qualify for the 15 percent premium, they must abstain from using cyanide and mercury. Worldwide, the Oro Verde miners are unique among certification programs in setting such high standards for their mining practices.

However, within the Colombian department of Choco, where the Oro Verde initiative is being carried out, a broad range of mining activities occur. Solidaridad's website shows the various forms of mining in this area. The major contrast is portrayed as one between artisanal panning for gold and semimechanized mining with excavators. The latter form of mining is presented as causing grave damage to the environment and as illegal, while the good gold comes from the panning sites. This representation also contrasts small-scale mining operations in terms of scale. The message is clear: mining with machines is bad, whereas manual panning is good. Small is beautiful. Although it is not Solidaridad's intention, this one-dimensional message prevails in the campaign. It is crucial to stress that the specific small-scale mining site portrayed in the campaign is simply very beautiful. This artisanal mining site, which has emblematic status, is run by Americo, a charismatic man. The website tells us that Americo started mining nine years ago and decided to work without mercury. The site he is working on is much older, and vegetation has begun to grow back on the beautiful stonewalls of piled-up waste rocks. Comparing Americo's site to the many small-scale mining sites we have encountered on different continents in the context of our respective research on gold mining, his site is by far the most beautiful site we have ever seen. Aesthetically, the stone walls and the rippling water of the little creek in the middle of the lush green forest are outright pleasing; this site is an icon for the Good Gold campaign. Oro Verde's official website portrays natural beauty, smiling people and a "place of love."[16]

The singling out of this beautiful artisanal mining site is exemplary for what James Scott (1998) has called "miniaturization." In *Seeing Like a State*, Scott (1998) points to the value of the aesthetic qualities of projects of improvement. Spatial arrangements must be visually appealing to be recognized as exemplary of high modernist projects for development. This requirement explains the attention to layouts and spatial designs in urban planning as well as in projects in rural areas. Moreover, Scott argues that specific project sites that live up to such aesthetic criteria will become emblems for the whole field of similar interventions. In practice, this means that the aesthetically pleasing sites will be visited in the contexts of project evaluations and the like. Miniaturization occurs in this showcasing of selected attractive examples of development projects, with the suggestion being made that these are just one or a few of many similar examples.

Miniaturization isolates beautiful icons from the context. Indeed, the context in which Americo makes his choices, and the way in which his mining operation is embedded in the wider context of land use, mining, political claims, and violence in the region are not visible. While this contextualization deserves attention, it falls beyond the scope of this chapter. Here, we want to analyze how the requirements of developing a consumer market set parameters for the representation of small, beautiful mining sites. The analysis of splendid isolation can be applied to the case of good gold and Oro Verde.

The small-scale sites are used to give an emblematic impression of what good mining looks like, and of the beauty of smallness. These mining sites seem to represent what the gold jewelry itself embodies as well: both the source and the product epitomize a "marriage of ethics and aesthetics." This relational identity comes out most prominently in Bibi van der Velden's exegesis of her jewelry design, which was inspired by her visit to Choco. The design explicitly encapsulates the beauty of the artisanal miner. Van der Velden's description shows how her design aims to embody the morals of small-scale mining communities as well as the fragility of the environment:

> Bibi van der Velden has designed a jewel produced entirely from Good Gold and inspired by her journey to Colombia. The core of the jewel is a rough nugget of nearly 50 grams of gold, a rare find for Choco miners. A small polished gold figure embracing the nugget represents the miners. The miner's embrace foregrounds the dependence of the communities on mining, but this shining little man also symbolises the driving force towards clean mining. The fact that the nugget and the figure of the miner are made of the same material emphasizes how gold resonates in the society. In addition, the forms of a pan and the fragile, local plant Dormidera are also present in the jewel. The jewel as a whole symbolises fragility of the gold mining process.[17]

The marketing of ethical jewelry repeatedly foregrounds this sharing of identity between the source and the consumer product. The slogan of Solidaridad's Good Gold campaign brings home the wishful bonding between the sites of production and consumption: "If something is mined with love, it can be worn with love!" This idea has wider currency. Vivien Johnson of the ethical jewelry brand Fifi Bijoux formulates the two-way directionality of effects when she explains, "we believe in luxury as it should be; without the blood, sweat or tears."[18] Ethical jewelry campaigns insist on a process of mirroring production and consumption; both must be characterized by the marriage of ethics and aesthetics. The social bonding as it occurs in consumption work (Foster 2008) must be matched by positive social bonds on the production side.

The small is beautiful, and the processes of miniaturization are materialized in an encounter between Americo, the artisanal miner, and Bibi van der Velden, ambassador-artisan. In her capacity as an ambassador for good gold, van der Velden paid a mediatized visit to Colombia in 2011. In a YouTube film that was also featured at the Amsterdam launch, she can be seen visiting Americo's mining site.[19] In addition to emphasizing the need to raise awareness, this film highlighted the professional bonding between artisan designer and artisan miner. Van der Velden acknowledged that prior to her involvement in the Good Gold campaign she had not realized how dramatic the circumstances of miners were; she explains that the surge in gold prices, and the associated gold rush, make the situation worse. Through her journey to Colombia she hopes to increase awareness for this issue.

Van der Velden met miners such as Americo who operate Oro Verde, the first green artisanal gold mine worldwide. She took part in the panning activities and offered Americo the bracelet she had designed. The visit inspired her designs, which seek to incorporate a sense of the splendid scenery of the Choco region. The visit clearly celebrated the encounter of artisans: artisanal miners meeting the artisan artist. The imagery is one of a bonding of artisans. Van der Velden's visit to the source of the gold she wants to work with is styled differently from the visits of other ethically oriented celebrities, such as Katja Römer-Schuurman in *Return to Sender,* or American celebrities going to Haiti after the earthquake of 2010 (Goodman 2010). In the latter cases, the celebrity can be seen as expressing the concern the world of wealthy consumers may have for poor people and producers. The celebrity represents the care of the privileged home society as a whole, and the fans/consumers can mirror their own empathy in the spectacle of the celebrity's do-good visit (Goodman 2010: 104). Bibi van der Velden's visit portrays a different type of relation based on mirroring. The YouTube film emphasizes her professional connection to the poor; she is a colleague also located on the gold-to-jewelry value chain. She is not just bonding with the poor, she is engaging in face-to-face contact with professionals situated at the other end of the supply chain. The act of sourcing the rough material that she will use as artisan–designer foregrounds the bonding with Americo, with whom she shares a relation of identity: the artisanal miner and artisan designer mirror one another.

These images of smallness and artisanal production, which are so central in the marketing of ethical jewelry, may have two negative consequences. First, the attempts to brand places may have unintended consequences, as the chapter in this volume by Meredith Welch-Devine and Seth Murray on eco-chic marketing of the Basque country also underlines. The sociogeographical source of production may be portrayed in ways that inadvertently run counter to the goals that fair trade has set itself in the first place. These sites become a miniaturized emblem of beauty with which distant audiences can identify. To facilitate feel-good associations, these places and the people who live and work there must be presented as purified, and in isolation from worlds of corruption and violence. "Celebrities, logos, symbols and landscapes are overtaking fair trade's previous bent of and for transparency and constructing a much less rich visual and textual language around the producer/consumer relationship" (Goodman 2010: 112).

Second, the message that small is beautiful may be appealing to consumers; it should not confine artisanal miners to small scales of mining only. Such restrictions would be at odds with a central goal of organizations such as Solidaridad, that is improving poor people's livelihoods. It is easy to see that the mode of mining celebrated here entails hard work and generates relatively limited revenues, in particular when compared to working with excavators. Information provided by Solidaridad shows that Oro Verde obtains 12 kilograms of gold annually.[20] To contribute to improving the livelihoods of impoverished artisanal miners, Solidaridad should do its utmost to prevent public relations (PR) campaign images from becoming straitjackets for producers. The goal of improving miners' livelihoods should not be sacrificed to PR agendas or to a single-minded focus on sustainability. Indeed, by putting pressure on producers to sell themselves as sustainable (Goodman 2010: 105), the current emphasis on sustainability runs the risk of confining artisanal miners within the parameters of small-is-beautiful, confining them to scales of operation and techniques that may be good for the environment, but bad in terms of the arduous working practices and limited revenues endured by the miners.

Policymakers and campaigners urgently need to consider the possible effect of PR campaigns on mining practices on the ground. For good gold initiatives to positively affect miners' lives, scaling up the programs' techniques and social innovations must remain possible for their participants. It should be possible for such initiatives to be attractive to wealthy consumers, without blocking the road to mechanization and increased production for impoverished producers. Solidaridad acknowledges the complexity of the world of gold production and these issues of scale. The model exemplified in the pyramid of change shows how Solidaridad seeks to diversify its programs with gold producers and designers working at different scales. This model should be used not only to design separate programs for producers operating at different scales, but also to provoke reflection on exactly how different scales are articulated. It can help to identify strategies for producers to jump scales (scaling both up and down) and elaborate how scales are linked to power relations more generally. Indeed, while Solidaridad may emphasize small-is-beautiful mining sites in its PR campaigns, it should simultaneously capitalize on its broader linkages to different types of small-, medium-, and large-scale producers to move beyond the tunnels and trenches that seem so characteristic of the gold mining sector.

Conclusion

The launch of the good gold designs in Amsterdam brought together people representing key actors in the value chain of jewelry: miners, designers, and elite consumers. We have shown how this form of fair trade is part of wider trends of eco-chic consumption and ethical capitalism. The Good Gold campaign should be understood in the context of a wider social field in which producers, firms, and NGOs partner up in projects to improve corporate, socioeconomic, and environmental practices. Solidaridad plays into this varied field, and the Good Gold campaign is only one of the modalities pursued within the broader range of improvement schemes Solidaridad promotes. The image of the pyramid of change captures Solidaridad's position and its strategic options within this wider trend of operating from within the formerly reviled system of capitalism. The current form of ethical capitalism tends to blur the market and the gift in the promotion of doing good. The fact that gold is represented as the gift par excellence amplifies this blurring tremendously in the context of the Good Gold campaign.

Our analysis focused on how the idea of good gold epitomizes the social good. On the consumer side, gold acts as a fetish that is capable of creating social good. A gift of gold symbolizes the qualities of positive, enduring social relationships. In contrast to this fetish use, we have seen that FT/FM entails a form of defetishization. For gold to be a good gift, it has to be mined under fair circumstances. To analyze the shape of defetishization, our discussion connected aspects of consumption work to the commodification of fetishes. The purity and eternity that gold appears to embody intrinsically becomes an overall message that affects all of the relations along the supply chain. The social good on the consumption side becomes the mirror for the portrayal of fair production. Drawing on Scott's notion of miniaturization, we have demonstrated how local mining sites and artisans involved in the supply chain are represented in the promotion of this form of ethical consumption. The beautification and isolation of mining sites, together with an emphasis on small scale, typify the images of good gold production. This splendid isolation risks obscuring the violence and misery that are often present as well. Moreover, this portrayal of gold's places of origin may restrict miners to small-is-beautiful practices.

Finally, we showed how the relations between producers and consumers are mediated by another professional involved in the value chain: the celebrity designer. Our analysis of the performance of the ambassador of the Good Gold campaign, designer Bibi van der Velden, shows how processes of value creation and branding build on the bonding between artisans. Bonding appears to be the norm not only on the side of consumption work and on that of production work, but also in the bonding between artisan colleagues along the value chain. Despite this emphasis on solidarity and commensurability, eco-chic also celebrates capitalism and shares its basic attitude to charity: doing good to others must do you good as well. The consumer should be allowed to do good in a world of comfort and options. Jort Kelder's ironic message ("the drinks are more important than the good gold") brought home a major point of eco-chic consumption work; it is primarily a matter of individual choice, with not too many strings attached for the consumer. Consumers want the right to engage in ethical consumption, as a (small and beautiful) part of their social world: this form of consumption adds value to individual lives that are already overwhelmingly rich, worthwhile, and full of choices.

Part II
Spatialities and Temporalities

–5–

Marketing the Mountain
The Emergence and Consequences of Eco-Chic Practices in the Basque Region

Seth Murray and Meredith Welch-Devine

Introduction

In this chapter, we turn our focus to eco-chic producers, rather than consumers, to highlight a crucial and distinct component of the commodity chain. We draw from two complementary long-term research projects in the Basque region of southwestern France to examine the emergence and consequences of eco-chic practices and ideologies among farmers there who principally produce sheep's cheese (see Figure 5.1). A number of convergent factors have enabled the emergence of new alternative markets for agricultural products produced here, including an active social engagement centered on ecological issues, a wariness of, and certain resistance to, mass consumerism, and ethical preoccupations with the modern productivist model of farming wherein cost efficiency and maximization of profit are de rigueur in the production process, even if these may come at the expense of healthy, quality goods. Overall, these factors resonate with wider consumer concerns about the quality, traceability, and authenticity of food products, many facets of which are explored in other chapters in this volume.

We focus our attention on how the conceptual rubric of eco-chic encompasses an array of strategies and practices that cheese producers employ with varying degrees of success. Basque cheeses can be found in specialty shops around the world, and their premium prices reflect an added value that comes from adhering to strict standards for quality control. In the examples that we present here, multiple forms of production may be interpreted as eco-chic, and each has its own historical and political reasons for coming into being and its own set of regulations by which producers must abide. These differing forms of production suggest an intersection between the historically situated politics of place and a public articulation of Basque identity that raises issues of authenticity. We also consider how European environmental policies that ostensibly entail restrictions on agricultural practices can simultaneously provide new opportunities for farmers to expand their economic opportunities and improve their social

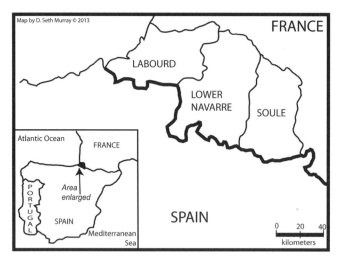

Figure 5.1 Overview of the Basque Region in France (map by Seth Murray).

standing by providing a space for farmers to assert particular cultural and political agendas.

Our analysis of the production and marketing of eco-chic goods cautions that the branding of an entire place, people, and set of economic activities may carry with it heavy consequences: the character of rural producers may be distilled and essentialized to generate a blurry ethnic caricature of Basques, thus allowing the co-optation of identity and place in the service of profit. This branding may also in some cases obscure unsavory or contentious aspects of production. At the same time, we conclude that the deployment of eco-chic practices can be a powerful tool for the improvement of economic, cultural, and political conditions and that they can—in certain cases—elucidate the linkages between producers and consumers and are thus important tools for economic development, as well as cultural and political activism.

Marketing Eco-Chic Commodities and the Politics of Place

Identifying a product with an explicit reference to place—be it a specific farm, village, region, or nation—is a common marketing tool. Most wine consumers are familiar with the term Protected Designation of Origin (PDO), sometimes known by its original French term—*Appellation d'Origine Contrôlée*. Similar designations exist for many other food and beverage products in Europe and, increasingly, around the world. In addition to guaranteeing the origin of a product, other designations exist that speak to the ways in which these products are grown or manufactured, such as with organic or hormone-free labeling, or the European Traditional Specialty Guaranteed. Identifying the origin of a commodity, particularly when it is a consumable food product, may connote a sense of quality, safety, traceability, and even authenticity for the consumer, as well as for the producer. PDOs, or geographical indications in general, are labels that classify a particular product that is linked to a particular location and embedded within a particular history. This place-based system of identification connects producers to consumers and transmits a set of messages—both explicit and implicit—about the inherent qualities of the products at hand, as well as the process in which they are created. PDOs must thus be approached in their specific social, economic, political, and even environmental context. If a specialized label helps to differentiate PDO products from generic, mass-produced commodities, it is because quality and authenticity are increasingly desirable characteristics for many consumers.

In this chapter, we focus not so much on a single item that is being marketed as eco-chic, but an entire area or region. While we primarily use the example of food products to illustrate how the region is marketed, other examples of products marketed with reference to the chicness of the region include experiential activities, such as hiking excursions and farm stays, that emphasize traditional landscapes and lifeways. This commodification of place depends on an idealized image that this place connotes in the minds of the public consumer (whether they be market-goers or tourists), even though that representation may be highly contested among the actual residents of the place in question. In a sense, it is the essentialized representation of a place, rather than the physical place itself, that becomes a commodity to be marketed, sold, and consumed. Our illustrations in this chapter highlight the connections between commodities and place that are involved in "marketing the mountain"—a phrase that for us refers to the branding of territory to enable a specific mode of production. Such branding problematizes the politics of place and, we argue, may lead to a simplification or overgeneralization of the identity politics of producers.

As forays into "market environmentalism" (Berthoud 1992)—that is, the use of market-led capitalism to ameliorate social or environmental problems—have increased, Marx's (1867) concept of commodity fetishism has been applied to the study of a variety of efforts to use market forces to protect the environment or to conserve biodiversity. Intensification of commodity fetishism has serious implications for our abilities to address the social and environmental costs incurred by capitalism. This chapter questions whether eco-chic practices can provide an opening to undermine the commodity fetishism that disconnects consumers from producers by defining and clarifying the relations of production, or whether they instead serve to further obscure the social relationships between producers and consumers (Carrier 2010; Hudson and Hudson 2003). Kosoy and Corbera (2010) argue that market environmentalism, particularly when dealing with ecosystems and ecosystem services, erases complexity and denies other ways of understanding and valuing what is being marketed. They caution against such marketing because it can reproduce existing inequalities, serving as a tool of injustice rather than equality. This critique of market environmentalism stands in contrast to the expansive research conducted on fair-trade products, such as coffee or cocoa, which have the potential to disrupt commodity fetishism (West 2012). In principle, fairly traded products are supposed to increase farmers' direct profits, reduce the oftentimes disruptive role of market intermediaries, and improve consumers' access to information about the goods they purchase. The traceability of fairly traded products is an important component to this system in which the origins of the product are verified or certified by external agencies to guarantee the authenticity of the product before it goes to market and to ensure its traceability. Alternative trade regimes, such as fair trade or direct sales, offer the opportunity to "remove the veil" by making the conditions of commodity production more visible, and by clearly articulating their effects on social and environmental systems (Hudson and Hudson 2003: 414).

Terroir is a concept that connects place, quality, and authenticity. At its very heart, *terroir* combines the biophysical elements of a place—its climate, a certain soil type, the terrain—with the intangible elements of local culture, regional history, and a producer's technical knowledge. Although *terroir* was originally associated with high-quality wine production, most notably in Bordeaux and Burgundy, it now includes a wide variety of food and drink products not only in Europe, but increasingly around the globe (Pitte 1999; Trubek et al. 2010). The concept of *terroir* occupies an important place in European agriculture, in part because of the economic value of products associated with a specific *terroir* (Demossier 2011). While it is an attractive concept to producers who seek to add value to their products, it also appeals to those individuals striving to maintain or redevelop certain traditions or historical methods of production that may have fallen into disuse. Similarly, *terroir* also seduces the consumer who seeks out products that are imbued with—or at least perceived to have—a sense of quality and authenticity. Thus, the concept of *terroir* is tightly linked to the production and marketing of eco-chic goods, and in this sense, *terroir* is a potent economic and cultural tool that enables the commodification of place.

The practice of marketing eco-chic goods can have mixed results, elucidating some aspects of the relations of production while obscuring others. It seems likely that whether the practice of eco-chic marketing ultimately contributes to or undermines commodity fetishism is very much dependent upon the item being marketed, and the particular social and political conditions in the locality or place of its production, marketing, and consumption. This ambiguous effect may essentially result in a false sense of security among those consumers who believe that their participation in a particular form of market environmentalism, such as with fair trade or direct sales, obviates the underlying dynamics of market capitalism. But, of course, it is nearly impossible to engage in ethical consumption without ethical production. To provide a clearer understanding of the strengths and weaknesses of the eco-chic concept for encouraging ethical production, in the following sections, we draw from ethnographic data collected with farmers to present two examples where food products, namely sheep cheeses, are enmeshed in practices of eco-chic marketing that are linked to a specific place, the mountains of the Basque region of France, and to expressions of a particular cultural tradition. We extend our analysis to the new opportunities for eco-chic marketing afforded by the creation of environmental protection areas in the region.

Ossau-Iraty and Marketing Eco-Chic Food Products
in the Basque Region of France

Although the Basque region has never constituted a formally recognized nation-state, it has endured as a distinct cultural region. The Basque region occupies a distinctive place in the Pyrenees Mountains, separating the Iberian Peninsula from the rest of continental Europe. The Basque language, *Euskera,* is a distinct non-Indo-European tongue and an important, enduring element that continues to substantially define Basque cultural identity (Bidart 1980). There is also a long history of resistance on the part of many in the Basque region to being incorporated into either the French or Spanish states. This traces back at least to the Carlist Wars of the eighteenth century and the 1936–39 Spanish Civil War (Watson 2003). After an 1848 treaty normalized the permanent borders between France and Spain, the Basque region of France had to directly contend with a powerful, centralized state that slowly but ineluctably affected many aspects of Basque social, political, and economic life (Murray 2003). On either side of the political border that separates the Basque region, there persists a strong sense of cultural identity. For some, Basque identity is marked by the importance of Euskera and its use in public life; for others, it is a contested political expression aligned to varying degrees with nationalist sentiments (Douglass and Zulaika 2007). But Basque cultural identity in most of its manifestations relies on an idea of authenticity that is grounded by a historical distinction from its French and Spanish neighbors.

Over the past three decades, France has embarked on a gradual process of transferring some powers from the central government to the regions. In the case of the Basque region, however, this transferal has had little visible political effect, because there is no formal recognition of the Basque region as an institutional entity in France; in fact, the Basque region constitutes one half of the Pyrénées-Atlantiques department, whose prefecture is located in Pau. This lack of political recognition differentiates the Basque region of France from its southern counterpart in Spain that includes the Autonomous Basque Community, which enjoys significantly more institutional, fiscal, and political freedoms.

However, the Common Agricultural Policy of the European Union has had a marked economic impact on the Basque region over the last half-century, particularly on those communities located in France that are more rural and agricultural. For centuries, pastoralism has been the dominant economic and ecological force in this part of the Pyrenees Mountains (Braudel 1988; Galop 2005). Small-scale pastoralism and cheese production in the Basque region is seen as a form of farming that has persisted over time and is now closely associated with an authentic expression of Basque cultural identity. However, demographic shifts, economic market forces, European Union regulations, and changing social norms are driving a shift toward larger herds and more specialized farms, pushing the agropastoral system toward increased agricultural intensification. Farmers now face a political and economic reality wherein rapid changes in the marketplace can potentially destabilize their farming operations, and thus the practice of labeling and marketing their agricultural commodities, most notably cheese, may be interpreted as a means for contending with this increased uncertainty and instability. Many other discussions of labeling products by origin or other criteria focus on the idea of products of quality (Barham 2003; Bérard and Marchenay 2004; Bowen 2010; Trubek 2008). However, in this chapter, we add the dimension of authenticity that emanates from a politics of place to this wider discussion.

Beginning with the first PDO of Ossau-Iraty cheeses in 1980, the Basque region rapidly established itself as a place where small family farmers adopted value-added modes of agricultural production, focusing on quality products rather than volume as an important strategy for economic survival and success. This focus on quality products extends beyond PDO-labeled products and now involves nearly 40 percent of the farmers in the Basque region (Welch-Devine and Murray 2011). An emphasis on quality products has thus become an important marketing tool and is a way for rural areas to reinvent themselves by appealing to the eco-chic citizen conscious of the implications of their consumption patterns. The production of sheep cheeses under the PDO Ossau-Iraty, so named after two valleys in the Pyrenees Mountains, connotes a craft-produced or artisanal food good. These cheeses can either be purchased directly at the farm from the producers themselves or purchased from retailers. At its heart, the intent of the PDO label is to explicitly link product, producer, and place—a connection established through the concept of *terroir* (Teil 2012). The emphasis connoted in *terroir*, of course, is on quality production for the purpose of quality consumption, which makes agricultural products particularly fitting because they may be linked to an individual animal herd, to a particular farmer, or to a single village. A small-scale mode of production is well suited to iconic foods such as sheep cheese, which can be associated with a place such as the Basque region to conjure up a potent image of quality and authenticity.

The PDO Ossau-Iraty is today one of only two sheep cheeses (the more widely known Roquefort is the other) with this highly visible and recognizable brand in France. At a county fair in October 2004, a former president of Ossau-Iraty explained that the original motivation behind the creation of their PDO was to "highlight the tradition and authenticity of our [cheese] products, to prevent them from being considered an inferior product, and to provide a brand to our Basque goods." These ideas of tradition and authenticity are explicitly coupled with Basque identity to build a brand and to establish and project the idea of *terroir*. This comes through in Ossau-Iraty's marketing campaigns, which often conjure up stereotypical images such as, for example, the cover of a 2005 promotional brochure for PDO Ossau-Iraty products, which featured a broad-shoulder Basque farmer with ruddy cheeks and sporting a black, wool beret, the herd of sheep scattered across the hillside behind him. The brightly colored, italicized caption underneath this photo proclaimed that this PDO product "evokes an authentic countryside, cheeses with the earth's savor and strength," which conjures up a laudatory but somewhat vacuous image. These marketing instruments certainly constitute eco-chic practices on the part of producers who are generating a message that explicitly conveys ideas of tradition and authenticity in ways that are familiar and recognizable to consumers.

The normative criteria that farmers must follow to obtain the right to label their products PDO Ossau-Iraty are quite stringent, requiring candidate farms to adhere to rigorous guidelines and to carefully record their procurement and production procedures. These requirements supplement those required by the European Union's Common Agricultural Policy. The PDO Ossau-Iraty brand restricts the breeds of sheep that can provide milk used for making cheese to one of the three breeds indigenous to the western Pyrenees Mountains, specifically rejecting the use of exogenous breeds that may produce more milk. Most, if not all, animal feed must be either raised by the farmer or purchased from neighboring communities (although some exceptions are permitted in the case of shortages due to regional droughts, for instance), so as to better thread the idea of *terroir* throughout the cheese-production process. Finally, the PDO Ossau-Iraty brand also dictates many of the methods permitted in transforming sheep's milk into a craft cheese product, forbidding, for example, the pooling of milk from multiple sheep herds to make cheeses collectively. This idea that these cheeses must be made from milk collected from a single herd of sheep reinforces the overarching goal of PDO Ossau-Iraty to reflect a specific region and a specific farm and, ultimately, to produce a commodification of place.

In 2007, 29 percent of the total sheep's milk produced in the Basque region of France ended up as PDO-quality cheeses and involved 37 percent of the area's sheep farmers (AND International 2007). However, the expansion and marketing success of PDO Ossau-Iraty over the past three decades has not met the expectations of all Basque farmers who originally participated in this branding effort. Many farmers saw the PDO Ossau-Iraty not only as an economic development tool, but also as one that would allow them to make a specific social and political statement. Early on, the two main farmers' unions in the Basque region—Euskal Herriko Laborarien Batasuna (Farmers Union of the Basque Country, or ELB), which is affiliated with the Confédération Paysanne at the national French level, and the Féderation Nationale des Syndicats d'Exploitants Agricoles (National Federation of Farm Workers' Unions, or FNSEA)—were at odds over some of the production criteria involved in determining what was permissible under PDO Ossau-Iraty, namely which sheep breeds could be raised. ELB, in particular, saw the inclusion of exogenous sheep breeds as potential threats to the idea of a traditional and authentic manner of farming. In this sense, including exogenous sheep breeds would not only disrupt an eco-chic marketing strategy, but also run counter to historically important farming practices associated with their Basque identity.

Resisting Eco-Chic: The Idoki Farmers Association

The PDO Ossau-Iraty brand has certainly aided in marketing the mountain in general, and in the marketing of Basque cheeses in particular, by establishing a more visible connection between product, producers, and place. However, within a decade of the creation of the Ossau-Iraty brand, a number of Basque farmers had grown dissatisfied with its implementation and operation scheme and opted to create a new farmers association under the brand Idoki. Founded in 1992, Idoki developed a membership charter that claimed to "only support and defend small, human-scale producers... who love the Basque country,... and who prioritize the direct sale of their products to the consumers" (Idoki 1992). While it is worth noting that Ossau-Iraty and Idoki both place an emphasis on the value of small family farmers within the region, members of Idoki prioritize the connection between small-scale producers and consumers through direct, on-farm sales, and typically do not make use of retail outlets. Indeed, the Idoki charter authorizes a single intermediary in the supply chain, thus eliminating the use of wholesalers. This is an important point of difference with PDO Ossau-Iraty products, which are sold internationally through multiple levels of wholesalers and vendors. While a connection to the global market may often be seen as a sign of economic success, it does not always sit well with those Basque farmers like those of Idoki, who emphasize local production and local consumption. For instance, when told that Ossau-Iraty cheeses sold in American grocery stores for as much as three times the price per kilo as in France, a Basque farmer in Soule replied: "That's crazy. Those Americans. It's going to get to where Basques can't afford to eat Basque cheese."[1]

Idoki incorporates a specific social and political objective in their membership charter that speaks to the relationship between Basque farmers and their homeland. The Idoki charter explicitly calls on its members to be farmers "who love the Basque country" and to not solely content themselves with producing and selling their goods, but to also participate in nonmarket activities that nonetheless provide an added-value to the region. While there still is an explicit concern with the quality and authenticity of their products, Idoki's declaration departs from the types of eco-chic practices discussed so far in two important ways. First, there is an intentional articulation of the producer's patriotism that is absent in Ossau-Iraty's materials and arguably from that of most other PDOs. This serves to exclude those farmers either who do not identify as Basque or for whom politics closely associated with a nationalist movement are anathema to their eco-chic marketing strategies. The second point of difference is that Idoki's charter also urges its members to not only be concerned with economic objectives, but also be socially and politically active in their communities. In this light, conventional ideas of *terroir* are supplanted by a different sense of place, one that is explicitly mobilized for social and political purposes.

The reference in Idoki's membership charter to patriotism and nonmarket activities is not innocuous, but one that connects to a deeper social and political movement among farmers that has evolved over the past three decades and includes the emergence and rising popularity of ELB among Basque farmers (Murray 2009). One middle-age farmer explained his decision to abandon Ossau-Iraty after nearly six years of membership to join Idoki by downplaying the economic aspect of his decision: "I'm betting on quality, craft production rather than mass production. I believe that labels like Ossau-Iraty need to closely monitor the production of craft and industrial cheeses; otherwise craft Basque cheeses run the risk of being overwhelmed by low-quality, industrial cheeses."[2] This farmer expressed his belief that Idoki excelled at controlling the quality of their cheeses and did a better job of differentiating between craft-produced cheeses and industrial, or large-production, cheeses. But he also emphasized his feelings that the PDO Ossau-Iraty failed to distinguish between the types of producers that belonged to its organization, welcoming both farmers who market the mountain out of economic convenience, and those who were involved out of a sense of patriotic love. It is within this strained relationship that the practices of marketing eco-chic in the Basque region ebb and flow. In this light, Idoki may be seen as a movement that purposefully generates a relationship between producer and consumer that is distinct from PDO Ossau-Iraty, enabling the farmer in Idoki to not only make a living, but also make a conscientious statement about how they want to interact and connect with those who consume what they produce.

Market Environmentalism and Eco-Chic Possibilities in Natura 2000

In the aftermath of the Second World War, European farmers were tasked with feeding a population burdened with rebuilding a continent ravaged by conflict. Farming was a respectable profession, and rural dwellers enjoyed a certain social and political preeminence. Over the last half-century, however, farmers and other inhabitants of rural France have seen their social status steadily decline. Farming has become associated with environmental degradation, and farmers suffer an adversarial relationship with urban citizens and policymakers who increasingly scrutinize their practices (Alphandéry and Fortier 2001). The numerous, and rapidly proliferating, agricultural and environmental policies that farmers must integrate into their daily practices entail a modification not only of farm practices but also of the profession itself, and the role of farmers has shifted from simply being producers of food to being the guarantors of heritage, rurality, and the environment (Szarka 2002). One notable example of this shift is the 2003 Luxembourg Agreement on the second pillar of the European Union's Common Agricultural Policy, which decoupled direct-payment farm subsidies from production quotas, instead incentivizing other activities that fall under the rubric of ecosystem services, such as water-pollution mitigation practices or the maintenance of hedgerows as wildlife corridors.

Demographic shifts and intensification of farming are poised to dramatically alter the mountain landscape in Soule, and there is a desire among many to address pastoral practices with legislation. One of the most widely discussed environmental measures in the easternmost Basque province of Soule has been Natura 2000. The Natura 2000 measure was designed by the European Union as a coherent ecological network of areas managed for favorable conservation outcomes. Its two enabling pieces of legislation, the 1979 Birds Directive and the 1992 Habitats Directive, both use protected areas and conservation measures on private lands to protect some 200 habitat types and 700 species deemed "of Community importance" by the European Commission in 2002.[3] Agricultural land is strongly represented in Natura 2000, making up 41 percent of the network in France (Ministère de l'Ecologie du Développement et de l'Aménagement Durables 2007). This amounts to 2.78 million hectares, or 9.6 percent of the country's agricultural land. The process of transposing the two directives into French law was finalized in April 2001, though not one of these sites has yet been fully established in Soule.[4] Whether the appropriate course is to support agriculture in this region or to regulate it remains contentious. The Habitats Directive ostensibly seeks to do both: encouraging the continuation of farming in the region by promoting practices seen as relatively environmentally benign and reigning in those deemed harmful. Natura 2000 sites cover the mountain pastures of Soule almost in their entirety (see Figure 5.2).

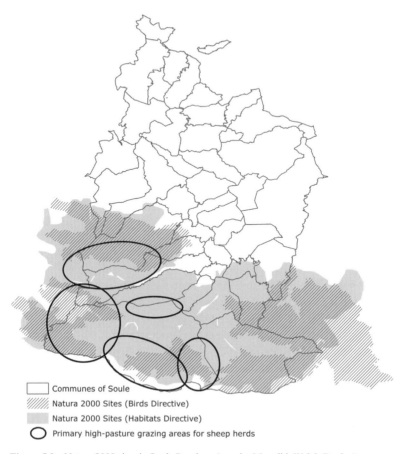

Figure 5.2 Natura 2000 sites in Soule Province (map by Meredith Welch-Devine).

Natura 2000's reception in the Basque province of Soule has been chilly at best. There is a lot of uncertainty on the part of farmers as to what changes Natura 2000 will entail, and there is fear that it will clash with traditional management practices. Most importantly, perhaps, farmers resent the feeling that the mountain is being protected from them rather than by them and that they bear disproportionately heavy constraints in service of this protection. "For us, it's 'alter your entire mode of production and deal with the bears.' For them, it's 'don't use so much water when you brush your teeth and get a low-flow toilet.'"[5] What enters into this dynamic as well is a strongly felt rural–urban divide, with the sense that the urban elite are dictating rural practice through policies such as Natura 2000. The mountain has ceased to be a productive and cultural landscape that belongs to the Basque farmers and has become the playground of the urban tourist and a global good for its environmental benefits.

In reaction to this, we have seen the appearance of a strong discourse linking traditional herding practices with sustainability, in an attempt to short circuit those using environmental discourses as a way of dispossessing farmers of their mountain landscapes. Farmers in Soule position themselves not only as caretakers of the land and landscape but also as its creators. They argue that their ancestors have raised animals in the Pyrenees since "before time" and that if there are rare species and valuable habitats in the high pasture it is due to and not in spite of their management practices. The farmers use this romanticized image of themselves as caretakers of nature to argue that they have no need for state intervention. Farmers repeatedly said such things as: "Our practices are what make the mountain beautiful" and "If it's beautiful here, it's because we've made it that way. For generations we've shaped these landscapes, and if there's something here worth protecting, it's because of us, not in spite of us."[6] In many ways, there is much truth to this linkage of traditional practices with sustainability, but it elides some important environmental issues—such as overgrazing and nutrient overloading in streams. As much as the farmers seek to present the mountain as a place where practices are homogeneous and benign, there are many approaches to herd and land management, and some appear more amenable to labeling and marketing as eco-chic than others.

Despite local resistance to the ever-increasing outside intervention in the mountain area, some Basque farmers have realized that Natura 2000 is a *fait accompli* and have turned their attention toward ways to live with the initiative and to turn it to their advantage. As in other parts of Europe, farmers in Soule are discussing the creation of a Natura 2000 eco-labeling scheme for products produced within their Natura 2000 sites (IIEP 2002). This represents an attempt to capitalize upon the implementation of Natura 2000 not only to provide new economic opportunities but also to assert their own political and cultural agendas, which may or may not conflict with Natura 2000. Although both PDO Ossau-Iraty and the Idoki farmers association have members in the area, neither organization has yet successfully articulated a policy position toward Natura 2000 that garners a consensus among farmers. This latest application of marketing the mountain, therefore, continues to be very much a work in progress.

Already, Basque cheeses are available in specialty shops across Europe. Cheese marketed under the label PDO Ossau-Iraty can be readily found in the cheese sections of certain upscale grocers in Sweden, Japan, or the United States. The effort to secure and use a Natura 2000 label for the cheeses produced in this region is an attempt by the farmers to financially capitalize on the tastes of urban elite markets and the ethical or environmental consumer and to garner a further price premium for these cheeses. At the same time, it is an attempt to assert farming as a respectable profession in France by highlighting the Basque farmer as an admirable steward of nature and its resources. As one farmer put it: "Having a label gives me some recognition for what I do. A Natura 2000 label would show consumers that I have adhered to certain procedures, that I am a steward of the environment. I want people to know that I'm not a destroyer of nature."[7]

Conclusion

The focus on creating and branding quality products in the Basque region of France now extends well beyond PDO-labeled products and involves nearly half of the farmers in the area. The illustrations that we offer here suggest a repertoire of production strategies that on the surface appear to draw from a single set of concerns and motivations. Indeed, much of the branding and marketing of goods produced by farmers may look identical to one another and evoke the same notions of authenticity and territory. However, it is not clear to us that these examples embody the same politics of place and identity. The values and attitudes expressed by PDO Ossau-Iraty producers center primarily on the issue of product quality and a rigorously defined production process tied to *terroir,* whereas farmers selling food goods under labels such as Idoki appear to act in terms that privilege their social and political engagement with Basque culture and identity. At the same time, Idoki purposefully unsettles and attempts to reconfigure the relationship between producer and consumer that is characteristic of neoliberal capitalist markets.

By focusing on the producers of eco-chic goods rather than on the consumers, this chapter brings into focus many of the issues surrounding the impact of production, marketing, and branding on those who themselves are producers and who share a region, a cultural identity, or other branded feature. There are inherent risks and consequences to marketing a rural place and way of life, because the creation and marketing of a place as a brand affects the people living and working in that place, even when they are not producing or consuming that good. These average citizens become what Robert Foster calls the "enduring publics" that are affected directly or indirectly by the practices of marketing eco-chic products. If, for example, images of farmers wearing black berets with sheep cheeses in hands, standing against the backdrop of an idyllic mountain landscape, are repeatedly deployed through advertising and promotional materials, then this marketing and branding constantly reinforces consumers' emotional expectations of what they perceive to be symbols of cultural Basque identity. This branding of Basque identity as rural and agricultural, for example, may be seen as an oversimplified and homogenizing caricature of a diverse people. At the same time, eco-chic marketing raises the question of the extent to which the market has taken over from the political arena in "achieving goals that have typically been civic matters" (Foster 2008). The branding of the Basque man—and it is almost always a man depicted—may also be seen as sanitizing Basque identity, attempting to replace the stereotype of the Basque bomb-thrower with that of the strong, rugged farmer. This image of the Basque farmer, and by extension the Basque region, may not be as contested as other elements of Basque (nationalist) politics have been, but the image is nevertheless a contentious portrayal, relying on images of and ideologies about rural farmers that are both wrong and damaging to rural producers. These ethnic descriptions produce and reproduce stereotypes of the Basque farmer that many of them may wish to leave behind.

Marketing Basque products as eco-chic may similarly obscure differences in practices among farmers that in turn may have negative consequences for the land and resources. In many ways, this branding does promote the quality of Basque agricultural products, by encouraging good practices to receive the desired designation of quality. However, because standards must be written in a way that they can be broadly applied and because they cannot address every aspect of production, labeling may hide some of the environmental costs incurred in modern-day farming, such as overgrazing, nutrient loads in soils and water, or the proliferation of less-desirable or invasive plant species. Consumers in

Paris may pay a price premium believing they are supporting environmentally friendly practices, yet the practices of one farmer might be quite different from those of his neighbor. Those differences are unlikely to be reflected in the remuneration that the farmer receives if they both fall under the labeling scheme. Farmers are thus in some senses incentivized only to do just enough to qualify and no more.

An emphasis on quality products is an important marketing tool and a way for rural producers to appeal to the eco-chic citizen conscious of the implications of the consumption patterns. We would go so far to say that the connections between agricultural product, producer, consumer, and place often disproportionately rely on urban consumers' nostalgic ideas of rural places and their search for authentic products. Although the emergence of eco-chic ideologies and practices may promote more sustainable and ethical patterns of consumption and be powerful tools and incentives for rural development, eco-chic marketing may also blur the distinctions between groups of rural producers and obscure the politics of place. We suggest that marketing the mountain in the Basque region in reality obfuscates some of the very practices highlighted by this branding. This chapter points at weaknesses and costs in a system that attempts to brand an entire place, people, and set of economic activities. But our critique should not undervalue the importance and place of eco-chic branding in local actors' repertoire of tools to improve the quality of the food products themselves, local environmental sustainability, cultural and political advancement, and farmers' economic livelihoods.

Acknowledgements

The authors would like to thank this volume's coeditors, Bart Barendregt and Rivke Jaffe, for originally including us in the 2011 conference sponsored by the European Science Foundation in Linköping, Sweden. Various components of our research have been supported by, among others, the U.S. National Science Foundation and the French Ministry of Culture, whose support we gratefully acknowledge.

–6–

Green Is the New Green: Eco-aesthetics in Singapore

Chris Hudson

From Changi airport and shopping malls to hotel lobbies and the lavatories at upscale restaurants, the city-state is festooned with delicate flowers, so it is hardly surprising that late last year Singapore hosted the World Orchid Conference. To say this event is a riot of colour is to say George Clooney is not bad looking. (McCabe 2012: 1)

Green Is Good

The airport terminal—that steel and glass paean to technological advancement and culture's domination over nature—is an unlikely place to find a thriving patch of Southeast Asian jungle. Yet, Terminal 3 at Singapore's Changi Airport houses a greenwall, a huge vertical equatorial rainforest of lush tropical plants, a butterfly garden, and a nature trail, alongside the standard global chain stores and other consumer outlets obligatory for airports. Visitors to Singapore are confronted even before they leave the confines of the terminal with two of the most important dynamics of consumer capitalism today: the aestheticisation of everyday life and the "green is good" ethos. This chapter examines the ways in which the conjunction of aesthetics and environmentalism can generate an affective force. In Singapore, this force has been mobilized in the interests of state building, national cohesion, economic development, and place making. Green is not only good, it is beautiful; as a global cultural imaginary, it can accommodate itself to the moral and ontological underpinnings of multiple state, commercial, community, and individual projects.

The green turn as an outcome of the environmental movement spearheaded by Greenpeace, Friends of the Earth, and other global institutions has transcended scientific concerns about permanent climate change and planet destruction to pervade the cultural imagination. A global discourse of saving the planet has precipitated a new vocabulary of metaphors and figurations that have emerged since the 1960s to reconfigure products, processes and behaviors as environmentally friendly, sustainable, or green. Green has become a designation for consumer production and consumption that claims to prioritize the environment. Sue Thomas lists *eco-chic,* and related terms such as *eco-fibre, eco-T-shirt,* and *eco-jeans,* as descriptors invented to reference some environmental connection (Thomas 2008: 531) and to render the product more attractive to the environmentally conscious. She dates the beginning of the eco-fashion movement to the launch of the Esprit Eco collection in November 1991 (2008: 530). The advantage of such prefixes and neologisms that allude to environmental awareness and concern for the future of the planet is that they are sufficiently general and semantically unclear enough to be transferable to other contexts. Green suggests any positive attributes connected to the pretext of a sustainable future. The 2006 issue of *Vanity Fair* announced that "Green is the New Black," thereby linking the fad-based consumption patterns of a global elite with the future of the planet. Daniel Esty and Andrew Winston have produced a handbook for turning "green into gold" by seizing competitive advantage through strategic management of environmental challenges (Esty and Winston 2009: 3), otherwise known as eco-advantage (2009: 26). Esty and Winston ask: "Why not use the eco-advantage to stick it to competitors? The 'green wave' that is sweeping the business world" (Esty and Winston 2009: 3) can be ridden to increased profits.

As Stephen Forshaw, vice president of public affairs at Singapore Airlines, notes: "You don't have to make environmental issues sexy: they already are" (Aitken 2008: 16). Noting the emergence of a slew of new terms such as *eco-sexy* and *ecolo-chic* to accompany the consumption of organic wine, bamboo dresses, hemp shirts, $300 eco-jeans and so on, journalist George Black wonders whether a better term would be *eco-narcissism* (Black 2007). Consumption, and the construction of lifestyle, are key features of identity performance, and consumption choices are "not only about how to act, but who to be" (Giddens 1991: 81). Rebecca Tanqueray's instructive book, *Eco Chic: Organic Living,* advises readers on how to render their homes eco-friendly without sacrificing chic. It foregrounds chic to the point where it is so dominant in the discussion that it is not merely fetishized, but has become a node of ontological security (Tanqueray 2000).

In addition to the promotion of the ethics of green, the environment itself is a marketable commodity. The rising popularity of eco-tourism in the form of adventure tours, jungle treks, nature discovery tours such as the orangutan tours of Borneo, and other experiences in which the tourist interacts with nature and consumes the environment through embodied action continue to proliferate and generate profits. For those who want an interaction with nature a little less vigorous than whitewater rafting in the Amazon, the environment can be consumed visually—a process now widely known as the tourist gaze (Urry 1990). John Urry (1992) has argued that the raising of an environmental consciousness and the growth in tourism are both effects of the increased importance of visual consumption. As an economy based on mass production gave way to post-Fordist flexible production, and mass consumption was superseded by forms of specialized consumption such as tourism, nonmaterial forms of production precipitated an economy of signs and space (Lash and Urry 1994). Use value was usurped by symbolic value and the consumption of signs rather than material goods became key features of the global economy. Central to this is the aestheticization of everyday life (Featherstone 2007).

In this economic regime, the production and consumption of place through tourism practices are associated with two forms of desire connected to environmentalism: (1) the search for symbolic values, such as sustainability and eco-friendliness, and (2) the aesthetic gratification, the sheer delight, and sensual pleasure of being in a beautiful natural environment. Virginia Postrel explains:

> Aesthetics is the way we communicate through the senses. It is the art of creating reactions without words, through the look and feel of people, places and things. Hence, aesthetics differs from entertainment that requires cognitive engagement with narrative, wordplay or complex, intellectual allusion…Aesthetics shows rather than tells, delights rather than instructs. The effects are immediate, perceptual and emotional. (Postrel 2003: 6)

In Nigel Thrift's terms, "aesthetics is an *affective* force that is active, intelligible…it is a force that generates sensory and emotional gratification" (2010: 292, emphasis in original). In the current climate of green is good and the global anxiety about permanent environmental damage, goods, events, experiences, and other forms of engagement created by forms of aestheticization may be intelligible within the wider cultural framework of environmental sustainability. Where environmentalism meets green aesthetics, the effect is what Sharon Boden and Simon J. Williams think of as "the channeling of affect through the calculative deployment of emotion in the service, or under the guidance of rationality" (2002: 498). The logic of the market—the rationality to which they refer—is wedded to the emotion invested in consumer goods, and the economy of desire in general, in an "arranged marriage" (Boden and Williams 2002: 498). In the context of the rising green economy, reason and emotion—desire in the service of capitalism—may also collaborate so that the rationality of the market and the drive for sustainability may together manipulate emotion and desire to encourage consumption not only of goods, but also of places, through aesthetics. One site where the imperatives of sustainability can collaborate with the profit-driven demands of the tourist industry to sell destinations is in the deployment of nature as aesthetic capital. In Singapore, economics collaborates with nature to enhance not just the environment but also private interests through the creation of an affective ecology.

The Greening of Singapore

In the 1960s urban slums, dilapidated and makeshift dwellings, and squatter populations were still common in Singapore. Traditional Malay-style *kampongs,* or clusters of communities, within the urban boundary were a feature of the young postcolony. Early in its developmental phase the government established the Housing Development Board (HDB), which demolished kampongs, Chinese shophouses, and other forms of domestic arrangements and replaced them with high-rise apartment blocks. Some 80 percent of the population now live in these ubiquitous high-density housing estates.

The construction of high-rise apartment blocks on estates constructed by the HDB was an important symbol of Singapore's transition to modernity. C. J. Wee has argued that Lee Kuan Yew[1] and his People's Action Party (PAP) engaged in a form of statist modernization and introduced a program of homogenizing social engineering of which the "bland postcolonial urbanism" epitomized by HDB towers is a concrete example (Wee 2007: 77). Along with industrial estates and downtown renewal in the form of demolition of traditional bazaars and their replacement with shopping complexes (Wee 2007: 81) and other forms of gentrification, HDB estates represent an "authoritarian urbanism" (Wee 2007: 79).

The homogenization of the urban environment and radical modernization to which Wee alludes (2007: 77–78), however, did not entirely denature the environment in its drive to engender a form of statist modernization grounded in instrumental reason and the devotion to functionality; rather, it actively relocated the natural environment as part of the developmental agenda. As the natural world was cleared to accommodate the built environment, new green areas, such as parks and park connectors, were "constructed" (Yuen, Kong, and Briffett 1999: 323).

These days, tourists leaving Changi Airport drive past the high-rise housing estates and industrial parks on routes lined with tropical vegetation. In fact, the vegetation not only lines the route, but on the busy Pan Island Expressway—a prime arterial road that runs across the island from Tuas in the West, to Changi Airport in the East—a median strip also provides space for nature to thrive. Visitors feel as if they are surrounded by green. This gives the impression not so much of a tropical jungle as of a well-manicured park, a regimented form of nature that reflects a resolute and highly managed strategy of a state intent on good governance and the creation of a disciplined citizenry. It represents the new green, a form of aesthetic capital in the service, not only of ecological sustainability, but also of cultural and economic sustainability.

The pervasive sense of environmental order is the result of a tree-planting program that was begun in 1963 by Lee Kuan Yew, in parallel with the razing of kampongs and construction of apartment blocks. An annual tree-planting day was instigated in November 1971 and has been a national day of importance ever since. It was not only an attempt to regenerate and sustain the eco-system in an industrializing nation, but also part of the nation building exercise. Lee had visited industrially advanced societies and observed that order and discipline were accompanied by a well-managed environment. An extensive program of the greening of Singapore was a crucial component of his development agenda after independence. Noting that most developing countries did not show due concern for the environment, Lee was unequivocal in his intention to deploy nature as capital for the nation-building project: "To achieve First World standards in a Third World region, we set out to transform Singapore into a tropical garden city" (Lee 2000: 175). He also commented on its economic consequences: "No other project has brought richer rewards to the region.... Greening was positive competition that benefitted everyone—it was good for morale, for tourism, for investors" (Lee 2000: 177).

The greening program, like a number of public campaigns launched since the 1960s for the purposes of social engineering, was also a campaign designed to modify behavior. Following the bans on the grazing of cattle in parks and streets in the 1960s were a number of other campaigns to improve urban space and generate respect for the environment.

These included the antispitting campaign, the antilittering campaigns, the banning of chewing gum, and the prohibiting of smoking in public places. Lee's long-term agenda to green Singapore was a comprehensive and forward-thinking project involving massive engineering works and the resettlement of people and relocation of activities. The Singapore River, once a polluted and stinking sludge, was cleaned up and revived. People who lived on barges on the river were moved and effluent no longer flowed into the river; fish returned. Three thousand people were moved from backyard and cottage industries to industrial estates, and 5,000 street food vendors were moved to regulated spaces where clean water was available and hygiene could be assured. Lee said of the greening program of the 1960s: "We planted millions of trees, palms and shrubs. Greening raised the morale of people and gave them pride in their surroundings. We taught them to care for and not vandalize the trees" (Lee 2000: 175).

The Parks and Recreation Department, which was responsible for Lee's clean and green initiatives of the 1970s and 1980s, was renamed the National Parks Board in 1996. Now commonly known by the abbreviation NParks, it was also instrumental in ensuring that the vision for a Garden City evolved into an all-encompassing concept: a mission to create a "City in a Garden." NParks has outlined six key areas of activity for ecological and social change to fulfill this vision: engage and inspire communities to create a greener Singapore, enhance competencies of our landscape and horticulture industry, enrich biodiversity in our urban environment, establish world-class gardens, optimize urban spaces for greenery and recreation, and rejuvenate urban parks and enliven streetscapes (National Parks 2011). A new intensified campaign of public engagement was launched in 2011. The chief executive of NParks, Poon Hong Yuen, was reported in the *Straits Times* commenting on Lee's project to mobilize the environment for development:

> The conventional wisdom is that development is achieved at the expense of nature. In Singapore our green cover, worked out from satellite images, has grown from 36 per cent in 1986 to 47 per cent in 2007, despite rapid economic and population growth. So rather than thinking our green drive is "artificial," I would prefer to say we have achieved something extra-ordinary through sheer will and decades of hard work. Officialdom's approach is more refined as well.... From ordinary trees that showcased our efficiency, we are now aiming for greater urban diversity and options for nature recreation that make Singapore a great city to live in. (Lee 2011)

Poon also noted that: "Mr. Lee saw greening as an integral part of nation-building. Well-managed greenery helped at that time to convince investors that Singapore was a place where things worked. It has instilled in Singaporeans a sense of pride that they live in the Garden City. These are benefits that cannot easily be quantified, but critical to nation building" (Lee 2011). It was a highly successful program, and today almost 50 percent of the island is covered with greenery. In an illustration of Singapore's commitment to the alliance of, on the one hand, rationality, measurement, and control, and on the other, the aesthetics of urban space, Poon observed: "No corner is left ungreened—not urban canyons or Chinatown, police stations or schools, overhead bridges or old estates.... Today, about two million trees have sprouted, and each is recorded in the NParks database" (Lee 2011). In addition to leaving no corner ungreened, Lee was so meticulous about the program and so involved at the ground level that he came to be thought of as "the Chief Gardner." Wong Yew Kwan, the first commissioner of Parks and Recreation from 1974 to 1982, reported that during the time he was commissioner he was flooded with memos and endless wish lists from the prime minister. He recalled Lee's obsessive involvement: "He likes walking in the Botanic Gardens in the evening. Then his personal secretary would call with requests. Mr. Lee might see pruned branches left on the side of the road. Or he wanted to know why leaves had fallen from a troubled tree" (Lee 2011). It is said that Lee Kuan Yew, still plants a tree every year.

Consistent action to green Singapore has, among other achievements, prevented soil erosion caused by tropical downpours, established a tropical/urban ecosystem, ameliorated the effects of the urban heat island, reduced air pollution, and created sustainable livability in a densely populated space. Han Fook Kwang, Warren Fernandez, and Sumiko Tan's volume on the ideas that drove Lee Kuan Yew makes the point that Lee wanted to transform Singapore into "a different city" (Han, Fernandez, and Tan 1998: 12). He did not want yet another Asian concrete jungle such as Hong Kong, nor a polluted uncontrolled sprawl such as Jakarta, and was not about to let climate or any other environmental factor get in the way. When the Singapore Botanical Gardens celebrated its 150th anniversary in 2009, Lee was there to reminisce about the strategy for greening. He gave his insights on the complexities of making Singapore into a "first world oasis" through transforming the environment and showing investors that Singapore was a well-organized place (Ministry of National Development 2009). He also observed that one of the biggest challenges was "motivating the public to change from Third World to First World behaviour" (Ministry of National Development 2009). The metanarrative of creating a first-world global city out of a third-world Southeast Asian semislum outpost of Britain involved the collusion of the economy with the environment. It was made clear by the Ministry of National Development at the 2009 celebrations:

> Today, the sight of tree-lined highways, manicured lawns and smartly-pruned hedges convey to visitors and potential investors, the message that Singapore is a place where things are done efficiently, where attention is focused on details, and where their investments would be well taken care of. The green environment also softens the harshness of urban living, uplifts the human spirit and improves the quality of life. (Ministry of National Development 2009)

Lee Kuan Yew has always understood the importance of control of the environment in the interests of livability. Cherian George has outlined his contribution to the development of Singapore through his introduction of a regime of climate control. George recounts the story, now legend, that when the *Wall Street Journal* asked several twentieth-century figures to nominate the most influential invention of the millennium, Lee named the air-conditioner (George 2000: 14) because it could transform a tropical environment into a temperate zone and, therefore, increase productivity and make Singapore competitive with the economies of colder climates. Singapore's society today is a blend of comfort and control (George 2000), an ordered society in which both citizenry and environment are centrally controlled.

Clearly, the greening program and its combination of strategies designed to create a sustainable environment and to represent Singapore as an efficient first-world economic success story have been an unqualified success. Singapore is an economic as well as an environmental oasis. The *Asian Green City Index*—a study commissioned by German company Siemens and conducted by the independent Economist Intelligence Unit (EIU)—designated Singapore as Asia's greenest city. The 2011 Siemens report alludes to the success of the Singapore project as a model of efficiency and good governance:

> Singapore City stands out in particular for its ambitious environmental targets and its efficient approach to achieving them.... The Asian Green City Index examines the environmental performance of 22 major Asian cities in eight categories: energy and CO_2, land use and buildings, transport, waste, water, sanitation, air quality and environmental governance.... "The study of Asian cities shows one thing very clearly: higher income does not necessarily mean higher resource consumption," said Jan Friederich, research head of the EIU study. "In addition, cities that performed well in the Index are characterized by their ability to successfully implement environmental projects and consistently enforce regulations," explained Friederich. (Siemens AG 2011)

Eco-aesthetics

The greening of Singapore was intended to change cultural practices and help to create a modern nation in a postcolony; it was designed to produce a more sustainable and livable urban environment; and it was about attracting investment by demonstrating Singapore's efficiency and control. It also had the effect of creating a new affective register. While green has always been green in Singapore, and is no mere fad, it is important to understand that a new sort of green affect has been created. Cities have an affective register, as Nigel Thrift (2004) points out, that can be observed in a range of behaviors, performances, and aesthetic practices. Aesthetic practices that can generate sensory and emotional gratification, produce "affective allegiances" and provide "the means of captivation" (Thrift 2010: 292) can take a number of forms. More importantly, they can also create "affective senses of space, literally, territories of feeling" (Thrift 2010: 292). Economies generate and mobilize affects to produce goods, services, and places that will captivate consumers. A green city is not just a more livable city, but also an economic asset because it conveys a sense of order and efficiency and appears as a safe place for investments; a green city represents aesthetic practices that generate "various mechanisms of fascination" (Thrift 2010: 290).

The greening program has meant that authoritarian urbanism and, some would say, the excessive management of social life by the government have acquired new forms of enchantment that create the affective allegiances necessary for the collaboration of reason with emotion. Since the 1980s the building of HDB blocks has been accompanied by the proliferation of high-end shopping malls offering goods and services favored by the global elite. It has been observed that this has produced a "national image closer to a coordinated shopping landscape than a political territory" (Chung et al. 2002: 217). Central to this image are what George Ritzer (2010: 7) has called "cathedrals of consumption," shopping malls with an enchanted, sometimes even sacred or religious, character. They are, in Ritzer's terms, "magical, fantastic, and enchanted settings in which to consume" (Ritzer 2010: 7). "Romantic capitalism"—a reenchanted world of dreams and fantasies driven by the romance of consumption (Campbell 1987)—is still a key feature of the economy in Singapore. Shopping—with its magical ability to create and fulfill fantasies—has occupied a central place in postcolonial Singaporean culture, so much so that Singapore sociologist Chua Beng Huat (2003) has argued that consumption is the culture of Singapore. Affective sense of place and various forms of emotional engagement are generated in these spaces. The city-state also has an enduring reputation as a paradise of shopping and eating. While shopping malls are ubiquitous and might obscure the image of a political territory, they cannot eclipse the intensity of the natural tropical beauty, the territories of feeling generated by omnipresent green. Orchard Road—Singapore's prime shopping precinct—differs from other upmarket shopping districts in Asia such as Tokyo's Ginza, Shanghai's Huaihai Road, or Hong Kong's Nathan Road in its dissolving of the boundaries between the urban and rural and the incorporation of nature into the cityscape. While the lure of shopping in the enchanted spaces of consumption might dominate the imaginations of visitors to Singapore, the greening program has made most of the island seem magical and enchanted. Elegant shopping complexes such as Wisma Atria, Plaza Singapura, Mandarin Gallery, Tang Plaza, ION Orchard, Ngee Ann City, and the Paragon are located in Orchard Road (formerly a nutmeg orchard), a well-greened thoroughfare; Vivocity is located on the beautiful Keppel Harbour. Through their association with shopping, spectacles, and performances designed to create Thrift's affective allegiances, and other forms of sensory pleasure, they have been transformed into landscapes of another sort; they transcend geographical meaning to become an ensemble of material and social practices in their symbolic representation (Zukin 1991: 16). "Natural" beauty, contrived through assiduous cultivation, the documenting and recording of every tree planted by NParks, and tireless attention to detail is now a crucial part of a new ensemble of material and social practices.

The Garden City Movement[2] has been influential in greening cities all over the world. Singapore has absorbed the ideas of the movement and the promotion of greenbelts in urban space to such an extent that these days the national image of Singapore is closer to a garden than the coordinated shopping landscape of Chung and colleagues' (2002) imagination. Recently, the Ministry for National Development and the NParks have escalated this project even further and begun to make the transition from "Garden City" to "City in a Garden" and to create a new lifestyle. The Ministry website declares:

> NParks aims to bring parks and green spaces right to the doorsteps of people's homes and workplaces.... NParks builds community ownership by enhancing lifestyle experiences in parks promoting the appreciation of greenery and nurturing a culture of gardening. (Ministry of National Development n.d.: 30–32)

The Gardens by the Bay project, which opened in June 2012, represents the ultimate transformation of a garden city to a city in a garden. The four gardens at Marina Bay present an eco-spectacle of immense ambition, scale, and beauty. The Gardens on the Bay is a park encompassing 101 hectares of reclaimed land on the edge of downtown Singapore comprising three green spaces on the waterfront: Marina Bay South, Marina Bay East, and Marina Bay Central. A display not only of environmental beauty, at once artificial and natural, it is also a tribute to the domination of culture over nature with its controlled atmosphere, cool climate, carbon neutral conservatories, the Cloud Forest (Figure 6.1) and Flower Dome, and a grove of eighteen supertrees. These are tower-like constructions, vertical gardens of climbing plants some 50 meters high that capture rainwater, filter exhaust, and act as ducts for the conservatories (Figure 6.2). Not content with environmental efficiency and green affect, solar panels provide energy for the supertrees to light up at night to create a new means of captivation in a sort of nocturnal tropical Disneyland, accompanied by a sound and light show. A walkway suspended between two supertrees allows an aerial view of the bay and an unobstructed view of the skyscrapers of Singapore, a reminder that it is a city in a garden. The Dragonfly and Kingfisher Lakes system channels run-off water from the Gardens and aquatic plants filter the water that is discharged into the Marina Bay Reservoir.

The Flower Dome, said to be largest climate-controlled space in the world, recreates a cool, dry microclimate to house plants exotic to Singapore, such as olive trees,

Figure 6.1   Cloud Forest, Gardens by the Bay, Singapore (photo by C. Hudson).

Figure 6.2 Supertree, Gardens by the Bay, Singapore (photo by C. Hudson).

date palms, and baobab trees. Gardens by the Bay was designated World Building of the Year at the 2012 World Architecture Festival. Wilkinson Eyre Architects, the winning team, not only expressed their intention to create a sustainable and energy efficient garden space, but also acknowledged the need to create affect. Paul Baker, one the architects, explained that they wanted to create "some real drama in a very flat landscape" (Dezeen Magazine 2012).

Every aspect of the combined urban and rural landscape of Marina Bay—reclaimed land, microclimates, artificial trees, event spaces, sound and light spectacles, and so on—is a manifestation of affective force, of emotion in the service of reason. Green affect and its accompanying sensory gratification have been described by visitors to Gardens by the Bay. One visitor's response to the experience of the gardens at night illustrates Thrift's means of captivation at work:

> As we walked across the Garden Bay bridge from Singapore's waterfront, the vision before us was unexpected and overwhelming.... [T]he first view of 18 Supertrees (some up to 16 storeys high) and two giant glasshouse biodomes (the largest the size of a couple of football fields) caused a physical reaction akin to that freaky first scene of the alien tripods emerging from the earth in *War of the Worlds.* The frequent forked lightning, thunderclaps and heavy skies of a tropical rainstorm only heightened the effect. (Liptrot 2012)

The extended space is suffused with lush vegetation, vibrant tropical blooms, and a luxuriant sensation of being in an all-encompassing garden. Only the most unimaginative visitor could fail to be moved by it.

Augmented by the Ministry's Community in Bloom program (part of a global movement promoting green spaces in communities) and given added buzz by the annual Singapore Garden Festival and the staging of the Twentieth World Orchid Show in November 2011—internationally recognized as The Olympics of Orchids—NParks has contributed to the increasing affect in urban spaces and to the means of captivation of residents and visitors alike. Excitement linked to environmental awareness has created territories of feeling that engage locals and tourists. The National Environment Agency has organized an annual two-day Clean and Green Singapore Carnival that encourages awareness, recycling, water and energy saving, and other measures individuals can take to help achieve a more sustainable city. This is accompanied by theatrical and musical performances in already green, eco-aestheticized spaces such as Gardens by the Bay, which both attract visitors to Singapore and create excitement combined with civic pride for residents.

The continued greening of Singapore is a key feature of this hyperaestheticized landscape where the consumption of nature coincides with the material culture of Singapore to create the tourist experience. The Ministry links knowledge of sustainability and aesthetic values with entertainment when it says that:

> the Gardens by the Bay will provide a new dimension to Singapore, encapsulating our City in a Garden theme. These gardens will provide colour, vibrancy and green space in which the best of our garden craftsmanship, horticultural displays and plant-based edutainment will be offered. It will capture the essence of Singapore as the premier garden city. (Ministry of National Development n.d.: 35)

The garden craftsmanship provided by NPark's team of professional horticulturalists is enhanced by the training in horticulture and landscaping provided by the Centre for Urban Greenery and Ecology (CUGE). Established by NParks and the Singapore

Workforce Development Agency, CUGE developed a mission to offer skill development to professionalize the landscape industry (Centre for Urban Greenery and Ecology 2011). Apart from horticulturalists and landscape architects, CUGE offers training for arborists, chain saw operators, park managers, and nature interpretation guides.

The National Parks Board has mobilized nature for the tourist gaze in urban space. The national newspaper, the *Straits Times,* reported on Lee Kuan Yew's observations as he inspected the progress of the Gardens on the Bay project in 2011. He reiterated his conviction that a beautiful, green, and sustainable city is also an economic asset and a competitive advantage:

> Mr Lee Kuan Yew, Singapore's former prime minister, gave his nod of approval yesterday as he took in the bountiful blooms in the Flower Dome, one of three sections in the Gardens by the Bay complex being developed by the National Parks Board....The journey to building this "world-class garden" by the bay can be traced back almost 50 years, recalled Mr Lee. "It was to make Singapore green...." Cities of concrete buildings, tarmac and pavements would be depressing and unpleasant to live in, he said. "You need to balance that with trees and flowers." Almost half of Singapore is covered with greenery, he noted, adding that "this has become an economic value to us...." But many countries also plant trees now and call themselves garden cities, he said, and to remain competitive, Singapore has a new vision: City in a Garden. (Wong 2011)

Conclusion: Eco-aspiration

The aim of aesthetic meaning, as Postrel points out, is to capture and convey identity and to turn an ineffable sense of self into something more tangible and authentic (Postrel 2003: 108–9). As the Green-is-the-New-Black ethos and the global desire for the eco-chic products demonstrate, green is also a class-based project, and eco an aspirational value for affluent consumers. Christopher Solomon reports on the ways in which the jungle adventure and hike into the orangutan rainforests—perhaps the identity project of young backpackers—has been transformed into less energetic and more indulgent experiences of eco-tourism:

> Not long ago the terms "eco-tourism" and "eco-lodge" tended to conjure up a rough image: an unwashed adventurer sleeping on the floor of an Amazon hut, frayed Lonely Planet guide for a pillow. Today the offerings under the eco tent have expanded hugely—and in some cases so have their price tags. From Australia to Nicaragua, travelers can find ever more eco-chic oases where they can have their close encounters with spider monkeys and eat their mango crème brûlée, too. (Solomon 2005)

Singapore offers plenty of opportunities for eco-chic consumption with high price tags, or what Van Jones calls eco-elitism (2008: 98). A newly opened hotel, The Parkroyal on Pickering, provides accommodation for ecological haves—that is, people who enjoy access to "healthy, morally upstanding green products and services" (Jones 2008: 53).

It offers luxury, aesthetic pleasure, and indulgence while it allows the affluent visitor to Singapore to identify with green values. With its guarantee to exclude the less well-heeled, it appeals also to the eco-narcissism identified by Black (2007). One website describes the Parkroyal on Pickering as one of Singapore's greenest hotels:

> The 367-room hotel redefines the metropolitan skyline with a unique hotel-in-a-garden concept offering 15,000 square metres of lofty sky gardens, and an exclusive rooftop Orchid Club Lounge…a dedicated wellness floor with terrace pool, spa and a garden walk high above the street level. Parkroyal On Pickering Singapore Hotel [is] one of Singapore's greenest hotels. (HotelClub 2013)

At its opening in January 2013, Parkroyal on Pickering appealed to consumer ego—the eco-narcissists and seekers of status affirmation—and the desire to be on trend when it offered the following opening special:

> Be among the first to stay at our hotel-in-a-garden, and get ready to explore our dedicated wellness floor with infinity pool, spa and a walking track high above the street level. At only S$278++, enjoy overnight accommodation in a Superior room with daily breakfast and complimentary Wi-Fi….Did you know that PARKROYAL on Pickering is one of the first amongst Singapore hotels to feature a solar energy system? All the glow lamps and sky garden night lighting are powered by the substantive 60kWp solar PV, thus reducing the consumption of precious non-renewable resources. (Parkroyal on Pickering Singapore 2013)

The state project of transforming a colony into a member of the geopolitical elite of first-world countries was one of the catalysts for the instigation of the greening program. Later, the establishment of Singapore as a global city—loosely defined in terms of its importance as a node in the global economic system—encouraged both elite and mass-market tourism. The conventional shopping and eating experiences offer an increasingly regreened urban environment where consumers can be captivated by the natural beauty of the island. Because the aesthetic capital constituted by nature cannot be controlled in the same way that price can be used to exclude people from elite consumer experiences, the enjoyment of nature, unlike the aspirational green of expensively retrofitted houses and eco-chic clothes popular in the West, can sometimes be independent of the constraints of class position. Low-rent and polluted and decaying industrial districts in any city are usually inhabited by citizens with little access to cultural or economic capital—Jones's "ecological have-nots" languishing in the smoke and fumes (2008: 53). Jurong Penjuru, a dormitory district for foreign workers in Singapore, is a grim and depressing industrial wasteland with little of the manicured tropical beauty found elsewhere and inhabited by the foreign workers who build the Gardens on the Bay, the HDB towers, and other projects. These foreign workers, however, are not without access to green territories of feeling, the constraints of limited resources and denial of citizenship rights in Singapore notwithstanding. Botanic Gardens and parks all over the world are usually free and allow for a popular engagement with a greened environment.

It is no coincidence that Gardens on the Bay is adjacent to the Marina Bay Sands hotel, casino, and shopping mall complex. This prime real estate is another example of the Singapore government's control of the natural environment. The process of reclaiming land has transformed the geography of the mouth of the Singapore River, expunging the Telok Ayer Basin and causing the river to flow into a freshwater reservoir rather than the sea. With water skiing and sailing now possible in a regreened urban landscape only a short walk from Singapore business district, Marina Bay is an articulation of the identity aspirations of the nation itself. *The Business Times* reported that: "The vision for Marina Bay is that of a high-quality, 24/7 live-work-play environment, one that encapsulates the essence of the global city Singapore is envisaged to be" (Ching and Ng 2008: 7). While the one hectare rooftop garden, Sands Sky Park, at the Marina Bay Sands Hotel can only be enjoyed by those with the financial means to cover the substantial nightly tariff, the affect generated by the neighboring Gardens on the Bay can be enjoyed by anybody regardless of class or income. The cost of water skiing and sailing may be prohibitive, but this does not preclude the exercising of citizen gaze alongside the tourist gaze.

The paradox of Singapore is that it maintains an obvious commitment to a sustainable environment while at the same time continuing its dependency on consumption. It is, of course, not unique in this respect. Singapore is still a place for the construction of self through its signature activities of shopping and eating. While hotel guests might feel themselves to be morally superior, and their sense of environmentally concerned self enhanced by staying in a hotel that uses solar power, the existence of the wellness floor with infinity pool and spa still speaks of self-obsessive consumption and identity fetishism.

In light of the transformation of Singapore through greening and the eco-aesthetics described above, it seems appropriate to revisit the analyses of Singapore's urban landscape by C. J. Wee and influential Dutch architect and critic of urban development Rem Koolhaas. Wee (2007: 77–98) identifies a homogenized, rather uninspiring, urban environment. Koolhaas, as Wee points out, condemns Singapore as a sort of fake, with an "inauthentic and no longer internally coherent existence that has created a decontextualized urbanism" (Wee 2007: 79). For Koolhaas, Singapore is a "city without qualities" (Koolhaas cited in Wee 2007: 79). It is clear that Singapore is not a city without qualities. While these qualities may be inexorably tied to the postindustrial economy and its dependence on commodity fetishism, the creation of lifestyle, and the aestheticization of the ordinary, they nevertheless appear in a continuum, a form of coherent existence.

It might not be going too far to suggest that in its transformation from colony to First World City in a Garden Singapore is unique. It would be hard to find another city so extensively and conscientiously greened. In this sense then, Singapore should be judged not on its authoritarian urbanism, but on its sustained beautification of the built environment. Lee Kuan Yew's endeavors to create "a different city" have also produced a different aesthetic, one that was not recognized by Wee or Koolhaas. The greening of Singapore has meant that the city-state has recontextualized itself and transformed a postcolony into something new, even authentic: a tropical urban landscape with a powerful affective allure in the register of the eco-aesthetic.

–7–

The Caring, Committed Eco-Mom: Consumption Ideals and Lived Realities of Toronto Mothers

Kate Cairns, Kim de Laat, Josée Johnston, and Shyon Baumann

Introduction

The idealized image of the eco-chic consumer is often a woman and a mother. Indeed, many studies show that women are more likely to be engaged with eco-consumption (Bellows, Alcaraz, and Hallman 2010; Starr 2009; Stolle and Micheletti 2006; Zelezny, Poh-Phung, and Aldrich 2000) and that mothers with young children are more likely to buy organic foods such as milk (Hill and Lynchehaun 2002). The realm of eco-consumption is also shaped by dynamics of social class, given the considerable financial and cultural capital required to achieve the performance of the discerning, environmentally conscious consumer (Cairns, Johnston, and MacKendrick 2013; Guthman 2003; Johnston and Szabo 2011; Johnston, Szabo, and Rodney 2011). In this chapter, we focus on mothers as eco-consumers. Specifically, we argue that eco-consumption is one contemporary form of caring consumption (Miller 1998; Thompson 1996) that North American mothers are encouraged to perform—a resource- and knowledge-intensive mothering project that operates as a gendered form of class distinction.

Caring consumption can manifest in various consumption choices where someone consumes with the goal of meeting the needs and desires of another. Although theoretically gender neutral, caring consumption has been studied particularly as a woman's responsibility, linked to gendered patterns of social reproduction (e.g., Thompson 1996). Eco-consumption serves this purpose when mothers seek to care for the nutritional and health needs of families, as well as the needs of the planet. While both modes of consumption are mediated by class, eco-consumption, in particular, requires access to privileged information concerning nutrition and the environment, as well as additional financial resources for expensive eco-friendly purchases. One's ability to enact eco-consumption is thus doubly circumscribed by class location.

The relationship between women's caring consumption and eco-consumption has not been thoroughly explored in prior research. By drawing from qualitative data exploring the choices of Canadian mothers who are green consumers, we are able to investigate the gendered dimension of eco-consumption. We ask the following questions: How does eco-consumption operate as a historically and culturally specific mode of caring consumption? What are the tensions between eco-consumption ideals and the lived experiences of shopping to express care for one's family and the earth? How are these tensions mediated or intensified by dynamics of social class?

Using the North American cultural ideals of gendered caring consumption as a theoretical point of departure, we investigate the lived experience of caring consumption in the specific realm of environmental purchases. Through focus group[1] discussions with fifty-six food consumers in Toronto, Canada, we identify an idealized figure—the Eco-Mom. This figure represents a set of ideals and norms that present sustainable consumption as a gold standard of good mothering. In North American media, mothers' caring consumption is dominantly framed as empowering, natural, and unproblematic (Bordo 1993; Douglas and Michaels 2004). By contrast, our focus groups with Canadian women consumers show that the experience of expressing care through environmentally sensitive purchases is often difficult to carry out—especially with the financial and time constraints many mothers face.

We argue that there are three key points of tension that characterize the lived experience of mothers who strive to fulfill the Eco-Mom ideal. Specifically, we identify tensions in how (1) information, (2) time, and (3) money factor into mothers' consumption choices. These tensions make eco-consumption problematic for the Canadian mothers in our study, because they require investments in resources that vary by class location and generate a gendered division of domestic labor that takes an emotional toll. Despite the predominant win-win frame of eco-consumption as pleasurable and easy (Johnston 2008; Johnston and Cairns 2012), our findings suggest that eco-consumption provides a venue where mothers are often left with the experience of failing to achieve yet another ideal of intensive mothering (Hays 1996).

Next, we review prior work on key concepts in this chapter, including intensive mothering, depictions of intensive mothering, and the caring consumption ideal in popular North American media and ethical consumption.

Mothering: Idealized, Intensive, and Sustainable

To understand the anxieties implicit in the concept of the Eco-Mom, we take as our point of departure research on motherhood in North America, as well as examinations of how motherhood and caring consumption are idealized in popular North American media. Following this, we address the way conceptions of maternal responsibility are extended through contemporary discourses of eco-consumption.

Caring consumption "is driven by feelings of responsibility for enhancing the well-being of others and a sensitivity to the interpersonal consequences of one's actions and choices" (Thompson 1996: 401). As a mode of consumption, it is representative of "intensive mothering" (Hays 1996), a hegemonic frame identified in feminist scholarship for understanding what and who constitutes a good mother in contemporary North American society.[2] Drawing on analyses of the gendered nature of housework and childcare (see, e.g., DeVault 1991; Hochschild 1989), Hays (1996) examines the contradiction between the rational, utility-maximizing role one is expected to personify in public realms, and the nurturing, selfless role that typifies motherhood in the private realm. She argues that the latter ideology has grown more prominent in North America over time, even for those women who must confront a self-interested, economistic ideology in the paid workforce. Indeed, the contradictory ideologies bolster one another and promote a moral dimension within conceptions of motherhood that emphasizes sacrificing oneself to one's children (Blair-Loy 2001, 2003). Intensive mothering is premised on the belief that childrearing is first and foremost the responsibility of the mother and is characterized by large investments of emotional time and energy into children's development. The net result is an intensified ideology of motherhood that is "child-centered, expert-guided, emotionally-absorbing, labor-intensive, and financially expensive" (Hays 1996: 8).

The commodity-centered ideology of intensive mothering takes on new meaning amid contemporary discourses of ethical consumption, especially its dominant North American manifestation as green consumption, or eco-consumption (Johnston 2008). Eco-consumption became a dominant fixture of North American food discourse in the late twentieth and early twenty-first century, visible in the proliferation of shopping venues like Whole Foods Market, the widespread popularity of films like *Food, Inc.,* and the adoption of alternative consumption discourses by corporate market actors (e.g., Wal-Mart organics) (Johnston and Cairns 2012). Within discourses of eco-consumption, individual consumer choice is imbued with collective significance as a means of creating change (Johnston, Szabo, and Rodney 2011); as such, mothers' shopping practices take on a new level of environmental significance. Given that women continue to do the majority of household shopping (see, e.g., Lachance-Grzela and Bouchard 2010), the rise of eco-consumption has prompted "a surge in green commercialism that primarily targets women" (Smith 2010: 67). Thus, feminist scholars highlight a gendered dimension within recent shifts toward what consumption scholars have dubbed the commodification of care (Goodman, Dupuis, and Goodman 2012). As a result, dominant North American understandings of maternal accountability now extend beyond the domestic sphere to include caring for animals, eco-systems, and distant others through conscientious purchases in a global economy (Cairns, Johnston, and MacKendrick 2013; Hawkins 2012).

In this context, we witness the rise of what we term Eco-Mom—an idealized mothering figure that reflects the discursive intersection of intensive mothering (Hays 1996) and eco-consumption (Johnston 2008). Exemplifying notions of maternal care and selflessness along with a sophisticated environmental awareness and commitment to ecological justice, the Eco-Mom selflessly consumes in the service of both child and planet. This historically and culturally specific articulation of caring consumption has a complex relationship to the dominant caring consumer. While eco-mothering emerges within the broader North American context of intensive mothering and caring consumption, the

Eco-Mom takes on the extra burden of caring for the planet, and this distances her from the average consumer in ways that reflect and reproduce class boundaries. While male shoppers are also enmeshed within a broader discourse of ethical consumption, the Eco-Mom ideal reflects the particular ways that household shopping responsibilities and familial health continue to weigh more heavily on the shoulders of mothers (e.g., Beagan et al. 2008). As a classed and gendered cultural ideal, the Eco-Mom models her commitment to ecological justice and refined knowledge of environmental sustainability, leading to an elite performance of caring consumption characterized by environmentally minded purchases that require both economic and cultural capital.

In keeping with the win-win narrative of ethical consumer discourse that is dominant in North America (Johnston and Cairns 2012), eco-mothering is idealized as a pleasurable consumption project easily attained alongside other maternal commitments, such as protecting family health. North American lifestyle magazines offer a seemingly endless array of "'simple' and 'easy' ways for women to 'go green'" (Okopny 2012: 135) while fulfilling caretaking responsibilities. While eco-consumption is positioned as an important element of elite maternal care work, sociological research suggests that the Eco-Mom ideal is rife with contradictions. Feminist scholars draw attention to how narratives of green consumerism work to privatize environmental problems through individual commodity solutions (MacGregor 2006; Sandilands 1993; Smith 2010). This privatization results in increased "expectations for women's domestic labour, encouraging women to educate themselves, learn new skills, and approach each day with heighted eco-awareness" (Okopny 2012: 135). Such awareness demands resources, as acquiring the requisite knowledge depends on cultural and human capital, while purchasing green and organic products requires financial capital (Cairns, Johnston, and MacKendrick 2013; Goodman, Dupuis, and Goodman 2012; Guthman 2003; Johnston, Szabo, and Rodney 2011). The process by which the intensive mother who is invested in ethical consumption becomes an Eco-Mom, then, is inherently classed.

While the Eco-Mom figure represents a seamless intersection of two powerful North American discourses—intensive mothering and eco-consumption—what is not clear is how mothers experience the Eco-Mom ideal in their daily consumption practices. What lived complexities are obscured by idealized discourses of the (middle-class) mother-consumer who skillfully shops, feeds, and cares for her family, while also promoting environmental well-being? We explore these questions through an analysis of Canadian mothers' focus group narratives of the lived experience of food shopping. Although some participants did not align their personal shopping practices with a narrative of ethical consumption, the Eco-Mom ideal emerged as a central theme in these discussions for most of the women we spoke with. Women frequently discussed efforts to feed their families in ways that expressed care for family members, but were also ecologically sustainable. It is worth noting that these food criteria were often interchangeably used in our conversations (e.g., talking about healthy organic food or delicious local food), and it was not always possible to parse out whether health, aesthetic, or environmental concerns were the dominant motivating factor in shopping decisions. While this chapter is not able to shed light on the relative balance of food motivations, we did clearly observe the presence of an Eco-Mom ideal in women's life worlds—a standard for food work that is green and healthy, sustainable for the earth, and nurturing for children's growing bodies. We argue that the Eco-Mom represents a particular kind of intensive-mothering project that demands significant information, time, and money—and consequently, often generates feelings of stress and inadequacy for women struggling to get food on the table.

Information, Time, and Money: Key Tensions for the Eco-Mom

In this section, we present an analysis of the ways Canadian focus group participants related to the Eco-Mom figure. The ideational foundation of the Eco-Mom is one in which mothers are presented as able to skillfully manage information, time, and money while satisfying children's needs alongside environmental ideals. We organize our analysis around these three themes. Canadian mothers' narratives of the lived experience of shopping sustainably while feeding children show how hard these women struggle to satisfy the Eco-Mom ideal. Information can be overwhelming and contradictory. Time is short. Money is not always available. These idealized standards provoke guilt in mothers facing pressure to care for children through informed, time-consuming, and resource-intensive food purchases that are ecologically sound. Moreover, access to each of these thematic resources varies by class, requiring privileged access to knowledge about ecological food choices, leisure time, and, of course, financial capital.

Information

Our focus group data reveals information to be a central theme in Canadian women's accounts of their everyday consumption. Many mothers described engaging in ongoing research to better understand the health and environmental implications of their food shopping. Women frequently incorporated insights from a variety of sources, including documentaries like *Food Inc.,* and writing about food politics by well-known American authors such as Michael Pollan *(The Omnivore's Dilemma)* and Jonathon Safron Foer *(Eating Animals).* They also drew guidance from eco-consumer guides like the "Dirty Dozen," a list of twelve foods with the highest pesticide residue put together by the Environmental Working Group, an American nonprofit organization. For example, Selena, who has a two-year-old daughter and is training to be a midwife, explains: "[My daughter] eats a bunch of fruits and vegetables, so anything that's in the top ten for pesticides I try to buy organic."

Access to knowledge is mediated both by cultural capital (e.g., knowing which sources to read and trust) and financial capital (e.g., using smartphone applications to guide one's purchases). Regarding the former, Matilda, a middle-class mother of two who works as a professional mediator, notes that:

[W]e read the alternative weeklies and all the free Toronto foodie magazines that tend to be around. And in there, they're all talking about local and organic and, dishes of this and that, or the other. So I mean, it's partly, it's not seeking it out so much as having the luxury to live in an area where that information is all over the place.

While information may appear to be all over the place, readership of food sources tends to vary by social location (Johnston and Baumann 2010: 224), and access to information about ethical consumption is not equally accessible to all citizens in all neighborhoods (Barnett, Clarke, and Cloke 2005; Johnston, Szabo, and Rodney 2011). Indeed, Matilda and the other members of this focus group repeatedly emphasized the ways in which their eco-consumption practices were facilitated by the rich opportunities for information-sharing available in their upper-middle-class Toronto neighborhood, which is known throughout the city for its high number of sustainable shopping venues, including organic grocers, ethical butchers, and high-end farmers markets (Johnston, Rodney, and Szabo 2012).

Food and shopping decisions are not purely driven by rational calculations or deliberate choices (Caplan 1997; Johnston and Cappeliez 2012), but it was clear in our focus groups that individual research projects shaped mothers' food practices. After researching industrial farming conditions and the potential health effects of hormones, several mothers described various ways they had reduced their meat consumption, a decision thought to have positive repercussions for family health and food system sustainability. Others, like Sue, a middle-class mother employed as a family support worker, described using a smartphone application to select ethically harvested fish for her husband and two young daughters:

> I can't remember what is the evil canned tuna and what's the good canned tuna! I can't remember that on my own. I would say that has affected our consumption of fish because you know, I am also anxious, especially anything that says ocean fish, as opposed to lake fish…occasionally you see Pacific wild salmon, and that is better than Atlantic farmed, but even then, the wild salmon when it is in season is ethically sounder than a farmed piece of Atlantic salmon.

Reliance on smartphone applications, and Sue's sentiment that she "can't remember" vital information on her own, underscores the burden produced by a surplus of overwhelming and sometimes contradictory information. Sue's comment about feeling "anxious" in the face of complicated shopping decisions resonates throughout our focus group data. Rather than engendering a sense of empowerment, the vast amount of information available left many women in our sample feeling overwhelmed in their efforts to consume in ways that would advance the well-being of their children and the environment. "I have magnified all the stuff you read in magazines," said Zahra, a middle-class freelance writer with a nine-year-old daughter; "so, hormones in meat and its effect on prepubescent girls…I've somehow come across novels about stuff like that." Many mothers echoed the sentiment that information frequently creates stress, rather than security.

Contrary to ideals of confidence and control associated with an Eco-Mom ideal, mothers' focus group narratives are punctuated by statements of uncertainty and anxiety as they attempt to decipher and filter complex information to fulfill their commitment to caring, conscientious consumption. What's more, they noted how navigating these competing environmental claims was a historically specific challenge. Lamenting how "complicated" shopping has become, Matilda remarked, "I don't think my mom sat there and thought, 'is it local, is it organic, is it ethical, am I supporting factory farms?' I mean, she just went and bought food."

Part of the stress associated with mothers' informed consumption is the challenge of navigating competing objectives and often contradictory information relating to various ethical and environmental factors. Put differently, having ample information did not always mean that the correct consumption path was obvious—particularly given the competing knowledge claims that characterize the North American foodscape, as powerful corporate actors vie for a piece of the eco-consumption pie (Johnston, Biro, and MacKendrick 2009). This presents challenges for all food shoppers, but our focus groups suggest that the complexities of green food shopping add an extra dimension of stress and responsibility to family foodwork patterns that are highly gendered and fall disproportionately on the shoulders of women (e.g., Beagan et al. 2008). It is not that fathers never care about sustainable food or experience pressure around family food work—although the standard is undoubtedly more flexible for fathers than it is for mothers (see Chabon 2010; Doucet 2006). Our point here is that the gold standard of good mothering gets ratcheted up by Eco-Mom; this version of the good mother not only provides healthy, delicious meals that her family loves, but also meals that are earth-friendly and sustainable (see Cairns, Johnston, and MacKendrick 2013).

Besides the problem generated by such elevated standards, the lived experience of caring for one's family and the earth through food choices is not always straightforward. Consider the case of Sadie, a thoughtful working-class single mother employed part-time as a city parks worker. Sadie clearly thinks that part of her maternal responsibility involves fostering ethical consumption practices in her two boys. However, this task is complex, and she describes the tension between local and organic as "a dilemma." This dilemma was experienced as a significant source of strife for Sadie, a committed environmentalist, but also a mother who is worried about the effect of pesticides on her children: "do you want something that's close to home but it could be full of pesticides? Or do you want something that's organic that's travelled thousands of miles to get to you?" For Sadie, ethical issues are always considered alongside questions of health, and she reports that she is "constantly concerned about buying my children the best quality stuff that I can find because then I feel like they will have a healthier constitution." Sadie described these kind of decisions as mentally and emotionally draining: "It's just exhausting! Constantly, analyzing similar foods and analyzing everything." Sadie's narrative disrupts idealized conceptions of the informed Eco-Mom who skillfully optimizes her shopping decisions. Furthermore, the fact that Sadie's research yields conflicting priorities also challenges the win-win narrative of ethical consumer discourse (Johnston and Cairns 2012). Contrary to celebratory claims about the ease of eating for change, our focus groups reveal ethical food shopping to be rife with contradictions—contradictions that create feelings of anxiety and uncertainty for women whose sense of maternal responsibility and ecological justice is channeled through their food-shopping practices.

Few mothers in our sample were able to dismiss the ideal of fully informed consumption, and many experienced emotional strain due to a pervasive sense of uncertainty in their food choices. Vicky, a middle-class artist and arts-educator, said "I worry about what's in the chicken, like, the meat...Cuz I worry about my daughter." Vicky's concern that her meat choices may have detrimental health effects for her adolescent daughter was exacerbated by the feeling that she is not adequately informed. "I don't feel I'm educated enough in all the chemicals," she said. Vicky presented the limits of her own knowledge as a personal failure in her role as mother, and added "I should educate myself more about this stuff." Even those who were highly knowledgeable about the food system expressed skepticism about the information available. Robin, a middle-class PhD student, shared her frustration with the challenge of researching the meat that she feeds to her young son, and said, "I want to know where it's coming from and a lot of times I find that it's opaque." This sense of uncertainty engenders stress for many mothers who seek ethical choices when shopping for their children—a far cry from the expert-guided intensive mother-consumer ideal.

Closely linked to the tensions arising from information pressures are the constraints mothers experience in relation to time—an issue we address next.

Time

In addition to the challenge of navigating a sea of contradictory knowledge claims, the mothers in our focus groups experienced time as a major constraint in their efforts to live up to Eco-Mom ideals. Consuming intelligently and responsibly was perceived as particularly difficult to accomplish when pressed for time. While the Eco-Mom invokes images of careful purchasing decisions made directly from farmers based on informed decision making, several of our respondents described harried shopping experiences in grocery stores—a place where many eco foods (e.g., organic foods) are purchased (Organic Trade Association 2010). In real-estate agent Manuela's words, "I think the tension at the supermarket is the time. Like I find myself running....So then, my decisions are not really smart because I'm rushing." Sue said that while she derives great pleasure from a leisurely trip to the farmers' market, most of her family's food is not procured this way. On regular food-shopping trips, the experience is often stressful and rushed; as Sue says, "I don't actually find it fun because everything is crammed into a day. So it's just like ah!"

When it came to the topic of gendered food labor and finding time to prepare food for kids, focus group participants expressed the idea that the responsibility for healthy, sustainable consumption fell squarely on their shoulders (as opposed to that of their partners). Expressing a common sentiment heard from women about their domestic division of labor, Selena says:

> I feel like I'm often like, [my husband will] look to me as like, the boss. He'll be like, "what can I feed her?"...And I'm like, "You could give her this, you could give her this and this

and this." And sometimes I'll get a little bit irritated if he'll just give her like, I don't know, some like white bread with cheese, like, three meals a day.... there are other things you can feed her!

Similarly, Matilda reported that her husband is concerned about food issues, but she noted that "he doesn't have that internal dialogue about, okay there's this many levels of ethical discussion about this or that." Both Selena and Matilda's comments suggest the imperatives of eco-consumption build on the complex calculations and consciousness so fundamental to gendered food work. Women didn't describe their male partners as fighting their eco-decisions in the grocery store; instead they more typically commented (or complained) that the men in their life don't seriously consider either health or sustainability when they carry out food work. Indeed, our focus groups show how eco-shopping responsibilities weigh disproportionately on women—especially those who are raising children, and suggest that eco-mothering is a time-intensive project involving seemingly endless research, planning, and preparation. "White bread and cheese" was understood as quick, but a cop-out—okay for dads, but not acceptable for good mothers. For example, Nancy reflected upon the distance between her own preference for food that is nutritious, local, and organic, and her husband, who "likes food that doesn't go bad. That's efficient, that's cheap." She noted that while her husband willingly shares in the food shopping for their family, "he doesn't know what this dialogue is in my head." As a result, Nancy, who works full-time as an education officer, must prepare extensive shopping lists that specify each exact purchase to be made, because for her husband to make these choices on his own, "I would have to change his whole values."

Like Nancy, many mothers in our study described spending significant time devising meal plans and shopping lists. They then ventured to multiple vendors to access food that satisfied their standards for health and ethics, and also suited family members' diverse preferences. Carmen's shopping routine is emblematic of this time-consuming project:

> I have this crazy system where, see we used to live on the Danforth and we would go to the veggie stores there, so like Fruit King and IGA and Sun Valley, and then we would also go to the organic store like the Big Carrot, and then a cheese store and then we would get our meats from the Mennonites. So, it's this big ordeal.

Carmen, a research librarian, noted that to sustain this complex system, "all the planning is like having another part time job." The framing of these responsibilities as a "job" is revealing, as the demands of eco-shopping amplify the gendered labor historically associated with mothering (DeVault 1991). While the broader discourse of caring consumption requires that mothers satisfy the nutritional needs and preferences of their family through careful shopping, the Eco-Mom is responsible for an additional level of planning relating to questions of sustainability—often requiring trips to multiple specialized shopping venues (e.g., to get naturally raised meat from the Mennonite butcher) and requiring time management to conform to farmers markets' less-convenient schedules—to fulfill the environmental commitments of eco-mothering.

In addition to the time requirements of planning and specialty shopping, eco-mothering also demands that women eschew convenience foods designed to make feeding children easier, such as prepackaged lunch items. Nina, an editor and middle-class mother of two young children, described an ongoing struggle in the face of child-focused marketing campaigns in the grocery store: "my son will be like, 'oh can we get that?' And it will be some kind of kid snack which is like cookies in individually wrapped packages, and they say it's perfect for kids' lunches. Well in fact it's not perfect for school lunches!" In addition to minimizing the harmful additives in her children's diet, Nina strives to limit the ecological impact of her food choices: "I use reusable packages for all my kids...I'm not about to buy something in a little hermetically sealed individualized pack to put in their lunch." Thus, not only is eco-mothering distinguished from the kind of feeding practices deemed acceptable for dads, but the Eco-Mom is also distinguished from a mainstream caring mom, who may treat her child with a hermetically sealed snack cake or package of cookies. While the ideals of intensive mothering and caring consumption are also time intensive, in practice, mothers invested in mainstream caring consumption often concede to serving processed foods to their children in an effort to balance competing demands for their time (Bugge and Almas 2006; Thompson 1996).

Ensuring that children consume only home-cooked meals made with whole ingredients aligns with environmental and childcare commitments at the heart of the Eco-Mom ideal; however, this was not a feasible option for all focus group participants, revealing the privileged resources required to sustain this performance. Elaine, who is middle-class and works as a research analyst, explained that she buys organic baby food for her son, because "I just feel more comfortable with something [where] there's no pesticides." She then added, "I know a lot of moms who make their own food, but I haven't gotten to that level yet." With the pressures of caring for a newborn baby, Elaine cannot take on the added work of making all of her son's food. Accepting store-bought organics as a second-best option, Elaine still faces considerable time pressures. Elaine does not own a car and organic goods aren't available at her local grocer, which is in a distant Toronto suburb. She must catch a ride with her father to a more affluent neighborhood hosting a large number of natural-food options—a trip that requires significant planning and coordination. Despite these challenges, Elaine still strives toward the Eco-Mom ideal and stated that "eventually I want to try to make my own food for him."

Time constraints sometimes cause mothers to make compromises in their consumption choices, and this can engender feelings of guilt or inadequacy—especially because the idealized Eco-Mom has time to do it all, and the eco-consumption narrative is typically a win-win affair. Nina reflected on the tensions that arise between an ideal world and the real world where she must manage time and satisfy children's nutritional needs and taste preferences:

> In an ideal world where I have loads of time, I would make [my food shopping] more political in a sense that I would act ethically, the way that I know to be ethically sound in every decision...but I think you end up compromising and it ends up being about making the choices, so with us, it boils down to, is it nutritious, is the packaging not disgusting in terms

of the waste, is it accessible, something the kids will like, but it isn't always....the choice isn't always as ethical as it should be.

Robin described similar compromises resulting from a "time-money-organization-availability sort of nexus." She explained that she "would love to be able to grow my own food, and I would love to be able to do most of my shopping at [farmers'] markets," but that "I don't always have the time to do everything." The time required to grow one's food was also raised by Sue, who framed gardening as a way of socializing her daughters as ecologically conscious eaters. "You want your children to know where their food comes from," she said, but "it is a lot of work."

Even when compromises resulted from practical limitations, mothers often experienced and understood these compromises as a personal shortcoming. For instance, Sadie described how she was particularly busy and forced to forgo her usual routine of farmers' markets and organic grocers to gather the ingredients for a carrot lentil soup that she had volunteered to make for her son's school. As she explained: "So I just went for [the nearby discount grocery store option] and made the lunch for the school out of that, you know? It was simple. I didn't have to go to four different stores and wait around idiosyncratic hours....But I didn't feel good about it." This tendency for mothers to feel badly about compromises necessitated by time constraints reflects the vast distance between idealized conceptions of eco-caring consumption—the mother who finds time to nurture both child and planet—and the everyday experiences of mothers who struggle to manage maternal and environmental commitments alongside a host of other family and work responsibilities.

Our focus groups reveal how the Eco-Mom ideal is continually negotiated within the constraints of everyday life, including the constraints of financial resources. For example, Zahra suggested that the degree to which one can fulfill ethical food ideals exists on a continuum, in that "it depends on where you are, what your head space is, what your day is like." As Nina observed, having access to the time this requires is a function of class privilege: "It is easy for Hollywood stars to drive their Prius cars and eat their sustainable food, well you know, because they have their own personal chefs and someone going out and buying for them every day" (see also Goodman 2010 on the role of celebrities in reinforcing eco-chic culture). By contrast, Vicky expressed exasperation that the weight of these complex issues should fall on her shoulders and that she lacked the time to comprehensively think through these issues in everyday life: "I'm not like, immersed in all this stuff to sort of be able to make educated decisions. My life is busy enough just trying to struggle and survive and pay my own bills." While time was a source of tension for nearly all of the mothers in our study, some faced the added pressure, or outright barrier, of financial constraints—our third analytic theme.

Money

Money constituted a key source of contention among focus group participants. Fulfilling the Eco-Mom ideal presumes the regular purchasing of expensive items such as organic produce and grain-fed, hormone-free beef, and women spoke openly about how one's class position enabled or constrained these practices. Some affluent mothers reflected upon how their own eco-shopping practices are facilitated by class privilege. For example, Sue noted that "there is a big class element about where you can get food and how much it costs because if you're trying to feed a family, or even yourself, and you're not making very much money, are you going to go and buy a six dollar head of broccoli from the farmer's market? Probably not because that's not enough calories." Reflecting further upon the issue of class constraints, Sue said, "that's the worry about this organic niche or the idea of sustainable and local is that it is all so very expensive, so it is not accessible."

Others critiqued the status displays associated with the Eco-Mom ideal, such as Manuela, who suggested that shopping at her local farmers' market is "a bit of an ego snob thing in our area," because "you want to be seen in the market, and the others want to be seen too! It gives you a few points." Lucia, another middle-class member of this focus group who is employed as a social worker, supported Manuela's assessment and joked that she calls it the "market for the rich hippies." Manuela laughed in agreement, then added "but you know what, I almost couldn't afford the bread. Like the bread was like five bucks." Manuela and Lucia's comments resonate with North American research documenting how eco-food is often sold in classed spaces (like farmers' markets), catering to values that are more readily practiced by privileged consumers (Guthman 2003; Johnston, Szabo, and Rodney 2011; Murphy 2011).

Thus, women in our focus groups were aware of how a mother's food shopping can function as a practice of distinction—a way of demonstrating the highest degree of maternal and environmental accountability. In stay-at-home mom Tammy's words, "when you are feeding your child out in public, you are advertising to people what kind of a parent you are." Another member of this focus group, Robin, agreed, adding "And we certainly see that a lot in this kind of neighborhood." Thus, Robin situates the status displays associated with eco-mothering as a common feature of her middle-class neighborhood, which is viewed as one of the more socially and environmentally progressive areas in Toronto, and is home to one of the most popular farmers' markets in the city. Tammy explained further: "Because I feel a lot of times that the way you feed your child is almost like a status symbol. Like, people are sitting around going, [assumes a pretentious tone] 'Oh, did you see these? They're organic.'"

Discussions about money and class privilege were not restricted to those with ample financial resources. Vicky drew attention to the gap between the Eco-Mom ideal and her lived reality: "When the discussion goes to organic, that is the ideal, but in reality the cost is too much for a lot of people. I cannot afford to buy everything organic, and have to go for stuff on sale at No Frills [a discount Canadian grocery chain]." This discrepancy between ideals and practices was also highlighted by Tara, a poor single-mother living on Disability Insurance. Tara said that if money weren't an issue, she and her teenage son would eat "all organic and fair trade and you know, all at farmers' markets, that kind of thing," but in reality, "sometimes I'm looking at something fair trade and then I have to get something that's 99 cents." While a few mothers in our focus groups weren't concerned about making ethical shopping choices, most were invested in the Eco-Mom ideal. This suggests that while this ideal is recognized across classes, engaging in this form of ethical caring consumption requires access to class privilege. As a result, money was a significant source of tension, particularly for poor and working-class mothers who felt constrained in their capacity to fulfill this ideal in their daily food shopping.

For mothers feeding children on a limited budget, eco-shopping decisions require a careful weighing of competing priorities. Sadie explained that a key reason behind her family's vegetarian diet is that "since having children I want to buy organic things, and I can't afford to feed them organic meat." Sadie's comment is in reference to the fact that, in North America, certified organic meat is always considerably more expensive than nonorganic options, and is associated with both environmental and health benefits (Johnston and Baumann 2010: 147–48; Johnston, Rodney, and Szabo 2012). Paige, a working-class mom with an infant daughter who works part-time as a food program coordinator, described a cost-management strategy of "choosing what products I'll just not compromise on and then choosing products that I'll compromise on." To illustrate this, she explained that she will "buy organic milk pretty much exclusively and eggs, too," but that for butter, "it's always just packages of just, shit." Also working-class and recently unemployed, Deb said, "I have to admit I'm very cheap about buying organic because sometimes it's very expensive." Nevertheless, since becoming a mother Deb has been researching food issues online, and this has motivated her to consider "buying more organic things like apples because of the pesticides, and to the degree that it permeates the skin of the fruit." Our focus group data demonstrates how financial constraints intersect with issues of information and time in ways that exacerbate these pressures, given the added research and planning required for eco-mothering on a limited budget.

These financial constraints generated emotional strain for many mothers, who experienced guilt, anxiety, and frustration in their shopping. Because care work and food work are closely intertwined, mothers described feelings of failure when they couldn't afford to shop in ways that match their environmental ideals. Paige shared that "sometimes it can be frustrating going to farmers' markets" because she can only afford to buy a few token items before heading to the discount grocery store. Selena, who is lower-middle-class, said, "I definitely have guilt." Like others, she drew attention to the discrepancy between her food ideals and her everyday shopping practices:

> I can imagine so many good things, like, "I only shop at farmers' markets" [said in a snobby voice] but like, it's so expensive to do that.... And like, I know how hard it is for the people to make farms actually survive. And I think every time I buy stuff that I know isn't supporting that model of agriculture I feel like, personally responsible for the decline of the single-family farm.

Despite the structural factors shaping these compromises, Selena experiences the discrepancy between her political ideals and shopping practices as a personal failure and feels guilty as a result.

Even as some critiqued its elitist underpinnings, the Eco-Mom ideal continued to hold appeal for mothers who strove toward an idealized model of caring consumption that extends beyond the family to include broader environmental objectives. For women struggling to feed their children on a limited budget, the Eco-Mom ideal remained an unachievable, though desirable, measure of good mothering.

Conclusion: Sustaining the Eco-Mom?

In this chapter, we have taken as our point of departure the predominance of the intensive mothering and caring consumption ideal in North American society (Hays 1996; Thompson 1996). We have examined how contemporary discourses of eco-consumption work to extend these hegemonic ideals of motherhood, inviting North American mothers to consume in ways that fulfill not only the needs of one's family, but also the needs of the planet. The additional financial, cultural, and educational resources required by mothers to pursue sustainability through their caring consumption, however, suggest that this mode of consumption occupies a privileged location. In the effort to enact it, the Canadian mothers in our focus groups are referencing—and approximating to various degrees—an idealized figure that we identify as the Eco-Mom.

To reiterate our answers to the questions set out at the beginning of this chapter, eco-mothering operates as an elite mode of caring consumption by reproducing and reinforcing class and gender distinctions, and it is accompanied by multiple points of tension. The idealized version of caring consumption emphasizes that mothers find care work satisfying, empowering, and effective. In practice, eco-mothering—consuming to express care for families and the environment—was generally accepted as an important goal to strive toward, but one that was often confusing, tiring, expensive, and typically a gendered burden. The specific points of tension—where ideals espouse something contradicted by practice—center on information, time, and money. On these points, discourse surrounding intensive mothering and eco-consumption reinforce ideals that mothers mostly experience as personal, individual disappointments.

Each point of tension, moreover, was intensified by dynamics of social class, serving to further underscore the ways in which eco-mothering acts as a distinctly classed form of caring consumption that mothers strive to perform. First, while information about how to best engage in eco-consumption is theoretically available to all, the mothers in our focus groups rely on foodie magazines, the writings of food authors like Michael Pollan and Jonathon Safron Foer, as well as smartphone applications, which presumes a degree of cultural and financial capital less readily available to those with less education and income. Second, mothers approximating the Eco-Mom ideal eschew convenience foods in favor of preparing organic, home-cooked meals, as the commitment to slow, unprocessed food distinguishes eco-mothering from mainstream caring consumption. Doing so entails the luxury of time and money and when these requirements are unavailable, many mothers experience personal feelings of guilt and inadequacy. Third and most obviously, a lack of money limits one's access to organic food and environmentally friendly household products, and consequently, one's ability to enact the Eco-Mom ideal. Even those lacking the requisite financial resources, however, acknowledged the value of striving to consume ethically, and they too experienced guilt in failing to achieve this measure of good mothering.

What are the implications of our findings for the potential of eco-consumption as a mainstream mode of consumption? On the one hand, the ideology of intensive mothering bolsters and naturalizes support for eco-consumption, and the broader category of caring consumption in which it is located. Informed, ecologically minded consumption can indeed help to nurture the health and well-being of children,[3] and for that reason, many educated, middle-class women are heavily invested in these ideas, even if they are critical of how difficult they are to achieve. On the other hand, this same ideology generates significant points of tension between ideals and lived experiences, producing guilt and disappointment among women in their efforts to enact Eco-Mom ideals (e.g., feeling guilty about not having a backyard garden and feeling responsible for promoting the decline of family farms). Guilt and disappointment may not be emotions that are likely to reinforce the behaviors associated with them, and may work to generate cynicism and detachment (as we indeed heard in some of focus group conversations).

We have attempted to demonstrate the ways in which eco-consumption is circumscribed by both class and gender. While there are many valuable studies that outline the class inequalities inherent in ethical consumption (see, e.g., Guthman 2003; Johnston, Szabo, and Rodney 2011), the very fact that this form of consumption is predominantly performed by mothers suggests that more attention should be paid to the gendered nature of eco-consumption. This is important both because it is problematic for eco-consumption within the family to be delimited by an unequal and gendered division of labor and because failure to achieve the Eco-Mom ideal results in guilt and anxiety for women who interpret these limitations as a product of personal shortcomings.

While the focus groups suggest that there are instances where mothers reject unrealistic ideals as they apply to intensive mothering and eco-consumption, these discussions also suggest that women mostly experience anxiety over not successfully managing the key issues—information, time, and money—that are central components of eco-mothering. Moreover, the idealized discourses of intensive mothering and eco-consumption provide a dominant cultural reference that others may in turn use to assess individuals and social contexts alike. The allusions to seeing and being seen suggest that, despite their own criticisms or jaded perspectives on eco-mothering, many mothers realize that their mothering practices are judged by others. Despite their best efforts, the mothers we spoke with report that the Eco-Mom is a figure that is difficult to either fully achieve, or ignore.

Part III
Bodies and Beauty

–8–

Afro-chic: Beauty, Ethics, and "Locks without Dread" in Ghana

Anna-Riikka Kauppinen and Rachel Spronk

Introduction

In Ghana, the hip fashion label Afro-chic proclaims itself as "[C]elebrating all the yummy goodness of Ghana: its people, its culture and its (far reaching) influences."[1] It is one of the many brands to emerge in the booming commercial beauty industry in the period of political and economic liberalization since the mid-1990s. In Ghana's capital, Accra, vendors of fashion goods and beauty services dot the urban space, from small wooden stands to high-end shops and beauty clinics. Apart from the open air markets selling fashion and beauty products and services, the streets are filled with billboards advertising imported beauty products, hairstyles, and fashion crazes. The hair business is especially prominent and provides a variety of hair treatments, such as chemical hair straightening and artificial hair extensions. In recent years, the marketing of beauty products made from locally sourced ingredients such as shea butter—advertised as healthy and natural in Ghana[2] and as fair trade, healthy, and natural in the global West (Chalfin 2004)—has become more discernible in the capital. In addition, the popularity of "natural hair" is slowly but steadily gaining ground. This chapter explores this turnabout in the Ghanaian beauty industry by focusing on the popularity of dreadlocks and twists among urban middle-class women.[3] We are specifically interested in how globally circulating ideas of environmentalism and naturalness are being recognized, reappropriated, and interpreted among upwardly mobile entrepreneurs and consumers in a rapidly growing African metropolis.

The Afro-chic marketing slogan quoted above suggests that fashion and beauty in Ghana are closely connected to specific ideas of local culture. In this chapter, we show how self-styling connects with wider processes of (post)colonial subject-formation (see Comaroff 1996) and historically rooted notions of Africanness. In the natural hair salons of Accra, dreadlocks are promoted not only as natural but also as truly African. The salon entrepreneurs brand the natural (and indigenous) base of their products, along with Africanness, as being two sides of the same coin. Natural is portrayed as African, and concepts of both natural and African are presented as authentic: that is, free from both chemicals and Western influence. As de Witte and Meyer remark: "Africanness thus becomes a matter of brand distinction, of lifestyle and taste" (2012: 60).

However, the branding of dreadlocks as a modern consumer choice rooted in natural, local origins also faces contestation. In Ghana and many other African countries, dreadlocks have been generally associated with backward fetish priests, criminal young men, and dirty Rastafarians, certainly not with successful middle-class women who are respected for their achievements. The question, then, is why these women and other young professional women in different African urban centers opt for dreadlocks (Spronk 2012: 63–96). Their choice is at odds with both normative ideals of appropriate feminine beauty, and certain class respectabilities (Shipley 2009: 649). As we will show, women justify their choice through a Christian discourse where, unexpectedly, notions of naturalness and Africanness also surface. These observations point toward a different trajectory of ethical consumption in Ghana, where religion provides an important index for everyday ethical contemplation (Lambek 2008: 148). Globally circulating tropes of ethical consumption, such as rootedness in authentic local culture and environment, are therefore embedded in a broader interpretative framework on the ground, which in the Ghanaian context also encompasses religious ethics.

The recognition of the value of a particular commodity as being "more ethical," and by association also "more African" than another commodity (see Graeber 2001: 45) cannot simply be assumed. It needs to be researched through detailed ethnography. Natural hairstyles in Ghana represent a form of consumption where globally circulating ideals of naturalness (see Jaffe, this volume), Christian sensibilities, and older and newer understandings of Africanness combine. Building on this premise, we suggest that any analysis of forms of ethical consumption in Africa, and more broadly the global South, must critically engage with contemporary debates about ethical consumption in the global West. Žižek (2009) has been one of the most insightful critics in relation to the very possibility of consumption as ethical. In this respect, he refers to the market's power to subjugate any critique of capitalism for its own benefit: that is, for the purpose of selling more commodities. The idea of ethical consumption has been effectively translated into the realm of the market, encouraging the idea of nonconventional (read critical) consumer choices, such as opting for an organic café latte. In this line of argument, dreadlocks could in Ghana be interpreted as an individualized expression of nonconformism. However, the assumption of individual autonomy that underlies the Western concept of ethical consumption and that endorses the idea that individuals, via their consumption choices, could be the environmental agents most able to save the planet Earth (Hickel and Kahn 2012: 221), is in some respects at odds with what Ghanaians might consider to be ethical considerations. Debates on the ethical dimensions of consumption, especially those concerning beauty and fashion, are not novel within Ghana and have regularly surfaced in the course of the national history.

Celebrating Africanness: From Cultural to Natural Consciousness

To understand how naturalness, Africanness, and authenticity come to be linked with the marketing of beauty products in Ghana, it is important to show how patterns of consumption have always been subject to lively debates. From dressing to skin creams and hairstyles, the individual consumer has had to position her- or himself in the debates where beauty has been concurred with social and political aspirations. In this chapter, we explore how contemporary middle-class women who opt for dreadlocks could be following previous generations of elite women in the sense that, in their day, those women too adopted styles that contrasted with the normative ideals of female beauty. Historically, cultural elites and urban middle classes have played an important role in spearheading new fashions, and in propagating cultural self-determination along with a sense of distinction and dignity (see Comaroff 1996; Schneider 2006). In the (post)colonial African context, the desire for cultural self-determination, together with ideals of beauty, has become associated with claims of authenticity.

Dress has always been used to express status, success, and wealth and to communicate self-confidence, agency, and dignity in Ghana. In precolonial times, much like the present day, while many people dressed in garments made of European and Indonesian cloth (Gott 2009), locally made fabrics remained important and popular. In fact, throughout history, Ghanaian dress has embodied customary values and aesthetic sensibilities (Akyeampong 2000; Ross 1998). Fabric designs with traditional significance, such as *kente,* continue to carry weight, especially at important social occasions like weddings, funerals, and political rallies.[4] Under colonial rule, the educated Christian elites, in particular, started dressing in European styles, partly because this was required by the colonial educators but also because this group saw itself as avant-garde. As 85-year-old Nana, one of the first Ghanaian females to earn a doctorate, told one of the authors:[5]

In colonial times we were brainwashed that European attire meant being literate and educated. During my time at Achimota [one of the most prestigious schools] I was proud to become like our [British] teachers. I had learned that only uneducated and illiterate women wear *ntama* [traditional costume, a cloth that is wrapped around the body]. But when I went to study in London [in 1949]...I was of course also getting proud to soon belong to an independent country with its own cultural identity, so I decided to only wear our own cloth. So that is when I started making *kaba and slit* myself [a suit of a top and a long skirt], as you see now being made by the most prestigious designers! It was not easy. In London I was admired by progressive Londoners and very much by other Africans, Nigerians...and by people from the West Indies. But back in Ghana...I remember that once the wife of a senior colleague of Peter [her husband] asked him why his fiancée was disgracing herself by wearing cloth and why she refused to dress properly. It was very unkind of her, but soon I was not the only one anymore, more and more women, you know, like me [educated and employed] started sewing their own clothes....For me, starting to wear *kaba and slit* was my contribution to our Independence, it was my expression of being a proud Ghanaian, proud of my cultural identity.

As the child of a mission-educated pastor, Nana had earlier in the interview process explained how as a girl she had felt proud of belonging to the first family in the area to live in a stone house and of being one of the first children to get formal education. The Achimota school she attended was "very English" and she had been proud to be part of this subculture and to "learn their ways." She had especially enjoyed learning to make music and play tennis. Only later on, when furthering her education in London, did she become more critical of the English presence and dominance in Ghana and how it undermined local customs. Dress became her way of positioning herself as a confident educated woman, a discerning colonial subject, and a proud Ghanaian.

As Comaroff (1996) has shown, in colonial settings the articulation of cultural identity and self-confidence became tangible in everyday material culture such as dress. For people like Nana, the connection between dress and cultural authenticity was a political matter: a personal statement of cultural sovereignty, of expressing pride of Africanness in the face of colonial subjugation. For colonial citizens throughout the continent, self-determination was expressed in African (rather than, for example, Ghanaian) terms alongside national projects. The intellectual and political elite from the colonies were in close correspondence with each other and with critical thinkers from the West Indies, such as Du Bois. They often met as students in England and formed a small continental elite in defense of independence.[6] They saw themselves as Africans vis-à-vis the racist non-African colonizers. The idea of an African culture (rather than a plurality of different cultures) was a central trope in the dehumanizing project of colonialism, and in reaction it became the prime instrument of political self-determination: Africanness had to be defended and hence became central to postcolonial notions of personhood (Mbembe 2001). Nana's choice of what we may term *ethical consumption* in relation to fashion points to a distinctive type of consumerist subject: a person who experiences her dressing choice as an expression of the newly independent African nation, but also as an expression of her agency. Africanness united both these expressions of self.

During colonialism, and even more so in the postcolonial era, both in Ghana and beyond, debates on Africanness became focused on skin color. These debates were closely associated with similar ones taking place in the United States and the Caribbean. As such, the counteracting of various forms of racism and the celebration of black skin was framed as foundational to one's being. Iconic African leaders like Senegal's first president Senghor (on Negritude), as well as Guinea's Sekou Touré and Ghana's Kwame Nkrumah (both writing on the idea of African personality), instigated debates against colonial oppression. They argued that through political coercion, people in Africa had been persuaded to turn away from their own culture and heritage and that this had had an impact on their self-respect (Nkrumah 1963). These leaders, along with their counterparts in the Americas, advocated the self-acceptance embodied in the slogan "Black is beautiful."[7] In Ghana, in relation to some women's practice of bleaching their skin with chemicals to achieve a lighter tone, the debate took a particular turn (Blay 2009, see also Pierre 2013: 101–22). Bleaching (like the straightening of black hair) was, and still is, presented as an unethical decision of self-enhancement that harms the person's mental and physical well-being. Since the emergence of this practice in the 1960s, every subsequent decade has witnessed fierce debates about skin bleaching. It has come to be understood as a symbol of white dominance and limited self-respect as black Ghanaians.

In the same vein, hairstyling has embodied ideals of both cultural heritage and post-colonial citizenship. Kwame Nkrumah's portrayal of Ghana as a model of African nationhood for other colonies to follow called for visual statements (Coe 2005: 9). In the wake of independence in 1957, Nkrumah framed heritage—most notably its aesthetic features such as drumming, dancing, traditional textiles such as *kente,* and hairstyling such as braiding—as the base of the new nation (Coe 2005: 62). Essah (2008) argues that hairstyling has represented a markedly feminine aspect of national cultural politics throughout the twentieth century. As such, the elaborately braided hairstyles of Ghanaian ethnic groups have been promoted as artistic cultural heritage. Hairstyles, different braiding techniques, and impressive attachments and headgear were considered to be authentic handicraft, which colonial officers had admired at cultural fairs organized during British rule (Essah 2008: 32).

From the 1950s onward, the import of artificial hair instigated a fashion craze of wig wearing. Like the practice of skin bleaching, wig wearing was vehemently debated in Ghanaian newspapers (Essah 2008: 158), with some journalists going as far as to call for a ban on wigs. According to Essah, "beauty from Ghana had to be 'original' and a 'cultural heritage,' but not of a primitive simplicity." Such debates show how politically charged the notion of beauty (and especially hairstyling) has been among Ghanaian political and intellectual elites. Hairstyles have been useful both for promoting African nationalism, and for debating the essence of African authenticity in the face of foreign influence.[8]

But decisions about dress and hairstyling have not only been influenced by anticolonial and postcolonial ideals of Africanness and personhood. The influence of Christianity on notions of respectability, decency, and dignity has been just as significant, especially during the social transformations in Ghana of the past twenty years. The General Jerry John Rawlings's military regime in the 1970s and 1980s was dominated by Nkrumah-style cultural politics of pan-African pride, as groups of African traditional religions fulfilled the public role of the national religion (de Witte 2004).[9] In the 1990s, the fall of Rawlings's regime was followed by the liberalization of the economy and a transformation of the social and political realm, which fundamentally changed the social dynamics in the Ghanaian public sphere. Charismatic Pentecostal churches, whose popularity had steadily increased in southern Ghana since the 1980s, harnessed audiovisual technologies to voice their vision of modernity and national development as grounded in Christian faith. Gifford (2004) speaks of a "paradigm shift" caused by Pentecostal churches and their sociopolitical role in effecting modernity in Ghana from the 1980s onward.

Ideologically the vision of national progress espoused by these churches was opposed to the state's cultural politics, which celebrated overt traditional forms of drumming, dancing, and dress. Christian actors did not consider these cultural portrayals of Africanness to be positive symbols of national sovereignty or progress. On the contrary, they explicitly demonized certain forms of tradition such as libation and ancestor worship (Meyer 1998), shrine worship, and the fetish priests with their naturally grown dreadlocks. The Pentecostal churches inspired many Ghanaians from all walks of life with their emphasis on this worldly success. In their interpretation of tradition, cultural elements, such as pride and the celebration of achievement were seen as crucial for embracing life: God will bless those who work hard. A (Pentecostal) Christian ethic has taken root in Ghanaian society, emphasizing the importance of education, responsible leadership, productive entrepreneurship, and the transformation of culture by casting away outdated traditions and embracing global developments. In the past few decades, the representation of Africanness has shifted toward an aesthetics inflected with globally circulating ideas.

This brief historical analysis gives an indication of how Ghanaian cultural elites have used beauty practices, such as dressing and hairstyling, to articulate political and cultural entitlements. Ethical condemnation of imported commodities, such as wigs and skin-bleaching creams, and positive evaluation of local and more natural hairstyles and products have featured since the colonial era. Interestingly, globally circulating ideals of ethical consumption as being rooted in locally sourced ingredients tie in with the existing historical trajectory in Ghana of valuing local products above imported ones. Informed by these continuities, we look next at the contemporary representation of dreadlocks as an ethical consumption choice, even though dreadlocks are associated with a kind of traditional Africanness seen by some as the antithesis of modern development. There are, however, competing claims for the modern acceptance of dreadlocks. As we will show, dreadlocks attest to a self-confident choice, and the idea of cultural authenticity can be modernized into a notion of the God-given body free of chemicals and artificial attachments.

Marketing the Natural

In the spring of 2010, a high-end Accra-based spa and wellness center, Allure Spa in the City (ASIC), organized a three-day international beauty expo. The expo was targeted specifically at small and medium-sized beauty shop owners and their apprentices, and members of the Ghanaian Hairdressers and Beauticians Association (GHABA). Many women came from Accra's numerous kiosk salons hoping to improve their professional skills, or perhaps just to enjoy a day out. Black beauty entrepreneurs from the United States and Ghana promoted products and gave workshops on high standards of facial, nail, and hair treatments and a workshop on dreadlocks. Throughout the three-day fair, the Ghanaian-born and U.S.-educated director of Allure, Dzigbordi Dosoo, marketed her skin product range Kanshi with the help of a Twi interpreter.[10] During the launch of the product on the first day of the fair Mrs. Dosoo, visibly moved, gave a speech:

> Authentically African means that this product is made by someone who understands Africans and the African skin. It's made by someone who was born in Africa, lived in Africa, grew up in Africa. Most of the time when you see products that come out of Africa, or have [a] natural base, they are not conceived by Africans but they are produced by non-Africans. Finally we have something that we can call our own.

Just as Nana chose dress in the form of the *kaba-and-slit* as her way of expressing her African rootedness, a beauty product was Mrs. Dosoo's way of doing the same.

Mrs. Dosoo's strategy for convincing low-end Ghanaian beauticians of the benefits of naturalness is to establish a direct link between the product and the Africa-based producer—in other words, to emphasize Africanness. This branding strategy is also a direct critique of the macroeconomic situation with foreign imports dominating the Ghanaian consumer market, as they do in many other sub-Saharan African countries. However, the expo visitors, namely ordinary beauticians, were less clear about their view on the benefits of the natural. They attentively listened to Dosoo's speech translated in Twi, but they did not further discuss the virtues of the natural, as one of the authors followed groups of beauticians in the expo after the speeches. This is most likely because for the wider Ghanaian population; concerns about natural African products represent a markedly Accra-based and middle-class form of discourse. This is confirmed by comparing the small number of natural hair salons to the thousands of mainstream hair salons across Ghana.

While the effect of Mrs. Dosoo's attempt to create unity through the use of natural African products may be limited, due also to the financial limitations of most Ghanaians, high-end beauty entrepreneurs like herself continue to promote a popular consciousness of ethical consumption rooted in African belonging.[11] Mirroring global consumer trends, their ideology stems from an appreciation of natural locally sourced ingredients such as shea butter and palm oil, infusing it with an emphasis on Africanness. de Witte and Meyer (2012) have argued that Africanness is increasingly mediated through visual aesthetics and that commercial arenas and entrepreneurs are crucial brokers in this development.

Another entrepreneur is "locktician"[12] Mikesh Afutu who owns two natural hair salons in Accra. He portrays himself as a well-traveled Afro-cosmopolitan (see also Shipley 2009; Thalén 2011), whose mission is to render Ghanaians "more African" by shaping their physical looks. His Mikesh Crown Natural Hair salons are located in two distinctive parts of Accra. One is Adabraka, an inner city neighborhood characterized by constant hustling and a heterogeneous composition of city-dwellers from young professionals to unemployed youth, mingling with homeless people walking around and sitting on the street corners. Mikesh's other salon is in East Legon, a distinctively elite neighborhood of gated residences, foreign-funded nongovernmental organizations (NGOs) and private schools. Besides locking the clients' hair, Mikesh's business involves the promotion of natural hair products from locally sourced ingredients, produced in rural areas outside Accra.

In both salons, the waiting rooms are bamboo-covered spaces separated from the rooms where the lockticians treat clients' hair. Treatment happens behind closed doors and darkened windows. Various slogans celebrating the benefits of natural hair hang on the walls: "Natural is good for the body, soul and environment," "Conscious black sisthren [sic] and brethren realize that natural hair is the anointed crown of God's Glory. No more perms of jerri curls,"[13] "Your hairstyle is your lifestyle." An image of a little boy in dreadlocks, looking at the camera with a determined face and arms crossed, commands attention in the room where the lockticians work. In the waiting room area, the eye is drawn to an artwork showing village women locking their hair under a mango tree, where a small wooden signboard pronounces "Mikesh Salon," along with Mikesh's logo, a golden crown. Mikesh was pleased to be asked about the artwork, which he had ordered from a local painter:

> That portrait is there, just like I told you, to tell people that whatever we do here is a reflection of the past. In the past, we don't use any chemicals or any relaxers in our hair. We just sit under the trees. There wasn't any salon, or a nice place for people to go and have their hair done. We do our hair under the trees, with the fresh air, with the plants everything around, the animals going around, and singing songs, that is how we were happy. But because we forgot too much of the natural, we started going to chemicals and all that. So what you see there is a reflection for people to know that whatever goes on here is also a reflection of the past, but, in the present.

Here, Mikesh directly connects Africanness with an untouched, glorified, past: an imagining that is shared by many Ghanaians and represented in the artwork featuring communal life in villages when beauty was still natural.[14]

The notion of an untouched past, that is, free from foreign influences, also finds expression in Sankofa symbolism, which is part of the rich Adinkrah tradition.[15] Sankofa,

Figure 8.1 Signs and artwork in the waiting space of one of the Mikesh Crown Natural hair salons (photo by Anna-Riikka Kauppinen).

the image of a bird that bends its neck to look backward while its feet point forward is commonly explained by the phrase "go back and take." It symbolizes the importance of appreciating one's cultural past in contemporary ways of life. The symbol was appropriated in postcolonial Ghanaian cultural politics—in both the Nkrumah and Rawlings eras—to persuade citizens that knowledge of the cultural past was not inappropriate (de Witte and Meyer 2012: 46). On the contrary, the citizens of the independent African nation were encouraged to feel pride in their cultural heritage. To this end the Sankofa became a powerful symbol that appears in various contexts including buildings, table napkins, and tourist artifacts. In the artwork in Mikesh's salons, the knowledge of the elders and ancestors refers to their presumed natural hairdressing practices. Mikesh argues that these practices are appropriate for present-day Ghana, because beauty markets are flooded by foreign chemical imports and include practices harmful to people's health. The fact that Mikesh decided to put up a billboard picturing his salon as located under a tree where women do their natural hair not only refers back into the past, but also implies a promise: the company renders a cultural past available in the present.

In Mikesh's version of Ghanaian culture, the cultural past and the celebration of its heritage in the present are transformed into both national and commercial resources. His concern, besides presumably making a profit, was the tendency of Ghanaian women to "copy the whites."

> You know we have been copying foreign cultures and all that, as Ghanaians. We don't really appreciate our cultures. But in other countries, they are very mindful about their cultures. Forgetting about your culture, you don't know your past, you don't know your future. So for a country to go on well, if we keep well our cultures, our cultures will invite a lot of foreigners, our cultures will attract a lot of foreigners. And you know it will also boost the economy. I am using the word *copy* because I can see the mix of foreign cultures coming in to mix up with our culture.

Indeed, in the course of daily observations in the Mikesh salons, lockticians did not hide their transnational orientation as Afro-cosmopolitans: the emerging urban, entrepreneurial mode of self-presentation in Ghana (Shipley 2009; Thalén 2011). Mikesh had gathered a dedicated group of young men around him who looked up to Jamaica as the unadulterated epicenter of African pride.[16] They were inspired by reggae music, Rastafarianism, and its theology of a natural lifestyle.[17] One morning a middle-aged woman emerged from the locking room with her long dreadlocks and started making up her face in the waiting area. As she was applying the foundation and eyeliner, one of the young lockticians came out to get a drink and remarked: "You should look natural today; why do you put on make-up?" The woman laughed and replied that she "could not do without make-up, ever." He looked slightly disapproving but did not pursue the matter further.

This exchange suggests that the ideal of naturalness held by Mikesh's Rastafarian-inspired lockticians is not necessarily shared by the female clients. However, it is safe to assume that through verbal exchanges such as this, and through the salon's interior design, including the slogans on the walls, the Mikesh ideal of naturalness enters into public circulation. While clients may not entirely agree, sooner or later they have to posi-tion themselves vis-à-vis the idea of naturalness as an ethical value, whether in terms of health and well-being, or the macroeconomic benefits of patronizing local products, or pan-African anticolonial cultural pride. In their many visits, clients become familiar with their lockticians and friendships may also develop. Such personal exchanges are likely to lead clients to view the hitherto uninteresting topic of naturalness with greater favor.

Mikesh's salons are a manifestation of the newer understanding of Africanness, pro-moted as a cosmopolitan and markedly modern consumer choice that also creates collec-tive emotional attachments through sensory engagement and experience (de Witte and Meyer 2012: 62). This overtly global orientation connects with the more familiar Ghanaian ideal of appreciating the cultural past as the base for progress and a viable future.

Polishing Africanness: The Christianity of Locks

As we have outlined, discourses of Africanness and Ghanaian heritage have a long and rich history that include shifts in their response to political, economic, and social transformations. The most recent turn in this history is a market-driven representation of "African heritage" with an explicit focus on visual style and design (de Witte and Meyer 2012; see also Comaroff and Comaroff 2009). This helps Mikesh to brand dread-locks as sophisticated, respectable, and sensible—a style with distinction. In doing so he has to carefully maneuver his way around the negative associations of dreadlocks with Rastafarians and reposition the style as respectable, even for successful urban Christian women. A crucial element in how Mikesh frames his marketing lies in the connection he makes between the naturalness of dreadlocks and the idea of the God-given natural state of humankind. His framing can be interpreted through the lens of what Coe (2005: 93) calls "polishing Africanness," that is, bending dominant discourses on Africanness to new situations such as the beauty industry in a strongly Christian country.

Mikesh's salons are stylish and tranquil places where busy women take a break from their hectic schedules. He has fashioned them as havens for natural products, natural style, and, above all, natural persons. In the waiting room space, clients sit in comfortable bam-boo chairs watching satellite TV. The lockticians are smartly dressed in jeans, Mikesh Crown t-shirts, and black Mikesh-branded vests. In the fully air-conditioned and tidy lock-ing room, clients sit in comfortable leather chairs, their bodies covered in shiny black cloth. Women praised the atmosphere and appreciated the effort he made to make the salon a comfortable space. Despite slogans on his wall that seemed at first sight to be inspired by Rastafarianism, Mikesh stated that he did not want to be associated with Rastafarianism as a religion. He was quick to correct the ethnographer who labeled dreadlocks "Rasta hair":

> Here, we don't call them Rastas, we call them locks. Rasta is a religion, just like Christianity, and Muslim. Our hair cannot be Rasta. We were created to have this, not religion. You don't have to go through religious beliefs to be able to be a locks person. That is our way of life that God gave to every black man in kind.

Mikesh was careful to avoid associations with Rastafarianism and appealed to the unity in the major religions: the existence of God. His decision to drop the word "dread" from dreadlocks in his marketing slogans is a significant symbolic act: any association with ugliness, dirty street youth or fetish priests had to be avoided. "It is your natural hair, how could it be fetish?" he responded when asked the reason for the change.

Mikesh was unequivocal about his position as a believer. While he was not proclaiming his own Christian identity, slogans and objects in the salons persuaded clients of the inherently godly character of naturalness as a modern lifestyle choice. In his salons, Christian books were prominently placed on the salon tables next to lifestyle magazines. In the East Legon salon waiting room, a colorful children's Bible lay open on the biblical story of Samson, who was forbidden to cut his hair by God. The message for clients was that the divine spirit and power that resides in the hair had to remain unaltered. There is also a slogan displayed in the salon that pronounces naturalness to be divine of origin. The implicit message is that artificial hair and chemicals belong to an inferior spiritual realm. Thus in the overall marketing of his salon and beauty products, Mikesh has blended Christian sensibilities to present dreadlocks as both modern and deriving from God.

People like Mrs. Dosoo and Mikesh function as cultural brokers in the anthropological sense (Barth 1963; Cohen and Comaroff 1976; James 2011; Szasz 2001). These agents mediate multiple ideals of naturalness: the globally circulating ideals of ethical consumption as rooted in appreciation of natural ingredients; notions of Africanness where natural hairstyles are political statements; and finally religious discourse where naturalness is understood as God's original creation. Mikesh incorporated the familiar postcolonial narrative of cultural self-determination, where cultural pride and the refusal to copy the whites is a central aspect of the ethics of consumption choices, by branding deadlocks as the latest mode of distinction. On many occasions, he repeated how dreadlocks can fit "so many different lifestyles." This allows dreadlocks to be invested with many promises: faithfulness to God's original creation, freedom from the use of chemicals harmful for one's well-being, independence from Western dominated beauty ideals, and integral to the emerging transnational collective of Afro-cosmopolitans.

We now turn to the female salon clients themselves and assess how these promises relate to the values of their everyday lives.

Enacting Africanness: From Naturalness to Godliness

In Accra, women's hair speaks to a way of life that is accurately described as the salon cycle. Whether women opt for braids, artificial attachments, or hair straightening, they have to regularly visit the salon to groom their hair. The salon cycle is an integral part of many urban Ghanaian women's lives from the moment they cease wearing their hair the typical children's styles—cornrows or cut short. Many women said preoccupation with one's hair shows that one is a "true lady" who knows how to look after herself. Hair is a woman's pride and can be a statement. When one of us complimented a friend on her new, and quite voluminous, long and fuzzy hairstyle, she responded: "Thanks, I felt like being Beyoncé [the popular female American musician known for her sensual looks], I felt like doing a little wild." Her colleagues looked disapproving and closed the matter with a "Ah, she again." Indeed, this woman was known for being unconventional, if not controversial, although she was also respected for being a generous and dedicated colleague. However, she always had to navigate the boundaries of convention carefully so as not to lose her status as a respected person. The popularity of dreadlocks among predominantly Christian middle-class women is, therefore, intriguing, given that the style is associated not only with dirtiness, ugliness, and harmful spirits, but also with a lack of proper femininity. For instance, Emma, in her early twenties and working as an NGO professional, told us how she had to convince her friends that her hair was clean and that she was taking care of herself: "They don't believe I put water inside, but I say I can even wash it at home." Washing your hair at home is presented here as a luxury because women who use artificial hair or chemicals always have to wash their hair at the salon.

Hair is a particularly useful part of the body for projecting explicitly class-determined forms of respectability and dignity, which also involves its own ethics. For these women, dreadlocks were beautiful for many reasons: for being sophisticated, hip, natural, God-given, and a tribute to Africanness. Elizabeth, a 27-year-old unmarried insurance sales representative, explained how tired she had become of going to salons and chemicalizing her hair and how dreadlocks made her "feel free." However, when she started growing and twisting her hair, the neighbors approached her father, asking why he allowed his daughter to wear a hairstyle that made her look "like a bad woman." They felt she no longer looked like a lady, which was especially problematic considering that she was not yet married. Many women with dreadlocks described similar public condemnation and vividly recalled incidents where their hair was subjected to collective scrutiny in their families, workplaces, and churches (see Ross 2000). Their experiences of publicly having to defend their aesthetic choices echo the experiences of earlier generations of predominantly elite women in Ghana, such as the narrative told earlier by Nana. Whereas for the older generation of women self-styling is closely tied to cultural and political ideas of Africanness, for younger women Africanness is a style that connects with globally circulating ideas of aesthetics and sophistication. For both groups, dress and hairstyle express inherently ethical choices that entrench Africanness as integral to a culturally self-confident person. "Why don't I have my natural hair? Why do I have to put all these chemicals in it and try to look like you, have this silky hair?" one woman said, referring to the long straight hair of one of the authors.

Dreadlocks must also be understood in relation to more common hairstyles in Ghana, and the distinctions that those styles indicate among middle-class and elite women in particular. Since the late 1990s, young professional women in Ghana, like others on the continent, started wearing nonconventional hairstyles as a way to distinguish themselves as "sophisticated" (Spronk forthcoming). They opted for very short hair or the fixed-to-the-skull cornrow braids, which are typically worn by children or impoverished women. Around that time, these sophisticated women also started wearing dreadlocks. Such daring hairstyles signified their financial independence, their relative social independence and, interestingly, their avant-garde position as professional women for whom nonconformist dressing choices were almost expected. As Gott (2009) argues, a wealthier, financially independent woman is assumed to visibly show off her status. This is not considered nonconformist in Ghana, but instead indexes the woman within the hierarchy of the broader community. Display itself is socially productive among African Christians (see Haynes 2012), and hence dreadlocks as natural hairstyles symbolize (relative) wealth and success.

Eunice, a 42-year-old single mother, recalled the time at the beginning of the 1990s when she was a successful young businesswoman: around that time, she cut her hair and dyed it yellow blonde and experimented with synthetic hair attachments and relaxers. However, her lucrative dress-making business did not survive, and at the time of our study, she was looking for a new business. One morning, when leaving her home compound, Eunice wanted to lock the roots of her hair before going to daytime prayers. She dressed in a beautiful long, cotton dress with Adinkrah symbols that she'd had made by one of her trusted local tailors. She explained: "In this hair and this dress, no one knows I'm poor. No one in the church has to know." Although financially Eunice had fallen out of the middle-class, she carefully hid her plight and wearing dreadlocks was part of this concealment. Newell's (2012) Ivorian informants call such consumption practices bluff: the visible surface of the body becomes the primary site for reclaiming respect in a situation where economic inequality is rampant. Part of Eunice's explicitly Christian social identity was to maintain her status as a successful professional in the eyes of her church community. As she remarked with a hint of satisfaction in her voice: "People in the church would never believe I have no money. They ask me for help all the time." Moreover, dreadlocks were relatively cheap compared to the latest salon trends. Thus dreadlocks can communicate respectable social personhood and hierarchy, which historically is an important aspect in Ghanaian women's dressing practices (Gott 2009).

For many women, dreadlocks also had religious meaningfulness, boosted by the story of Samson in the Bible. One such of these women was Ama, twenty-nine years old and working in marketing:

> Me, I feel proud. Some of the Christians say it is no good. Some say it is a sin. But it is even written in the Bible that no one should bring down the hair. And chemicals, they use it. Even for Samson, God said that he shouldn't comb his hair. God knew, he had a reason for saying that. If God told that to Samson, why don't I do the same thing? The way it is in the Bible, it says so! But perm, it's not in the Bible. It's good for my body not to touch with comb or scissors.

Ama took a leather-bound Bible from her purse and pointed to a page that refers to long, untreated hair as containing strength and spirit. In fact many women had shown this section to their pastors because textual, sacred evidence was important for them. The idea that natural human hair entails spiritual presence is also present in the Ghanaian Ashanti traditional religious belief that human hair is the locus of a person's spirit (de Witte 2001: 201). However, despite the biblical justification of their choice as being in accordance with Christian ethics, women explained that they still covered their hair in church. Paradoxically, for some women the church was also the place where dreadlocks were most vehemently criticized.

All of these narratives demonstrate the many layers of meaning that a single hairstyle, dreadlocks, can entail in one ethnographic context. The style indexes appreciation of naturalness and aesthetics. Natural hair is recognized as better for personal health and well-being, and a powerful symbol of African belonging and pride in a distinctively modern sense, while dreadlocks can also index success, confidence, and respectability. Such confidence is needed to have the courage to have a natural hairstyle in a country where the "salon cycle" is the rule.

Conclusion

Since colonial times, and even earlier, fashion has signaled competitive accumulation, symbolic innovation, and social distinction (Comaroff 1996: 28). As we have argued, the debates on fashion and beauty are connected to a much longer ideological history related to the desires and ideologies of belonging that materialize on the surface of the body.

Dreadlocks are iconic of the contradictions faced by the modern Ghanaian wearer: they show how the person ties into global flows while also marking a locally crafted identity. Fashionable people wearing dreadlocks display a particular pastiche of Ghanaian and global elements, which captures precisely the paradoxical relationships of difference and sameness that Ghanaians constantly have to negotiate. As the history of consumption in Ghana testifies, fashion bears with it the threads of a macroeconomy: it is a means of engaging people in the global market, but the particular terms on which this is done are constantly being renegotiated. The ethics of fashion consumption have been and continue to be part of cultural and political processes. In unforeseen ways, dreadlocks in Ghana comment on the possibilities presented by a commodity-driven culture: they represent an effort to limit dependency on the coercive expectations of the global market and the fashion system. In the restless urge for advancement through ongoing consumption, and structural economic and political regulation, and amid the unevenness of commodification, dreadlocks take an unexpected position. Wearing dreadlocks is economically more viable than all the artificial hair styles (they are cheaper) and a very clear statement on Africanness.

Women with natural hair in Ghana are few in number compared to the huge majority with relaxed or artificial hair, yet natural hairstyles and beauty products sourced from locally grown ingredients have sparked public debates related to what is ultimately important about Africanness. The high-end beauty entrepreneurs interviewed here have taken a specific route in the negotiation of what constitutes the ethical aspects of Africanness by connecting the naturalness of human bodies to natural products. Their aesthetic presentation of dreadlocks, naturalness, and Africanness compose a single set of meanings, even if their salon clients are less emphatic about the particularly African qualities of naturalness. Be that as it may, the initiation of an ethical consciousness that associates naturalness with the inherently African qualities of products and styles is currently ongoing.

For future research, we encourage more attention to local campaigns that highlight the qualities of domestically manufactured products, which shifts the perspective away from analyzing Western consumers in relation to African producers (Berlan and Dolan 2013; Dolan 2009; Leissle 2012) toward Africans as consumers themselves. We also invite reflection on how people from different class backgrounds position themselves in these debates in rising African economies. This requires attention to distinctive historical trajectories that embed globally circulating values of environmentalism and ethical consumption with more situated concerns and sensibilities. We wonder, for example, how people in Africa configure the focus of ethical consumption: whether environmentalism will begin to figure prominently or whether the emphasis will fall, for example, on employment for the multitude of unemployed youth. It will be intriguing to follow how Afro-chic articulates with eco-chic, and what kind of ethical reasoning such a path may engender

Acknowledgments

We thank Marleen de Witte for support and helpful comments on the first draft of this chapter.

–9–

Ital Chic: Rastafari, Resistance, and the Politics of Consumption in Jamaica

Rivke Jaffe

In Jamaica there exists what I call *ital chic:* a cross between ethical consumerism and the marketing of cool that represents an aesthetic repertoire and a commercial strategy based on Jamaican countercultures, most explicitly the African Caribbean socioreligious movement of Rastafari. Symbols and aesthetics of a Rastafari lifestyle, also known as ital livity, are mobilized to market a variety of products and services, ranging from restaurants and hairstyles to candles, clothing, and cosmetics. In this chapter I make an initial exploration into the implications of this phenomenon for Jamaica in terms of class and cultural politics, as well as its relation to the politics of sustainable development. While ital chic's producers come from diverse backgrounds, its consumers are mostly middle class or elite. There is, therefore, a risk that this mainstreaming of Rasta elements is not necessarily a progressive move toward the transformation of Jamaican society. Here, I will explore the political stakes of ital chic and consider to what extent the capitalist logic and the classed strategies associated with ital chic may imply the commodification of resistance or even a pacification of the dread.

In Jamaica, the entire range of elements that make up eco-chic are present, in a specifically local manifestation that I have dubbed *ital chic.* Similar to eco-chic, ital chic is a form of consumption that combines environmental, ethical, and health concerns with a luxurious, chic sensibility. However, this form of eco-chic is articulated principally through the indigenous practices, philosophy, and aesthetics associated with Rastafari. Much attention has been paid to Rastafari as a countercultural form, its focus on Africa and revaluation of blackness, its status as a "new religion," and its connection to popular culture. One of the less studied but central tenets of this African Caribbean socioreligious movement is ital livity. Ital has been described as "a commitment to using things in their natural or organic states" with an emphasis on harmony between humans and nature and a rejection of the artificial in favor of the natural (Edmonds 2003: 60). This is witnessed for instance through the propagation of a largely vegetarian diet (ital food); the avoidance of tobacco, alcohol, and drugs (except ganja, which is considered not a drug but an herb); a preference for herbal healing; and the (semi)organic agriculture practiced in rural Rastafari communes. Associated with this commitment to the natural is a broader rejection of the industrial, the imported, the capitalist, the materialist—Babylon. Livity refers to a socially committed lifestyle that encompasses "self-reliance, cooperation, natural organic living and peaceful coexistence, [and] provide[s] critical alternative ethical and even economic approaches that oppose the unmitigated market-centered, selfish individualism and rampant materialism of contemporary globalization" (Meeks 2002: 166).

While Rastafari has long been a counterculture, and Rastafarians are still often regarded as somewhat disreputable or dirty, Rastafari has become increasingly accepted and recognized. The symbols and aesthetics of a Rastafari lifestyle, or ital livity, have begun to trickle up. References to Africa, the Lion of Judah, and the colors red, green, and gold, as well as a focus on natural and ethical living, traditional healing, and vegetarianism, are used to market a variety of products and services. Ital chic merges an eco-friendly stance with a back-to the-roots ideology, colored by a strong black consciousness. Where Asian forms of eco-chic invoke ancient local traditions that precede colonial rule by centuries, ital chic often alludes to an imagined Africa in its "return" to preglobal, precolonial ways of life. It also has a tendency to draw on ideas of a rural old-time Jamaica that cannot, by definition, be precolonial but nonetheless successfully conveys the desired conjunction of nature, local culture, and the authentic.

What was previously considered very unrespectable now looks fashionable and cosmopolitan, even as it allows consumers to feel comfortably nationalist or locally grounded. The reframing of Rastafari elements as fashionable happens in part through the global recognition and validation of Rastafari and the international trends toward slow, natural, and ethical living. In addition, the incorporation of Rasta also assuages feelings of cultural dislocation and domination through a philosophy advocating a local, traditional (or neotraditional), and back-to-basics lifestyle.

At its most popular, however, ital chic may be described as Rasta lite, a diluted version of Rastafari principles and practices. The consumption of ital chic generally does not require behavioral changes that are unstylish or uncomfortable or that carry social sanctions. More often, this form of consumption promises individual wellness—that is, health, beauty, and spiritual benefits—achieved tastefully and comfortably, with ethical or environmental spin-offs that are an added bonus. Those countercultural elements that made Rastafari disreputable before are still mostly shunned; what was previously unrespectable is still largely unrespectable. Specific procedures of sanitization and distancing—for instance, through new spatial contexts and increased prices—are necessary to make Rastafari acceptable, to ensure that its broad idioms are marked as clean and proper. While ital chic professes a strong attachment to the local and to traditions dating back to before the globalization era, its aesthetics have often been endorsed in foreign contexts, usually the United States. Similarly, some ideas of what the local is and looks like appear to be filtered through the lens of tourism, and this involves a certain level of self-exoticization. This does not appear to diminish the sense of authenticity or nostalgia associated with some ital chic products and services, nor does it detract from their aura of cultural self-determination. As ital chic is in many ways a class project, its high price is as important a marker as extranational validation:

for a product to move from ital to ital chic entails moving into a different price range and a different sociogeographical space.

Jamaican Class and Cultural Politics

Jamaica's middle classes have tended to display externally oriented, cosmopolitan consumer habits, as have similar class groups in postcolonial societies elsewhere (e.g., de Koning 2009; vom Bruck 2005). This outward orientation has served as a marker of class distinction. Kingston is a divided city in terms of class—and color—and spatialized consumption patterns have served to reinforce these divisions. A middle-class uptown position is confirmed and displayed through consumption and mobility, through the association with specific commodities, and through a differential use of urban space. Through ital chic, the middle class's external, global, high-tech consumer orientation loses ground to simpler, locally rooted lifestyles. That these local patterns are also "blacker" than previous ones is most likely not coincidental. As Deborah Thomas (2004) points out, recent decades have witnessed the blackening of the Jamaican nation, displacing creole multiracial nationalism.[1] While a lighter (browner) skin is still often associated with a more advantageous class position, blackness has become an increasingly important marker of ethnonational belonging. Given the long-standing correlation between class and color, this has also meant a significant shift in middle-class orientations. Where in the early to mid-twentieth century a racist ideology was prevalent among Jamaica's brown and black middle classes (Chevannes 1998: 68), by the early twenty-first century this has largely changed, as modern (rather than folk) forms of blackness have become central to Jamaican belonging. While Thomas and others (e.g., Edwards 1998; Stolzoff 2000) have explored the contribution of popular culture to these new, blacker definitions of the nation and of cultural citizenship, the centrality of material culture and consumption to the ethnically imagined Jamaican community has been explored much less. I want to suggest that we might understand ital chic as an element in the performance of blackness that has become increasingly critical to being Jamaican. From this perspective, ital chic consumption can be seen as central in the reconfiguring of identities and belonging to the Jamaican nation. It can function as a conservative class strategy that offers middle-class Jamaicans a way to acquire the moral and cultural capital associated with Rastafari without having to critically examine their own class position or deal with poverty and social exclusion—a combination of appropriation and distancing that at times requires something of a balancing act.

The embrace of Rastafari by the middle class is not completely unprecedented. A similar enthusiasm was evident in the 1960s and 1970s among middle-class youth who were politicized by the activism of the time; the middle-class, respectable character of the Rastafari group Twelve Tribes of Israel also goes back a number of decades (van Dijk 1988). While ital chic, in the early twenty-first century, presents itself as an apparently apolitical trend, it is in fact quite political, but in a way that is more or less the opposite from the activism of the 1960s and 1970s. Ital chic represents a significantly conservative politics, because it dislocates ital from the complex and contested domain in which it originated.

Consumption and the Politics of Sustainability

Ital chic also represents something of a conservative politics in its relation to sustainable development. In a time of global environmental crisis, finding an effective way of achieving development that "meets the needs of the present without compromising the ability of future generations to meet their own needs" appears increasingly urgent (World Commission on Environment and Development 1987: 43). The term *sustainable development* itself, having gained sociopolitical recognition and global circulation from the 1980s, is "deeply, perhaps inherently ambiguous" (Rydin 1999: 468) and is interpreted in multiple ways, from radical calls for cultural revolution to very mild gestures toward technological or managerial change. However, radical forms of sustainable development that critique accepted notions of economic development and the emphasis on the constant acquisition of material goods appear to have lost ground over the last few decades (Williams and Millington 2004: 102). Milder light-green forms of environmentalism appear to be dominant, and forms of sustainable, green, and ethical consumption fit well within these less radical attempts at sustainability.

Sustainable consumption choices can certainly have an effect if operating at a large enough scale. Political consumerism has become a formidable global force, with consumer choices emerging as an easy-access form of market-based politics. Reflecting the neoliberal turn, the market has become an important site of politics, collective action, and ethics, where citizen-consumers are mobilized to incorporate noneconomic values (such as the environment, social justice, and human rights) when selecting products and producers. This politicization of the market—and the concomitant privatization of politics—is sometimes seen as providing a more effective answer to economic globalization than old politics. However, others have pointed out the potential dangers of this shift toward the market: for instance, it may restrict the realm of politics to those with money. Moreover, environmentally friendly and other political consumer choices may turn out to be only temporary changes in purchasing habits that can be substituted for the next trend a few years down the road, or abandoned when consumers' income levels slump (Micheletti 2004; Spaargaren and Mol 2008). Ital chic, I believe, highlights an additional danger in its ambiguous, apolitical form of sustainability politics. It is an attractively packaged form of consumption that implies that it can achieve positive social and environmental effects. Yet as long as it remains unaccompanied by any real political action and reshaping of Jamaican political ecology, it may only serve to reinforce class distinction.

Examples of Ital Chic

There are a number of categories in which ital chic seems evident, relating to hairstyles, wellness, fashion, and food. Following are illustrations of each of these categories. One of the most obvious examples of ital chic may be the phenomenon of Sisterlocks, a form of very fine dreadlocks that need to be done according to a specific patented technique with a specially developed tool. In contrast to the messier, matted kind of dreadlocks some Rastas wear, this hairstyle offers a more elegant, polite form of dreadlocks. Not co-incidentally perhaps, Sisterlocks originates from the United States, where it is marketed as a system of natural hair management. This system was founded in 1993 by JoAnne Cornwell, an associate professor of French and Africana studies at San Diego State University (Bell 2007: 138). Because some associate hair straightening with a lack of racial pride, all over the Internet, women are endorsing this natural hairstyle that does not involve chemical processing. Sisterlocks is described as an ideal neat hairstyle for the professional woman: finally, a form of dreadlocks that one can wear in polite company and to a corporate job. There is, however, a drawback. Getting this type of locks in Jamaica, even if it is not done by a certified Sisterlocks consultant, will cost around J$20,000 (approximately US$235)—for a session that might take up to thirty hours—while a tightening session will cost at least J$3,000 (approximately US$35).

Of course, there are many reasons someone would choose to wear Sisterlocks—interventions in one's appearance are related to one's gendered, ethnic, and class identifications in various, complex ways. But given the cost and the association with a professional lifestyle, might we regard Sisterlocks as uptown dreadlocks—a fashionable middle-class way to reaffirm one's black or rootsy identity in a mildly nonconformist way, without being a dirty Rasta?[2] Has the dread associated with locks been pacified (see Frank 2007)?[3] While the answer might seem at first to be a straightforward yes, the politics of black female hair remain complex. To wearers such as Tracy, a professional botanist in a management position at one of Jamaica's government agencies, Sisterlocks represents a way to assert a black self (see Figure 9.1). Tracy grew up with a mother who stressed black pride, and throughout high school Tracy wore her hair natural. However, after high school and moving on in higher education and her career, she "did the processing thing," though she never really liked it. After years of processing her hair, she went back to wearing it naturally, in twists. Twisting is a time-consuming process, and Tracy's sister helped her with the upkeep. However, when her sister moved farther away, Tracy could not find anyone who was willing to help her do it on a regular basis, and Sisterlocks presented itself as a way of keeping her hair natural while requiring less work. To women like Tracy, Sisterlocks is not so much a trend; rather, it signifies: "I'm comfortable with my black hair."[4] Wanting to express this cannot be wholly apolitical. But while it is an intervention into the politics of color, it does not join this to the politics of class, religion, or nature, as is the case for Rastafari and traditional locks.

Two other good examples, in the wellness category of ital chic, are Starfish Oils and Ital Blends. These aromatherapy companies' main product lines feature bath products and scented candles. For Starfish Oils, the bath products include bath salts and handmade soaps (see Figure 9.2). The descriptions and packaging of these products stress their artisanal manufacturing, the use of local products, the age-old traditions they draw on, and their beneficial effects on health and spiritual well-being. The Sweet Jamaica Bath Bar urges the buyer: "Lively up your bath experience with Sweet Jamaican vanilla and nutmeg—essential oils of island spices that soothe your sense and pamper your soul.

Figure 9.1   Sisterlocks (photo by Wayne Modest).

Relax and create your very own Caribbean getaway." The use of lively up is a gesture toward the Jamaican Creole vernacular—and quite likely a sly Bob Marley reference—while vanilla and nutmeg, as local products, are used to invoke nationalist sentiments and are touted for their beneficial effects. Yet this localism is balanced by the use of self-exoticizing tourist tropes and terms such as "the islands" and their purported sensuality.

Figure 9.2 Starfish Oils products (photo by R. Jaffe).

The reference to a "Caribbean getaway" is also a little curious—how does one get away to the region one is already living in? The body oil in the same scent is even more explicitly tourist-tongued, promising that it will transport you "to a warm, flavourful space of mind, overlooking a crystal blue Caribbean sea." To be fair, the company sells locally but also targets an international market. The True Lavender Aromatherapy Spa Bar boasts that it is "cold processed by hand with the most nutritious vegetable oils and enhanced only with 100% pure essential oils and herbal botanicals." Lavender's "history of herbal healing" is asserted, as is its ability to "promote the growth of new skin cells, relieve nervous tension and relax the mind and body." Besides these constant allusions to wellness of body, mind, and soul, references to nature and the environment are also ubiquitous. The soap packages, for instance, are all marked with the slogan "Earth. Nature. You." Other texts encourage us: "Touch the earth. Get back to basics. Smell beautiful. Be a star. Be a fish. Be natural."

Starfish Oils' scented candles include a line of Bob Marley candles. The Natural Mystic Candle is marketed as an "all-natural, aromatherapeutic candle [that] evokes the spirit of Marley's Rastafarian roots and the music he left behind." Other candles are based on traditional Jamaican products such as Blue Mountain coffee, ginger, ortanique, and mint tea. The Jamaican Ginger Tea Candle is "hand-poured in Jamaica" and carries the following text: "Knowledge of the healing powers of ginger is as old as the first recordings of man. Jamaican ginger is known for the strong and distinct flavour, which we proudly capture in this candle." The lid of this candle depicts laborers harvesting ginger in straw baskets. Again, the emphasis on pride in artisanal production, local products, and age-old traditions is evident.

Ital Blends is a newer company, with products that also target both a local and an international market. Their 100 percent goat's milk soaps—that are "all natural" and hand crafted"—include the Lively Up Yu'self, the Pure Niceness, and the Cease N' Settle series (see Figure 9.3). These products place ital in a central position and give a definition of ital as "anything that is organic, natural or wholesome." The Blue Mountain Moment soap promises "an opulent woodsy aroma that grounds [the user] to mother nature," while the Jamaican Gypsy soap presents itself as "a euphoric aroma"—"Spirits carefree, souls forever young. Dance to the tune in your soul."[5] The name of the Blue Mountain Moment soap is both natural and nationalist; that of the second soap localizes gypsy, in Jamaica an external signifier for wild exoticness, while drawing indirectly on a carefree no-problem image of the island. On removing the soap from its packaging a small card

Figure 9.3   Ital Blends soap (photo by R. Jaffe).

drops out, with the words "honor nature" printed against the backdrop of a verdant scene, presumably Jamaican nature. The company's website proclaims, while playing reggae Muzak: "It's our mission to take you back to the natural grassroots of skin care." As with Starfish Oils, we see a neotraditionalist attitude (taking you back), a connection between nature, spiritual wellness, health, and beauty, bolstered by a mildly nationalist use of Jamaican vernacular and reference to the grassroots.

In fashion, two brands representing ital chic are CY Clothing and La Pluma Negra.[6] Both sell mainly t-shirts. CY Clothing, formerly Cooyah, presents itself on its website as a company that has "embark[ed] on a fashion evolution geared towards uniting all people as one, while supporting the global conscious evolution towards healthier lifestyles." CY Clothing's products—"with natural Bamboo and Hemp fabrics, printed with green friendly inks and dyes"—make ubiquitous use of the Rasta colors of red, green, and gold and symbols such as the Lion of Judah and Haile Selassie I, and are printed with slogans such as "Jah Army" and "Rasta Lives."[7] La Pluma Negra means "the black feather" in Spanish. According to its website, this company "was born out of the need for a Jamaican brand catering to the more discerning customer who needs a classy, comfortable t-shirt." This reference to a "more discerning" clientele speaks to an intention of elite branding, while cultural nationalism is made explicit as well: "La Pluma Negra is all about cultural nuance; it glorifies its culture like no other brand in the country."[8] This glorification goes for about J$2,000 (US$24) per t-shirt, and interestingly takes place on t-shirts produced by American Apparel, a US company with an explicit ethical production policy. Cultural pride is again evident in the use of Rasta colors, and in slogans in Jamaican Creole that refer to Rastafari and to local Jamaican products or sayings. Examples are "Souljah," "Nuff Okra Roun' Mi," "Ganjahmekya," and "Me Run Tings, Tings Nuh Run Me."[9]

My final examples are two vegetarian or ital restaurants, Livity and Ashanti Oasis. Both are located in uptown Kingston. Livity moved from Hope Road to the business district of New Kingston, in part because of continuing problems with parking space. While its previous location, close to two universities, pulled a partly academic crowd, the current site attracts—based on their attire—a variety of professionals, including businesspeople from the nearby office complexes. Awaiting the completion of a larger outside seating area—constructed using wood, bamboo, and palm fronds—customers either take away their food or eat it at one of the tables in or around the main building. This building's exterior is painted in red, green, and gold, while inside the walls are decorated with Rasta wood carvings and glossy depictions of some of the menu items, such as "Yatties: a variety of delicious fillings in a whole wheat crust."[10] Other decorations included pictures of Haile Selassie I, signed promotional posters of a large range of reggae artists, and framed versions of Livity's values and the restaurant's mission statement. The general atmosphere is cool yet colorful and rootsy. A friendly Sisterlocked young woman takes orders from behind the counter, which also serves as a display for several healthy roots drinks. The dishes and drinks served at Livity express a Rasta and black consciousness. One special dish was the Marcus Garvey Stew, which featured a blend of red, black, and green beans.

Ashanti Oasis is located in the heart of Hope Gardens, one of the city's few large public green spaces. The restaurant has a breezy open construction, and customers can dine at small tables circling an abundance of green plants and a small bridge over softly gurgling water. The yellow walls and green woodwork match the colors of the restaurant's logo, which adorns the uniforms of the wait staff who comes to announce the daily menu. African references are evident in the name Ashanti, in the traditional Ashanti stool featured in the logo, as well as in the Egyptian print on the wall next to the kitchen. Ashanti is owned by Yvonne Hope, a longtime Rastafarian in her mid-fifties. Figure 9.4 shows Ms. Hope standing proudly in front of her restaurant, accompanied by one of Ashanti's uniformed waitresses. In the past, Ms. Hope grew her own food in the hills outside of Kingston, making her own soy milk and using "nothing from Babylon." Ms. Hope claims she started the restaurant in part to disprove the stereotype of Rastas as dirty and disreputable.

She has seen a change in Jamaican society, noting that where vegetarianism was seen as dangerous and countercultural in the past, people have moved toward an embrace of such a diet and lifestyle. Nonetheless, she told me that many people cannot believe that she created Ashanti—they rather expect a brown, uptown male to be its creator.[11] The restaurant's atmosphere does have an uptown association—a local journalist described

Figure 9.4 Yvonne Hope and waitress in front of Ashanti Oasis Vegetarian Restaurant (photo by R. Jaffe).

Ashanti's "ambience of simplicity, calm and serenity [as] just what one needs if you work in New Kingston" (Parkison 2003). Ms. Hope described her patrons as a mix of businesspeople and Rasta *bredren,* who tend to come later on in the day; during a recent visit, around one o'clock in the afternoon, the parking lot was dominated by large SUVs, normally associated with the wealthier classes.

Both restaurants draw on Rastafari elements in their cuisine, names, and decor, while drawing a mostly upscale crowd on the basis of their location and ambience. They promote a vegetarian diet as a healthy choice, while combining traditional Jamaican ingredients and dishes with internationally popular healthy products such as tofu and wraps. Both restaurants have hosted a variety of Rasta-related cultural events, such as book launches, poetry readings, and meetings. Their aesthetics draw on that of Rastafari in their choice of colors, symbols, natural materials, and references to Africa. Yet the styling of the vegetarianism and the Rasta elements is such that, bolstered by their uptown locations and cost, both restaurants attract a largely middle-class, professional clientele.

Conclusions: Commodifying Resistance?

Ital chic is a form of consumption that revalorizes local, preglobal tastes and traditions in a very modern, global way. It draws on Rasta aesthetics and symbols as it promises beauty, health, spiritual wellness, and cultural pride. As the sharpest Rastafari elements are pacified or at least sanitized, ital chic may provide middle-class Jamaicans with a currently fashionable way to embrace a locally rooted lifestyle without sacrificing a cosmopolitan orientation in terms of comfort and style. They can partake in their identification with a Jamaicanness that is increasingly framed as black, lower-class, and downtown without leaving the spaces of consumption delineated by capital and class.

A number of drivers behind ital chic can be located. On the one hand, we are witnessing a gradual trickle-up of grassroots Rasta initiatives, as is the case with Ashanti Oasis. At the same time, it is not difficult for entrepreneurs with no historical or cultural grounding in Rastafari to co-opt its revolutionary symbols for profit. The recent embrace of Rastafari by the Jamaican government could be indicative of either or both phenomena. Policy documents such as the Natural Cultural Policy include Rastafari as a cultural expression to be recognized, protected, and promoted (Ministry of Education, Youth, and Culture 2003). Given Rastafari's countercultural, antistate tradition, and a long history of state oppression of the movement, this may seem hypocritical. Such inclusion may indicate the broad reach and influence Rastafari has gained through its struggles in the last several decades. In broader terms, this turn in Jamaica's cultural policy can be seen as a state response to the popular blackening of the nation, in which Rastafari has played a central but not exclusive role.[12] However, the Jamaican government's endorsement can also be interpreted as an economic move that encourages the commodification and sanitization of Rasta as a tourist product and as a basis for the country's cultural industries.

Just as there are multiple ways to understand the production of ital chic, there are multiple ways to interpret its national popularity as a consumer product. This popularity may have to do with middle-class brown angst or with genuine environmental and health concerns. From an optimistic perspective, ital chic means that Rasta, the archetypical counterculture, has succeeded in transforming national values. It provides a divided society with a shared Rasta-colored space where uptown and downtown, black and brown, believe in a national vision based on ethnocultural pride and environmental concern.

Ital chic, then, demonstrates the ways in which consumption, the state, and Rastafari have come together at a specific point in Jamaica's history. The phenomenon can be analyzed as a capitalist manifestation of a global eco-chic trend that dampens the resistive power of a movement. However, it can equally be taken to demonstrate the culmination of a national shift in political economy, the fashioning of which was strongly predicated on the ideas of Rastafari: Pan-Africanism, autonomy, and self-pride.

The political stakes of ital chic, as they relate to both the Jamaican middle class and Rastafari, are ambiguous. Ital chic is clearly a part of a classed consumption repertoire, providing a new space for those middle-class consumers who prefer a more Jamaican flavor. However, it can also operate as a conservative mechanism of class distinction. As a specific class strategy, ital chic can be interpreted as a market-based way for "browns" to claim blackness and belonging, and with these their right to (continue to) speak for the nation. As a political consequence strengthening the role of the middle class, this would be antithetical to the aims of Rastafari. The potential consequences for Rastafari, though, are mixed.

It is tempting to call out "Judgment!" on the diluted form of Rastafari that ital chic presents. The sanitized repackaging of Rastafari themes and aesthetics appears to exploit the movement's revolutionary appeal for economic gain and can be taken as a sign of the continued encroachment of market forces into the domains of religion, ethics, and politics. Yet the idea of commodification is somewhat complicated by Rastas such as Yvonne Hope. She is part of a longer tradition of selling the ital; Rastafari already has a commodity base of its own. To her, ital chic is not a trend—through the promoting of her group's practices she is able to make a living while encouraging others to live right. As Rasta attitudes of resistance and ital livity are brought into a middle-class sphere, an acceptance and appreciation of these stances, even if in sanitized forms, may function as an opening to a truly critical position.

It is difficult to state with certainty whether the mainstreaming of Rasta elements is a progressive move toward the transformation of Jamaican society or whether what is at work is a capitalist logic that is commodifying resistance. This ambiguity perhaps represents the dilemma of lifestyle, or, more specifically, style: while style can be devoid of politics, it can also represent a space of education or serve as a platform for political mobilization. The transformation of the symbols and image of a movement of resistance into marketable commodities can, but does not necessarily, indicate the commodification of the counterculture itself.

There are various forms of Rastafari that exist in the twenty-first century, some of them more entwined with the Jamaican establishment, others more rooted in opposition to it. They are faced with global capitalist mechanisms that deftly incorporate and pacify the symbols of any counterculture that holds appeal to the moneyed classes. The national context is very different from that of the early and mid-twentieth century, with complexities including classed anxieties, shifts in the ways in which Jamaicanness is imagined, and neoliberal government priorities. The challenge, I think, is for the various contemporary forms of Rastafari to reposition themselves and maintain integrity in the face of these changing contexts. In any event, Rastafari have been successful in achieving at least some of their goals, in that blackness and humans' relation to nature are most definitely on the nation's mind.

–10–

Tropical Spa Culture and the Face of New Asian Beauty

Bart Barendregt

Western travelers, tourists, and scholars have for long perceived the Orient as authentic, sensual, and mysterious, and even today Asia is for many home to all what is lost to modern (Western) man. Such musings say much about the Western audience's longing for a sensual other expressed through a depiction of the East as a place of splendor, purity, and closeness to nature. However, more recently the Southeast Asian middle and upper classes seem to have tapped into such stereotypes as to retrieve an authentic life experience that, according to many, has been threatened by ongoing modernization, globalization, and, most feared of all, westernization. As an answer to these threats, a regional culture has over the last few years been up and coming that ironically uses the vocabulary, ideas, and images of an lifestyle of health, beauty, and spirituality that currently is so fashionable in the West. In this chapter, I focus on the most eye-catching manifestation of this New Asian lifestyle: the tropical spa.

Spas are often traced to the thirteenth century iron-bearing spring at the Wallonian town of Spa (Crismer 1989). Yet curative baths only became a trend in fifteenth century Renaissance Europe when scholarly treatises devoted to the subject first appeared and rudimentary spa directories were composed in England and Italy.[1] By the mid-seventeenth century, it was an accepted habit for European elites to spend their time at mineral springs or at seaside resorts, and in time these resorts also provided Europe's newly developing bourgeoisie with leisure time away from industrial life (Mackaman 1998). The three—the new rich, leisure, and spas—would from the nineteenth century onward be knit even more closely together. As spas became commercially interesting, water from curative springs was bottled and exported as far as the United States. In 1826, the first American spa resort opened in Saratoga, New York, the city's name being derived from the word for "medicine water" in Mohawk, the Native American tribe that had previously settled the area (Corbett 2001: 171). Within the context of the new American superspa, the Native American link not only was used to give credibility to the curative powers of the springs but also was soon appropriated in tourism—a strategy that ever since has been widely used in the spa industry. In the late 1970s the first truly modern-day spas appeared—a process that was given greater impetus in the 1990s by the wellness revolution, with its desire for slow living and an emphasis on bodily well-being.

The desire for slow living was accompanied by a return to more craftsman-like practices and an appreciation of local products (see Parkins and Craig 2006), as well as traditional and exotic prescriptions such as massage and Chinese medicine. This renewed concept of the spa attracted well-to-do visitors from Asia and, in the early 1990s, was also taken up by the first destination resorts in Thailand.[2] Since then the spa industry has been one of the fastest growing sectors in Southeast Asian travel and leisure—and has even been used as a component of development strategies.[3]

Today, *tropical spa* is a term that refers to resorts, most of them located in Southeast Asia (hence the adjective *tropical*), where well-to-do tourists from both the East and the West are pampered in luxurious, exotic, and often "mystical" settings.[4] Tropical spas offer myriad services including beauty, fitness, medicine, and spiritual relief. Whereas most but not all spas are open to both men and women, consumption seems highly gendered in nature and conditioned by the demands of industrial society (Hudson 2003: 287): men are generally attracted to services for their health and the functionality of their bodies, whereas women are more concerned with their appearance. However, in this chapter I am more interested in the differences in ways visitors from the East and West consume spas. I do so by paying attention to the ways the tropical spa is attracting Western participants through guides, coffee table books, and web directories—promotional tools that have their historical predecessors in sixteenth century spa listings, novels featuring well-known springs, and modern-day airline brochures. Additionally, I will show how the tropical spa phenomenon also serves to promote a New Asian lifestyle among the local well-to-do by stressing the spa as a tradition with local roots and by using elements of local landscapes that visually stress Asianness. In various ways, this New Asianism is expressed through ideas of health, beauty, and spirituality. Let us now turn to the first symptoms of this new Asian lifestyle.

Rise of the Wellness Industry or Emergent Regionalism?

Early 2005 saw the publication of Erlinda Enriquez Panlilio and Felice Prudente Sta. María's book *Slow Food: Philippine Culinary Traditions,* which not coincidentally is dedicated to the founder of the Manila chapter of the International Wine and Food Society. The book offers a lush variety of Philippine foods under headings such as "Pospas—My Mother's Legacy," "The Vanishing Tawilis of Lake Taal," and "Christmas of My Childhood," shading authentic dishes into the memories of a passing age. "Today one wonders about the future of Philippine cooking," the introduction notes. "Slow food...traditional food...food prepared from scratch with no shortcuts, using only the finest ingredients acquitted [sic] at the peak of their season, is a vital and valuable component of every Filipino's sense of self" (Panlilio and Sta. María 2005: 6–7).

Elsewhere, a Javanese businesswoman, Martha Tilaar, popularly known as the mother of natural based cosmetics, has launched her Dewi Sri line of body scrubs, which is now popularly advertised as "the Secret of the Tropical Goddess." Her website explains that "an old Indonesian folklore tells of an ancient remedy inspired by the Goddess of fertility and prosperity of rice fields and crop harvest. Her beautiful, healthy skin is the emanation of a timeless beauty ritual enhanced by traditional bathing. Based on this secret, a series of treatments was born."[5] Tilaar's recipes are believed to be based on the traditional ingredients used by the princesses of the palaces of Central Java, which only adds to the products' aura of mystery: these ancient secrets for beauty and health are now also available to ordinary women in both the East and the West.

Finally, moving eastward, the island of Bali was once called "the Island of Gods." Since the late 1990s, it has been the Island of Tropical Spas as it has gradually become more of a sanctuary for those looking for self-actualization. There are hundreds of spa resorts on the island, varying in size and services. One can partake in a traditional massage or aromatherapy, or simply relax, and afterward enjoy an al fresco organic dinner while listening to traditional gamelan music.

Filipino-style slow food, the ancient secrets of Javanese beauty, and the Island of Tropical Spas: these are but a few examples of the recent boom in Asian-style eco-chic. But what do these products have in common, and why are these and similar products suddenly so enormously popular throughout Southeast Asia?

Products that stress the local, the slow, and the natural are a current fad among the new wealthy of Southeast Asia's metropoles. The well-to-do often consider consuming such products to be indispensable in dealing with the alienating effects of the difficult-to-handle, abstract processes of globalization, modernization, and westernization. While the remedy is indeed very local in nature, this volume shows that similar phenomena can be found throughout the non-Western world, although both the intentions of and meanings invested in such practices may be very different from what is happening in the West. For this reason, the Southeast Asian middle and upper classes' current fascination with beauty, health, and all things natural can be seen as a distinct interpretation of global culture—an Asian response to the wellness industry of the West—especially among the nouveau riche, who until recently primarily defined themselves through their patterns of consumption, but otherwise lack a shared identity, and now seem to desire a more authentic cultural experience. At the same time, the preference for natural, local, and more authentic products confronts us with a rupture in global culture, as the Southeast Asian middle class suddenly no longer seems solely obsessed with consuming the Western symbols of modernity. On the contrary, it is now modern and fashionable to read the "Asian philosophies" of Deepak Chopra or to build a house based on the principles of Feng Shui or Vastu Sastra. Rather than fast-food chains like McDonald's or Pizza Hut, the latest buzz is local slow food: one eats *nasi kampung* (village-style fried rice) in posh restaurants and drinks traditional and organically grown coffees at Starbucks or local coffee bars.

These practices, which can be grouped together as Asian-style eco-chic, are modish combinations of lifestyle politics, environmental awareness, and an urge to get back to the natural and authentic.[6] More than that, they are increasingly part of the identikit of the well-to-do in Southeast Asia. In mimicking the lifestyle and shopping practices of their peers in the West, middle- and upper-class Asians seem to demonstrate their cosmopolitan consciousness, combined with an appreciation of local (read: regional and Asian) culture. One of the ironies of such global flows is that as a result Asia rediscovers itself through the West.

What are we dealing with here? Cultural nostalgia, self-Orientalism, or some sort of elite cosmopolitanism? It surely is a cosmopolitan consciousness, which is then expressed in often patriotic ways: Philippine food as a sense of self, Dewi Sri as an ancient Javanese secret, or, as we will see, the tropical spa as Asia's botanic and cultural heritage. In that case, one could speak of cosmopatriotism, a very rooted kind of cosmopolitanism (see also Jurriëns and De Kloet 2007). Being local in a globalizing world was long considered far from hip or modern, and thus locality had to be transformed and reinvented. Asian-style eco-chic offers such new opportunities for constructing community, and, as I will argue, has therefore become part of an All-Asian renaissance and an elite lifestyle associated with it: New Asianism. A similar stress on a shared pan-Asian culture can elsewhere be found in fashion, cinema, science, and politics. However, the consumption of Asian-style eco-chic is one of the most visible of these manifestations, and one that can be found in the everyday domain. It's in the ways the well-to-do dress, what they decide to eat, and more broadly in their approach to life. For many, New Asianism has become a preferred lifestyle, though one that is full of contradictions: it is one that most Asians can hardly afford; it is neither new nor solely based on the ancient secrets so often used in its advertisements; and it is a mixture of outright commercialism with a touch of instant spirituality. Importantly, it is neither fully Western inspired nor completely Asian. Rather, different audiences are consuming Asia in different ways and for different reasons, as the case of tropical spa culture here will illustrate.

The tropical spa is the place where ideas of a cosmopolitan lifestyle, eco-chic, and Asianism merge. Tropical spas are lavishly designed destination resorts where one can stay overnight and choose from an amalgam of beauty, health, and spiritual practices. It is perhaps more appropriate to speak of tropical spa cultures rather than of a unitary phenomenon because the spas are a conglomeration of different sorts of newly invented or old, often profoundly romanticized traditions and therapies. The resorts, which today are primarily found in Southeast Asia are aimed at the wealthy Western and East Asian traveler, but in many cases also at the local well-to-do. Although these groups might consume spa culture for various reasons as we will see below, tropical spas are seldom run either solely by Westerners or exclusively by Asians. These resorts are typically international ventures: the luxury resort Chiva-Som, for instance, has a Thai manager and a Swiss hotel director, which counters the easy accusation that this is merely an imported foreign phenomenon. Moreover, in its outward appearance and in line with other forms of eco-chic, the tropical spa culture stresses the local, either indigenous practices or well-known traditions from neighboring Southeast Asian societies. The past few years have seen an enormous boom in these tropical spas, and hundreds of them can be found in Bali alone. Bali, however, is but one of the many areas visited by the international leisure class that travels to similar resorts in Phuket, Kerala, Manila, or Singapore. Moreover, these spas have given rise to numerous derivative products, such as Martha Tilaar's Dewi Sri Spa body scrubs, CDs with spa lounge music, and beautifully illustrated coffee table books that promote the tropical spa culture as a New Asian lifestyle that also can be enjoyed by the less wealthy. Before looking at such derivative products and the ways they spread spa culture beyond the resorts, we must first look at the ancient tradition of healing waters. It will help us understand the current popularity of tropical spas.

From Healing Water to Asian Beauty

Although the idea of the spa is a modern import from the West, Asian societies have long been familiar with the healing qualities of water, especially springs. One of the most famous examples is the Godavari River. Shelter to Rama and Sita in the Hindu epic *Ramayana,* it is believed to flow underground, invisible to the human eye, where it is said to be connected to underground basins, flowing into fountainheads or bowls supplying holy water to India's many temples. Holy purification water, or *tirta,* is also central to Balinese religion (see Figure 10.1). The purification water is generally seen as a gift from the ancestral deities to their descendants, and almost every Balinese temple has its own source of water that is used to produce it. Tirta can help its consumers to remain conscious and free from sorcery, and it can even save someone from death (Ottino 2000). Hence, tirta is both vitalizing and purifying, albeit the latter function tends to be stressed nowadays.

In the aftermath of the growing worldwide popularity of the wellness industry and eco-chic, ideas of healing water have been reinterpreted, both in the West and in Asia, with luxury spas becoming Asia's hottest trend of the 1990s. Water is no longer the only medication used. Nevertheless some spa resorts, like the Begawan Giri ("noble hermit of the mountain") and Mandara (a reference to the mythology of the sacred center in Hinduism),[7] both located in Bali, are built next to what are, respectively, considered a sacred spring and the supposedly powerful confluence of two rivers.

According to Benge (2003: 15), it is exactly the focus on nature's abundance and her rich aromas that gives Asian beauty such an enormous worldwide appeal. In this, it falls in line with eco-chic's fashionableness; "while a deepening commitment to a kind of environmental consumerism now grips people in the West, it has been the mainstay of Asian culture until recent economic development" (Benge 2003:15). However contradictory it might sound, "back to the basics" is the new concept of modern beauty. At present, these spas, while focusing on traditional Asian beauty treatments, also include health therapies and ways to get back in touch with one's spirituality. Some spas, like the Banyan Tree spa in Phuket, explicitly embrace Buddhist philosophy. Others only make vague references to any of the world's religions or promote themselves as karmic resorts that offer programs to destress or overcome trauma. In some societies, spas more overtly address religious peculiarities. Responding to the emergence of an ever-increasing Muslim middle class and its need to publicly express itself, Muslim day spas have become a lucrative niche in the Indonesian market in places such as Jakarta, Yogyakarta, and Palembang. Muslim salon spas exclusively target a female Muslim audience with services that are roughly similar to their more secular equivalents, but promise a more serious and

Figure 10.1   Tirta Empul Bali (photo by B. Barendregt).

secluded atmosphere.[8] Emphasis also has slowly moved toward prevention rather than cures, putting beauty on an equal footing with health. A Los Angeles visitor summarizes the appeal of the Southeast Asian spa as follows:

> A must see for anyone who wants to witness paradise. I made my way up there...and found something so magical and beautiful that it was inspirational. I could not stop talking about it for days. The Asian Spas are so much more intoxicating and beautiful then [sic] the European Spas. The packaging of the products with natural fibers, banana leaves, lotus leaves, etc. are perfectly pleasing. They are politically correct and appealing. (Amazon.com 1999)

Tropical spas include Bali's pioneering Nusa Dua Spa, founded in 1994, where twenty-six therapists perform approximately eighty therapies a day. They also include the US$26 million Chiva-Som in the Gulf of Siam, a health resort that prides itself in blending well-being with exquisite luxury. One American visitor commented:

> If you are looking for a relaxing spiritual cleanse coupled with a daily workout program, this is the place. I woke up to yoga, had 3 great tasting healthy meals and a massage each day. I couldn't ask for more. I felt the staff was extremely accomodating [sic] and paid close attention to little details (they even presented me with a basket of beautiful roses and a small cake on my birthday—that was truly a surprise!) The menu of spa services was excellent—my most memorable was an hour consultation with a monk and an hour with a hypnotherapist. I had my first Thai style massage there also.[9]

Based on these quotes, critics might argue that what we are dealing with here is simply a successful commercial practice that is targeted at well-to-do, mostly Western tourists. The first part might be true, because like most lifestyle practices, tropical spa culture has definite commercial aspects that not only explain civilizations in terms of commodities, but also show that although many Asians despise Western liberal values, they embrace the modernity of late capitalism. Regarding the last part of this criticism, however, the Western affluent are not the only spa consumers; their Asian counterparts also partake in spa culture, albeit for different reasons. Western, but also East Asian, travelers visit spas because the resorts address the wish for an unpolluted, pure, and very consumer-friendly version of the tropics. The local well-to-do, on the other hand, seem to frequent spas to pronounce and revalidate their own cultural roots. Different needs and taste are also reflected in the sort of spa one visits. Whereas foreign travelers have a preference for destination resorts, where they can swim and enjoy a massage, while making the resort a background to their holidays, middle-class Javanese, as an illustration, seem to prefer day-spa salons. Such spas are often a place to prepare the bride and groom for an upcoming wedding, an occasion that in Southeast Asia may take up to several days, with the couple given ritual baths and donned in different clothing and make up for various events. Well-known spas, such as Martha Tilaar's salon, offer prewedding packages *(paket pengantin)*. Such packages generally include services such as *mandi Ken Dedes* (a 3.5-hour treatment that includes herbal baths, purification with scented smoke, and the use of romantic oils), facial treatments, and manicures. All of these services are offered at various occasions and to both the bride and groom.[10] These services can be enjoyed at the spa compound or at home. The latter variant does not differ much from the more traditional services offered by the *dukun pengantin* (traditional beautician for brides on Java) as described by Puntowati (1992).

In addition, many middle-class Javanese women regularly visit day spas to have a traditional cream bath or enjoy aromatherapy., To them, spas have become inherent to a modern, though very genuine, Asian lifestyle. In participating in spa culture, they have rediscovered treatments their grandmothers were fond of, but by putting them in the context of an international spa culture, such therapies have become very modern and no longer deemed backward, village-like, and, therefore, cheap. To these women (and to a lesser extent men), spa culture addresses various needs; it not only offers health, beauty, and spiritual practices—a place where one in a relaxed atmosphere can meet with like-minded people—but it also significantly addresses a much needed social function.

Over time, spas have come to emphasize leisure and wellness, and as a consequence, spa culture has become a favorite destination for many, both in the West and in the East. Although spas are said not to be traditional to Asia, centuries of its health and beauty practices are being used and repackaged. As one handbook for spa aficionados notes, the "worldwide vogue for spiritual and mental, as well as physical, fitness has been at the core of Asian beauty custom since the beginning of time" (Benge 2003: 11). Access to the spa resorts seems restricted to the happy few, for now. That said, there are other ways in which to share in the tremendously popular spa culture, ways that make an important contribution to the wider recognition of the spa ideals of beauty, health, spirituality, and New Asianism, of which spa culture is increasingly becoming a part. To study the ways New Asianism as a lifestyle is gaining ground among affluent Southeast Asians, it is informative to have a closer look not only at the resorts, but also at the ways spa culture has been disseminated through public media.

Spas Mediated, or Asia Brought Home

The tropical spa is in all respects a sanctuary for the senses: blending taste (cuisine ranging from after-massage snacks to Asian golden muesli), touch (a sensory journey consisting, for example, of a four-hand massage), and smell (aromatherapy is one of the most popular treatments), thus breaking with the adage that our age is primarily a visual one. Still, the visual continues to matter, because it is instrumental in spreading the spa culture's message beyond the resorts. Brochures, books, and websites tell the story of an elegant fusing of indoor and outdoor spaces, the modern and the traditional, the primitive (read: authentic) and the convenient, mixing five-star amenities with a local ambience. It is to these visual elements that I now turn.

Nowadays respected resorts have their private-label products, like the Spice Islands oils from Esens (available at the Nusa Dua Spa, Bali) or the Dewi Sri line of body scrubs, with which to recreate the spa experience in one's own home. One of the most eye-catching, or ear-catching, ways to do this has been the recent trend of repackaging traditional tunes as spa music.[11] Here, however, I will restrict myself to print magazines and coffee table books and the way they represent and disseminate tropical spa culture and associated eco-chic practices, as these are among the most important carriers of what is now fast becoming the trend of New Asianism. Without the authors possibly being aware, these books and magazines have historical predecessors in sixteenth-century spa publications, nineteenth-century guides and novels describing spa life in France (Mackaman 1998), and more recently, in-flight guides such as the 1960s Pan Am spa directory. Each in their way promoted spa tourism for a particular audience. Visiting any upmarket bookstore (or try Amazon.com), one will be struck by the thousands of titles that deal with the healing potential, power, and "holy order" of water. Titles include, among others, *SalonOvations; Day Spa Operations* (1996), *The Spa Encyclopedia* (2002), *Spa & Wellness Hotels* (2002), *Spa and Salon Alchemy* (2004), and *Spa & Health Club Design* (2005), all of which focus on an evolving worldwide spa culture. Many of these coffee table books are exclusively about Asian spas. They sometimes consider a particular national tradition, such as the *Japanese Spa* (2005) or the *Thai Spa Book* (2002), but more often portray it as a regional all-Asian phenomenon, such as *Spa Style Asia* (2003) or *Ultimate Spa: Asia's Best Spas and Spa Treatments* (2006).

In this section, I shall focus on two publications: Sophie Benge's best-selling *The Tropical Spa* published by Periplus in 2003[12] and the internationally available glossy magazine *AsiaSpa* (2004–present).[13] Both were published in Asia. Benge is a British expatriate who lived in Asia for seven years, while the editorial staff of *AsiaSpa* is made up of both Western and Asian journalists. Neither publication seems to exclusively address a Western or Asian audience. Rather, they cater specifically to the urban middle or upper classes. As important to *The Tropical Spa* as its explanatory text, and in line with the stress on the visual, are the stunning photographs by Luca Invernizzi Tettoni.[14] *The Tropical Spa* is in fact a catalog of some of the better-known Southeast Asian spas (although criteria for their selection are strikingly absent). The book also offers stress-releasing therapies under titles like "Rites of Massage," "Hair Story," and "Face Value," thus giving the reader access to a holistic and uplifting lifestyle at home.

AsiaSpa (not to be confused with the similarly named *SpaAsia* magazine) is one of the countless new lifestyle magazines in Southeast Asia that increasingly act as "missionaries of modernity" (cf. Heryanto 1999). The bimonthly magazine is now sold in Hong Kong, Singapore, Malaysia, Thailand, China, the Philippines, and several other Asian Pacific countries. Like *The Tropical Spa, AsiaSpa* magazine clearly caters to the wealthy, as can be concluded from its ads for Hyatt resorts, expensive chocolate, and Aston Martin and Rolls Royce automobiles. The latter items are typically aimed at a male market, and *AsiaSpa* in no way pretends to be a women's magazine, despite the gendered orientation of some of the spas found in Southeast Asia today. The magazine's upmarket orientation is confirmed by its use of English, chosen in this case not so much because of the magazine's international (e.g., Western) readership, but rather because English is the language of the new Asian middle class and, therefore, a marker of modernity and cosmopolitanism. The magazine is widely available in flight libraries, airport shops, and the lounges of various Asian airline companies, once again linking it with a wealthy leisure class and modernity. Large segments of society thus seem excluded from the world of *AsiaSpa,* but it can be argued that, like other glossy magazines, its readership acts as a role model, displaying a middle-class lifestyle that is aspired to by many.[15]

AsiaSpa magazine and its associated websites[16] are published by the Hong Kong–based AdKom. Their editorial staffs are composed of Asians and Westerners, men and women. Most of the contributors to this and comparable magazines are people who are involved in the wellness industry as journalists, consultants, or therapists. *AsiaSpa* magazine contains such regular features as SpaTalk, Urban Spa, Book Watch, Spa Finder, and Dare to Dream, the latter being a section on the ultimate indulgence, unfolding people's wildest dreams of consumption. It also has special features like articles on Angkor Wat revisited and, in the anniversary issue, an A-to-Z of Asian therapies.

To a large extent acting as advertisements for and by the industry, some modern-day guides are quite superficial and shallow. In their praise for a much-romanticized mythical past, everyone seems to have been healthier, more beautiful, and nobler in the past, and stereotypical images of spiritual traditions typically abound. Frequently, such descriptions include clearly invented traditions and misrepresentations of the people who supposedly practiced them. In describing the Datai hotel on Langkawi Island in Malaysia, *The Tropical Spa,* for example, comments that "with your third eye it is not hard to see a Dayak tribesman emerging from the trees to appear on the jetty of your spa suite. Stick to real vision and your visitor will likely be one of the many monkeys to whom this Malaysian slice of rainforest really belonged before the Datai [hotel] arrived" (Benge 2003: 40). Nowhere is it explained that the Dayak people actually do not live on Langkawi, but on the relatively far-off island of Borneo.

I now turn to considering the role such books and magazines play in shaping a New Asian lifestyle by providing the new visuals and stressing the alternative temporalities that tropical spa culture has become known for.

Spa-scapes: Visualizing Asia as Paradise

An important aspect of spa culture is the way the spa is turned into a part of a wider natural setting. Resorts are often located at scenic spots and are carefully designed in accordance with the natural surroundings. The Tjampuhan Spa in Bali, for example, is housed in the former guest house of the Royal prince of Ubud,[17] which was once home to international artists such as Spies and Bonnet and the starting point of the Western-inspired art movement Pita Maha.[18] Today, the resort offers open views of the river valley, "with all buildings enjoying the natural insulation of traditional Balinese thatched roofs and surrounded by tropical greenery and flowers" (from its brochure). Massage rooms are located along the water, where the sacred Oos and Tjampuhan Rivers meet, and situated just opposite the 900-year-old Gunung Lembah temple complex. Not seldom—and this is intentional—it is difficult to distinguish where the spa resort stops and nature takes over. If such a natural environment is not at hand, and many spas are nowadays found within larger Southeast Asian cities, such natural landscapes are artificially created, using organic materials, such as wood, stone, and flowers. Again it is a tropical image that is constantly invoked, but one that is cautiously adapted to the needs and taste of the modern urban visitor.[19] In either case, landscaping (i.e., adapting the resort to its direct surroundings) is an important process often undertaken by skilled architects and designers and inherent to the atmosphere created within the spa. In absence of other bodily experiences such as taste, smell, and sound, such visual cues are even more stressed in the magazines and coffee table books that represent tropical spa culture. It is through these visual cues as well that a shared Asian world seems to be drawn for both the Western and local readership.

"The pictures are just so well taken, you feel like you want to go there," one reader of *The Tropical Spa* wrote on an Internet review site. Indeed, some readers do so. A Singaporean girl wrote that she bought the book in Bogor (Java) at the Novotel gift shop while on vacation. During this trip, she visited the Chedi and the Mandara spas, where "foods are as portrayed in the book" (again, food is here merely reduced to a visual matter). Like a modern pilgrim, she further visited the San Gria Spa and Resort in Lembang (Java) and the Dharmawangsa in Jakarta, concluding: "having had spa treatments in both the U.S. and Indonesia, I have to say that Asia can do it best!" Julia, a Malaysian woman from Kuala Lumpur, was similarly convinced:

> Being Asian and proud of my heritage, I grew up watching my late grandmother prepare her own home-made facial products with natural herbs found in the forest. The resorts featured [in *The Tropical Spa*] offer travelers an incomparable and convenient setting for discovering the Asian secret to the ultimate relaxation and indulgence for the senses. A must have for all Spa lovers! (April 28, 2000)[20]

Needless to say, the spas do not always meet the visitors' expectations, Western or Asian, created by the books, magazines, and websites. A German tourist who visited the Chiva-Som, one of Asia's most luxurious resorts in the Gulf of Siam, complained:

> In contradiction to the pictures you see on Chiva-Som's website this hotel is not located on a quiet beach! These pictures must be very old... The hotel is surrounded by high apartment buildings (up to 20 stories), the beach is very dirty (also directly in front of the hotel) and I personally didn't want to swim in the ocean after looking at all the garbage, ... dead jelly fish, and leftovers from the dogs and horses. (August 19, 2005)[21]

The Tropical Spa, like *AsiaSpa* magazine and its equivalents, contains spectacular, visually stunning photographs, and in the tradition of coffee table books, it could be argued that Benge's text merely complements Tettone's photographs, rather than the other way around. The text on the dust jacket of the similar *Spa Style Asia* (Lee and Lim 2003) does not exaggerate when it states that "spa prices and services will appeal to destination-oriented travelers, while the extensive color shots of spa surroundings, both interior and

Figure 10.2   Inside a Javanese spa (photo by B. Barendregt).

exterior, offer plenty of ideas for homeowners who would create smaller versions of paradise." Or, as the brochure of the Balinese Wibawa Spa reads, "Designed as a Healing Sanctuary it is situated *seemingly away from everything*"(my emphasis). Both the tropical spa and its representation through books and magazines are therefore not so much trying to sell an outstanding reality but rather the dream of a different, more beautiful, yet-to-be realized world, outside of ordinary time and place. This image touches upon the representative possibilities inherent in the spa's depiction of both Asian nature and culture and the paradise-like qualities spa culture clearly wishes to invoke.

The Tropical Spa depicts a much-idealized world, or at least a miniature version of it, where it is "the mood of yesteryear [that] inspires the imagination and treatments somehow feel better in a truly authentic setting" (Benge 2003: 67). Spa architecture reminds one of representations of the "traditional" in World Expositions or modern-day heritage displays, and it makes possible "a world of images more real than real" (cf. Hendry 2000: 70). Whereas some tropical spas, such as the Oriental Spa in Bangkok, purposely invoke the somewhat decadent atmosphere of the colonial architecture of pre-independence Asia, the Oriental palaces of former eras seem even more popular as a source of inspiration. Carved and painted double doors in the Majapahit style are incorporated in some Indonesian spas, evoking a princess's chamber and referring to a glorious and mysterious past. So-called chambers of ethnic chic are added, again stressing the tropical or Asian aspect of the place.[22]

In some cases, whole traditional villages have been recreated at a spa resort. An example is the Balinese Jimbaran Spa, where landscape designer Made Wijaya combined English Cotswold architecture with a Balinese village layout. In other Balinese spas, Benge noted, "even that nostalgic image of maidens bathing naked at the water's edge is realized by the local village girls" (2003: 33).[23]

The Tropical Spa further states that the spas "adopt an earthy ambiance in tune with the powerful landscape surrounding them" (Benge 2003: 33). In fact, tropical spas are miniature landscapes or one might say spa-scapes, which play with the nature-culture distinction and often substitute one for the other in fusing indoor and outdoor spaces. Among spa culture's top attractions are, for example, *al fresco* dining—eating organic food outdoors rather than at home—and "offering that all-Asian frisson of showering naked next to nature" (Benge 2003: 43). Other spaces, too, have a supposed otherworldly quality, setting them apart from everyday life. This brings me to the second feature that spa-scapes seemingly share: its invocation of an Asian paradise.

The Nirwana Spa at the Meridien hotel in Bali, for example, is built on a much-contested site, although none of the spa books mention this. It is located next to the famous temple at Tanah Lot, which Benge in *The Tropical Spa* links to "a 16th-century Majapahit priest who suggested to local villagers that this was a sacred spot" (2003: 54). Similarly, *AsiaSpa* magazine's special feature for January 2005 describes Cambodian spas taking visitors "into the mists of time to Angkor Wat whose spiritual ambiance is recreated within the surrounding resorts" (Nicol 2005: 10).

"Creating your own paradise" is a very popular slogan on the dust jackets of spa books—"whether you're a traveler seeking the ultimate spa, or a homeowner seeking ideas for reproducing paradise in your own backyard" (Amazon.com 2005). Paradise in this case seems to be nothing less than Asia itself, or at least a landscaped and much-idealized version of the best Asia has to offer. Thus, the Divana Spa in Lang Suan, Bangkok, Thailand, claims that "On earth there is no heaven, but there are pieces of it," and such pieces are being shaped by ethnic chic, colonial style, and the glory of palaces of former eras. The same advertisement also promises the audience a twenty-first aristocracy, by "unveil[ing] the royal secret of wellness," creating a link between spa culture and a new Asian royal lifestyle that clearly deserves more attention.

Spa Time I: Twenty-first Century Royal Lifestyles

The pages of the January 2005 edition of *AsiaSpa* magazine contain a stylish black-and-white advertisement for the Intercontinental Spa in Hong Kong. A Eurasian woman is shown in profile, obviously enjoying the pleasure of water trickling down her nude body. The accompanying statement that "For once, it's all about me" further intensifies this sensual and intimate atmosphere. Indeed, *spa* seems to be a "mantra for the growing band of worshippers at the altar of self-preservation" as *The Tropical Spa* suggests (Benge

2003: 9). *AsiaSpa* magazine confirms that "your spa experience is all about you—what you enjoy and what suits you." These are not just empty slogans but are representative of the ways in which readers and wannabe visitors are encouraged to take time for self-actualization without having to be ashamed of the common association with hedonism. Not coincidentally, coffee table books always show individuals alone, in an isolated spa, clearly enjoying the supposed silence of what must really be a rather packed resort. Tropical spa culture thereby endorses the cult of individualization. Parkins and Craig describe people's urge to increasingly construct their own biographies in contexts where traditional ways of life and identities are under pressure: "appreciation of the knowledges, customs, tastes and pleasures of previous times are becoming part of the plurality of life options to individuals in constructing their own life narratives" (2006: 7, referring to the work of Beck and Beck-Gernsheim). But constructing one's own life narrative is the perquisite of the happy few, and Parkins and Craig add that nowadays "access to means of self-actualization becomes itself one of the dominant focuses of class division" (2006: 13, quoting Giddens).

Indeed, the newly rich of Southeast Asia are constantly looking for new ways to acquire cultural capital, not only by carefully selecting what to consume and which places to frequent, but also by adopting a particular lifestyle or being generally obsessed with lifestyle itself. Ariel Heryanto (1999) argues that these new Asian affluent classes are trying to restyle themselves as a new aristocracy by partaking in specific cultural events, such as poetry readings. A new Asian lifestyle that is partly based on regular visits to spa resorts might in this sense be a means not only for self-preservation or self-actualization, but also for self-aristocratization. Not very surprisingly the link with aristocratic values is indeed often made in spa culture, portraying the new leisure elite as all too willingly identifying itself with former elites and vice versa. Thus, in *The Tropical Spa,* Benge (2003: 51) describes how both the Mandara Spa at the Ibah hotel in Bali and the Tjampuhan and Pita Maha Private Villa Spa are the property of Balinese royal families. Elsewhere other aristocratic families have also transformed their former palaces into small spa resorts.

Similarly Benge describes how "many of the natural treatments that are now commonly used throughout tropical Asian countries trace their origins to the palaces of Central Java" (2003: 15). Traditional *lulur,* a body polishing process using spices and yogurt, has reportedly been practiced in the palaces of Central Java since the seventeenth century. Martha Tilaar, the mother of natural cosmetics mentioned earlier, is reputed to use it as one of her ancient palace secrets that are now available to the common woman in both the East and the West. Another example is Mooryati Soedibyo of Mustika Ratu, another famous Indonesian brand of natural cosmetics. Mustika Ratu's *jamu* (herbal medicine) and traditional cosmetics are based on recipes that originated in the Surakarta Hadiningrat royal palace, and President Director Soedibyo herself is described on the company's website as a princess-turned-businesswoman:

> B.R.A. Mooryati Soedibyo was born in Surakarta, Central Java on January 5th, 1928. She is a princess that grew up inside the Surakarta Keraton (palace) under the watchful eyes of her grandparents. The aristocratic traditions of the keraton were a part of the princess's daily

life from the very beginning. She was patient in her study of blending of ingredients to make Jamu and other preparations for health and beauty care, as well as giving careful attention to other traditional arts.

From her grandmother, B.R.A. Mooryati learned how certain plants could impart their restorative powers to those who use them in the proper fashion. This was typical of the kind of traditional wisdom that had long been known only to members of the keraton aristocracy. By the age of fifteen, the young princess had mastered the art of herbal making and making up faces. She used this knowledge in preparing the Bedhaya and Serimpi dancers for their performances at the Surakarta Keraton. At the same time, she was also trained in the Javanese art of body care-known as Ngadi Saliro Ngadi Busono as well as time-honored traditions of courtly ethics and manners.[24] B.R.A. Mooryati began a new chapter in her life in 1956. With her marriage that year, she left the charmed life at royal keraton and moved with her husband, Ir. Soedibyo Purbo Hadiningrat MSc., to the city of Medan in North Sumatra.

With this new life, came new opportunities. During her spare time, B.R.A. Mooryati began formulating her own Lulur (body scrub), an exfoliating masker designed to lighten the complexion. She also began to make Jamu according to traditional recipes. These she gave to the wives of her husband's colleagues. In 1978, Mustika Ratu's products began to be distributed to local stores through salons chosen to be the company's agents. The public became far more aware of the value of traditional health care and beauty products through magazine and advertising campaigns.[25]

Today, Mustika Ratu is an international bestseller, with its own spa resorts and a separate spa cosmetics line, "enchanting the world with royal beauty." Maybe, *AsiaSpa* magazine wonders, "it's time to consider your spa experience as a ritual rather than a luxury" (Yon 2005: 14), a ritual that provides the New Asian well-to-do with the aristocratic values and cultural practices so eagerly desired. Furthermore, spa culture in many ways seems to contribute to a new Asian lifestyle that is trying to come to terms with the fast pace of modernity without necessarily looking to the West.

Spa Time II: Alternative Temporalities

The Tropical Spa advertises the Jimbaran Spa in Bali as a resort "maintaining its indigenous sense of the exotic; gamelan music, eastern aromas and a soul soothing atmosphere where time has no role to play" (Benge 2003: 43). Yet there seems to be an overall obsession with temporality in spa culture, as the process of taking time, the experience of time, and past time are stressed. Using the splendor of ancient palace secrets, nostalgic nudes, and a premodern Asia where life seemed simpler and more pure, spa owners seem to consciously evoke the past. Following MacCannell, one could argue that "the final victory of modernity over other sociocultural arrangements is not the disappearance of the nonmodern world, but its artificial preservation and reconstruction in modern society" (1989: 8). In a similar vein, Benge (2003: 135) seems to overidealize a near but almost forgotten past in which nature is a place where times gone by can be retrieved. The book could be hinting at a way to cope with the uncertain future that many newly developing

Asian countries face nowadays, but part of it might also point at a more general fear of modernity itself, particularly the directions it should take locally.

Eriksen (2001) has pointed out the acceleration, typical of the Western information society, which threatens to eliminate distance, space, and time. While not a reality for most Southeast Asians, the new rich in Asia's metropolitan areas surely will recognize much of what Eriksen describes. Similar to their Western counterparts, they are unhealthily rushed and becoming victims of what Eriksen characterizes as the "tyranny of the moment." In the Western European context, Eriksen asks for a reappreciation of slow time, a temporal regime that differs radically from the fragmented, rushed regime that regulates so much of our lives. According to Eriksen, we need to take charge of our own rhythmic changes to get the best from both worlds—to balance between "the hyperactive, overfilled, accelerated temporality of the moment, and…a serene, cumulative, 'organic' temporality" (2001: 164). In its most extreme forms, spa culture, associated with eco-chic practices and the New Asian lifestyle that springs from it reminds us of a similar critique of an ever-accelerating global culture (see Figure 10.2). An attribution of positive value to certain kinds and uses of time seems to occur in spa culture, as it does in eco-chic generally: it is chic to be modern and to be modern is to be fast. At the same time, it is very eco to question this speed and to think of more conscious and sustainable modes of using time.

In spa culture, ideally an effort is made, even while only temporarily, to get "back in touch with nature and so with [your] spiritual souls, which have little role in day to day urban existence" (Benge 2003: 15). Most tropical spas employ a strict etiquette to ensure that their guests enjoy the promised peaceful sanctuary. This includes discouraging the avatars of global fast-life like mobile phones, pagers, and other electronic devices. In describing the atmosphere at the Bali Hyatt's spa, Benge writes, "like so many Javanese words, *leha leha* says it all succinctly.[26] It says peace, relaxation, daydreaming, an empty mind and lying prostrate gazing at the sky" (2003: 47). Spa time in this perspective thus hints at timelessness, and the therapies are described as having been used for centuries by Javanese princesses as an elixir of youth, "unchanged since Thailand's Ayutthaya period," or as one advertisement offering Kerala's 500-year-old *ayurveda* system says, "your trip to eternal youth."[27] "Taking time" is yet another often used expression that illustrates spa culture's advocating of a slower, if not different, temporality.[28] Time is taken, for example, in such sanctuaries of spiritual silence as the tranquil room, the quiet room, or the absolute void of the flotation tank, where half an hour's relaxation is equivalent to eight hours of sleep. These are the places where, as Benge puts it, "the sound is waves, the view is seashore, the smell is spicy and the mood is thick with calm" (2003: 27).

Spa time very much means retreating into the self, and by getting attuned with the surrounding spa-scapes, the inner landscape should be explored. Spa time is offered here as an alternative temporality, an articulation of the present and one's presence therein (cf. Parkins and Craig 2006). The visit to the spa thus promises an instant experience of spirituality that is so difficult to come by in modern life. It is an inner beauty, but achieved at the speed of an extreme makeover from the inside out.

Comparable to lifestyles based on New Age or slow living, spa time does not so much offer a complete break with modernity, nor a continuous parallel temporality, isolated from the rest of global culture, but rather is its obverse in that by slowing down just temporarily—as long as a visit or a holiday to a resort may take—one can recharge in order to cope with the speediness of everyday life. Or as *AsiaSpa* magazine puts it, "Being able to get away from the outside world, retreat inside and relish some well-deserved time out is vital for our physical, mental and spiritual health" (Nicol 2005: 10). Significantly many spa brochures, books, and magazines promise an explicitly modern experience, advertising urban spas where you can "maintain your equilibrium in the city" (*AsiaSpa* 2005: 28). *The Tropical Spa* shows people enjoying a hot stone massage while overlooking Shanghai's skyline, and the Thai therapists of the Oriental Spa are said to live as "Buddhists in the urban tumult of Bangkok," seeking to "understand the nature of tranquility" (Benge 2003: 61).

Spa culture, from resorts to books, websites, and other forms of advertising, excels in a reflexive negotiation in using the pleasures of previous times in the present, at times also projecting utopian possibilities, "in the sense of a longing for a different, and better way of living, a reconciliation of thought and life, desire and the real, in a manner that critiques the status quo without projecting a full-blown image of what future society should look like" (Parkins and Craig 2006: 8). Spa culture might serve here as a key to a new age, with Asianism as its preferred lifestyle.

Conclusion: The Spa as Source of a Future Asia

Resort companies increasingly seem to realize the potential of Asianness, praising the attention that natural health and beauty have traditionally received in local societies.[29] Besides the revaluing of local traditions, this also leads to newly created identities. One of these is cosmopolitan in character. The book *Spa Style Asia* uses the term *cosmopolitan* to refer to "a kaleidoscope of international cures" (Lee and Lim 2003: 79) consisting of such therapies and treatments as *lomi lomi,* Swedish massage, and the like. These are by no means associated with their original localities nor are they seen as exclusively Western. Rather, they are global and thereby rendered less threatening to Asian culture. The latest and most hip therapies are, moreover, advertised as being New Asian or again to quote the *Spa Style Asia* guide, "Asia's paradigms revamped" (Lee and Lim 2003: 71). Whereas "cosmopolitan focuses on international treatments which are offered by Asian spas (e.g. Western therapies domesticated)...New Asianism is devoted to traditional Asian treatments updated with a modern twist" (Lee and Lim 2003: 71), or as *The Tropical Spa* puts it, the spa is a concept "as old as the hill it springs from, rewritten for the contemporary scene" (Benge 2003:9). Many of the therapies variously known as Asian Approach, Oriental philosophy, or, more aptly here, New Asian, are therefore based on traditional oriental healing systems that have been practiced throughout history. *Watsu,* or water *shiatsu,* for example, is a Japanese form of massage reinvented in America but further developed as an aquatic body therapy for tropical waters by the Breathing Space

Company of Singapore. The Java wrap, as described by *The Tropical Spa,* is yet another example of "a global beauty phenomenon waiting to happen: an age-old process for a new age answer to slimming" (Benge 2003: 94).

Rather than focusing solely on local traditions, globalization has thus triggered a newly emergent regionalism in which the idea of Asia is used as a counter to the take on modernity and globalized fast life that the West is known for. As I have sketched here, eco-chic and, most notably, the latest trend of tropical spa culture are contributing to the New Asianism lifestyle industry. In the process, spa culture seems to have gained different meanings to different groups of visitors. Western but also East Asian visitors praise spa resorts for their paradise-like qualities and their consumer-friendly approach in representing the tropics of Asia, complete with its beauty, health, and to a lesser extent spiritual practices. However, spa culture is at the same time contributing locally to a new pan-Asian lifestyle that is eagerly consumed by the Southeast Asian new rich who are looking for the shared values they were hitherto lacking. New Asianism is, therefore, typically a process that occurs at the interface where cultures meet, and the tropical spa is its successful shop window. To quote Leo Ching, "Asianism no longer represents the kind of transcendental otherness required to produce a practical identity and tension between the East and the West. Today, 'Asia' itself is neither a misrepresentation of the Orientalist nor the collective representation of the anti-imperialists. 'Asia' has become a market, and 'Asianness' has become a commodity circulating globally through late capitalism" (2000: 257).

But why is the spa the popular choice in celebrating this new Asianism? Why health and beauty, practices that so often are associated with the Western evils of individualism and the cult of hedonism?

One explanation of the spa's popularity as a source for Asian identity construction might be the assumption that the spa is merely a popular-culture leisure activity and therefore a soft cultural form that is relatively innocent. At the same time, culturally it seems far more effective than the often-politicized Asian values debate[30] of the mid-1990s or today's economic approach of the ASEAN and similar organizations. In the aftermath of such top-down approaches, as Chua (2003) suggests, a genuine reinvention of Asian cultural identity is now being undertaken, not only by governments but also by intellectuals, artists, and commercial enterprises. New Asianism has led to new approaches in filmmaking, fashion, and media regionalism.[31] In this process, an Othering of the West takes place by stressing the uniqueness of being Asian, a feature that is also clearly present in the mediations of tropical spa culture. As such, Benge's *The Tropical Spa* characterizes Asian people as more intuitive, stating that "low touch Western society keeps tactile expression behind closed doors, while Indonesians touch all the time...they carry compassion in their hands" (2003: 99). Elsewhere the book notes: "In Indonesia, the birthplace of many tropical health and beauty secrets, there is an ancient Javanese expression; *rupasampat whaya bhiantara.* It roughly translates as 'the balance between inner and outer beauty, between that which is visible and that which is within' and it is the parable by which women in this part of the world live without even thinking of it" (2003: 11). This brings me to a second possible explanation.

Significantly, it is mostly women who are participating in spa culture and, therefore, mostly depicted in the mediations of spas. In their *Re-Orienting Fashion,* Niessen,

Leshkowich, and Jones (2003) allude to the construction of the feminine in Asia as the bearer and wearer of national tradition. In the spa publications, however, it is not so much a national as a pan-Asian identity that is stressed by the women portrayed. The photographs in *The Tropical Spa* and other coffee table books and in magazines like *AsiaSpa* mainly show women, both as visitors and as therapists. These women are rarely recognizably Western. Most often, they are Asian women of indeterminate nationality. According to Steve Kemper's (2001) study on advertising in Sri Lanka and Malaysia, these women may be called pan-Asian models. Kemper notes that during the heyday of the New Economic Policy, in the 1980s and early 1990s, advertising in multicultural Malaysia was not to privilege any single ethnic group (Malay, Chinese, or Indian), lifestyle, or profession. Advertising agencies, therefore, promoted an all-Malaysian identity by recruiting pan-Asian models whose origins were often complicated but who were mostly of Eurasian descent.[32] Away from a Malaysian context, in other Southeast Asian societies Eurasian or mestizo women continue to set the beauty standard (Rafael 1995), leaving those dark of skin to take recourse in whitening cream or other measures. Ideally, women are a bit of the East meeting a bit of the West; the pan-Asian models depicted in the coffee table books, therefore, seem to again highlight the complexities and contradictions present in new Asianism.

Lastly, the popularity of spa culture as the carrier of New Asianism might be explained with reference to the long tradition of adopting ideas on beauty, health, and spirituality in the Asian countries under study, but also the neighboring East Asian societies. Many of these ideas have been exchanged for centuries and could to a certain extent be regarded as cosmopolitanism *avant la lettre,* but also as an early form of a pan-Asian culture. They are an easily recognized hybrid that, again due to its outward innocence, can serve perfectly as the foundation of an imagined regional community.

The question remains to what extent New Asianism as a lifestyle and its associated practices of eco-chic and tropical spa culture will remain a minority cosmopolitanism, a new form of exclusion that helps the consuming classes to define what is hip and modern. Will it eventually trickle down to the now-excluded masses? If it does, it might well be incorporated as some sort of new ecology that, in addition to stressing pride in local produce and local identity, might also stress the much-needed sustainability and environmental consciousness that still seems to be lacking in many parts of Southeast Asia.

For now, the wellness industry, eco-chic, and the tropical spa cultures seem to be involved in constructing a possible new postnational imagery in which lifestyle and the leisure industry increasingly play a role. Here the new Asia is presented as collectively facing the West, a collectivity in which race, religion, and nation become mere nuances in an overall taste that is Asia. The New Asia is in many aspects still an idealized Asian landscape, a dreamt-of identity in a time when all identities seem increasingly to be under pressure. Above all, New Asianism is a way to reflect on a possible near future, a future that *The Tropical Spa* posits as a break with "a time, not so long ago, when the notion of beauty was literally skin deep...[but now] not anymore. Recent decades of materialism have given way to a caring millennium and new approach to beauty that stems from within" (Benge 2003: 111).

Afterword: From Eco-Chic to Eco-Smart

Sharon Zukin

The deeply grounded studies in this book pose a fascinating question: under what conditions could eco-chic consumption become the new normal?

Eco-smart consumption already resonates with many hopes and plans, from keeping the planet Earth alive to promoting a less toxic humanity, and from developing more authentic selves to ending economic inequality. But several issues may prevent these hopes from becoming a reality.

Most important, the corporate engine of economic growth is fueled by selling more products to more consumers in more places at more times. A big business that claims to promote ecological rules of production is a corporate oxymoron, for regardless of its pious pronouncements, its everyday operations, from sourcing raw materials to disposing waste, tend to deplete and pollute natural resources.

We have little chance to escape this iron cage. In the more developed countries where people use consumption choices to express their individuality, marketing gurus have already split the commodity atom into an infinite variety of niches and brands. If we don't like fat, they sell us lean. If we don't want to wear leather shoes, they make them from fabric. They call their factory-processed food products *natural,* and when we no longer believe that label, they change it to a vaguer claim like *fresh* or *quality.*

Moreover, shifting consumption preferences in the Global North make it possible to expand consumption in the Global South. Growing demand for eco-tourist sites in Costa Rica and Vietnam, organically grown, fair-trade, shade-grown coffee beans from Guatemala, and relaxing spas on Bali enlarge the scale of these activities, which in turn spurs transnational corporate takeovers of individual, domestic producers. Corporate control raises the financial stakes, which likely puts more pressure on land and water. If economic benefits flow down to the work force at all, they transform men and women who had eked out a modest subsistence into ambitious consumers who want better, and easier, lives.

Transnational corporations (TNCs) have leaped at the opportunity. With shifting consumption preferences and saturated markets in the Global North, TNCs direct their efforts to emerging markets in the Global South. KFC and Pizza Hut are building franchises throughout China and Cambodia, and obesity rates there are climbing (Gomez 2013). Global beverage producers SABMiller and Diageo are moving into Africa, selling small, cheap bottles of beer to low-wage workers and forcing individual home brewers out of business (Sonne, Maylie, and Hinshaw 2013). The Cheesecake Factory is opening branches in Mexico and Kuwait in partnership with local corporations (Kowitt 2013a, b). Do consumers in Latin America and the Persian Gulf states need more fast food in their shopping malls?

Consumers always say they want a choice. And desires, though socialized by norms and values, are hard to direct into ethical channels. A few years ago, animal-rights activists persuaded fashion designers to stop using fur. But today, rabbit-fur hats and raccoon collars are back on the runways, in the fashion magazines, and on retail websites and in the stores. "If it's cute, I want it," a teenager once told me about the way she shops. Empowering consumers has cultivated a sense of entitlement rather than a sense of responsibility.

For those who choose to live simply, their ethical beliefs have been commercialized, corporatized, and turned into an oxymoron, too. The slogan of the magazine *Real Simple* and its website is "Life Made Easier." Sometimes these media platforms preach the message that consumers should reflect on, reorganize, and relinquish some of the stuff they own. But they never say, "Don't buy." Instead, they promote the same programmatic steps to happiness as other lifestyle guides, soothing consumers' anxieties by submerging them in contradictions. *Real Simple* promises to show us "five ways to be patient," along with "15 quick fixes to make around your house, 15-minute projects that won't put a dent in your weekend." The media seem to know us better than we know ourselves. We want happiness, we will buy it if it is for sale, and we want it now.

If we believe what the lifestyle media tell us, *living simply* means buying *the right kind* of goods, which will raise our *self-worth*. With this in mind, *Real Simple* presents "9 food items you can feel good about buying" because a portion of the revenues will be donated to charity (http://www.realsimple.com, April 18, 2013). The partnership between buying well and doing good has become a quick-fix Protestant Ethic for the new era of consumer capitalism. But it erases the moral dimension of choice and hides economic inequality. It suggests that consumers help the poor when we buy more./

With no sense of irony, *Real Simple* promotes a list of products whose very names are a parody of eco-chic pretentions. We see Häagen-Dazs black cherry amaretto gelato, Jcoco Edamame Sea Salt Chocolate Bars, and Davidson's Tulsi Chai Tea, "a blend of Rooibos leaves and three varieties of holy basil,...caffeine-free...full-bodied and rich with minerals and antioxidants." There is a degree of self-righteousness, a conspicuous consumption of nature, and a sense of indulgence that recalls Thorstein Veblen's caustic critique of the leisure class.

The power of corporations to control our thoughts by media content and seductive advertisements is hardly new. But the co-optation of our better selves in the connected capitalism advocated by the former CEO of Coca-Cola is less transparent and even more effective than magazines and ads. Our living space is colonized by demonstrations of corporate social responsibility. On Earth Day 2013, for example, fashion boutiques in New York City featured installations and window displays to glamorize nature. Ralph Lauren's windows in the West Village showed "a composting station complete with bins and gardening tools to educate shoppers on fun ways to turn ordinary waste into rich, organic compost naturally" (Wilson 2013). And when corporations persuade us they are good, we internalize their brands. Coke, Whole Foods, Ralph Lauren: these are not just trusted products that we choose; they are *US*.

How can we escape the iron cage of brandization? Consumer goods corporations, backed by governments, control the global circulation of products, images, and values. When Bart Barendregt and Rivke Jaffe, the editors of this book, ask us to take a postcynical stand on consumption, they are pointing to the limits of consumers' moral indignation and, also, perhaps, to the limits of our social action. Effective action requires community support and a political infrastructure: more grassroots movements, less corporate sponsorship; more local networks, less Facebook.

To recruit believers, these new movements must combine ethics and aesthetics. This, after all, is the promise of eco-chic consumption: we can give up more while getting better. Though the appeal of less but better reflects a self-interested concern with happiness, it also represents a collective anxiety about constant change, about endless promises of abundance, and about visions of progress promoted by government and interpreted by corporations. Yearning for authenticity is one way of expressing the anxiety. But authenticity often becomes a weapon of those consumers who already have the financial resources to choose, whether they are foodies, gentrifiers, or hybrid-electric car owners. The next step is to connect individual choices to a production system that responds to, rather than manipulates, collective needs. A more authentic self is fundamentally a more social self.

Becoming more socially conscious consumers is an urgent goal. This requires us to develop new ways of seeing the world—and of seeing ourselves in relation to that world. Eco-chic says that making the right consumption choices is a matter of style. But eco-smart says that making the right choices is a matter of survival.

Notes

Chapter 1: The Paradoxes of Eco-Chic

1. An opposite but related trend is the Barefoot Bloggers Initiative, with its own practical guide that advises users on how to grow a sustainable, green blog and that features articles from some of the world's most influential green bloggers.

2. The Asian Tigers are commonly understood to include South Korea, Singapore, Taiwan, and Hong Kong, although reference is sometimes made to the Asian Cubs of Malaysia, Vietnam, and Thailand.

3. For Green Daoism, see Duara (2011). The UK-based "muslim lifestyle magazine" *Emel* published a theme issue on Green Islam in June 2009 using the somewhat provocative title "eco jihad," using the term to refer to Muslim environmental activists and invoking the Islamic imperative that posits humans as *khalifas* (stewards) of the earth. See also Abdul-Matin (2010).

4. CSR is usually shorthand for extra attention to corporations' responsibility to contribute to sustainable development, the welfare of the local population, and ecosystems of the landscapes in which they operate. CSR campaigns have long been favored by major Western companies such as Shell, Nike, and, in Robert Foster's contribution to this volume, Coca-Cola; they are currently becoming increasingly popular among corporate players in the South as well. Whereas some see CSR as a means to reinvent the very meaning of development itself (Blowfield 2005), others fear the (unintended) consequences of large companies becoming the engine for development.

5. For a genealogy of the concept and its latest resurrection as a global value chain, see Bair (2009).

6. Mowforth and Munt give the example of the WTTC, a global coalition of chief executives from all sectors of the travel and tourism industry, which encourages governments, in cooperation with the private sector, to harness the industry's growth while at the same time pursuing sustainable development through industry environmental initiatives such as the Green Globe scheme. They point out that, given the WTTC's location in the global North and the predominance of first-world members, such initiatives are doomed to help reproduce global inequalities.

7. In recent years, eco-fashion has increasingly been picked up by Asian designers, for example in Malaysia and Indonesia, where interestingly enough organic and natural clothing is often dubbed "ethnic," signaling a return to tradition rather than only nature.

Chapter 2: Adversaries into Partners? Brand Coca-Cola and the Politics of Consumer-Citizenship

1. "Culture jamming" refers to the disruption and subversion of commercial media, often by using a medium itself (especially advertising) in ironic or satirical ways.
2. By contrast, Micheletti seems to have become more optimistic; see the 2010 revised paperback edition of her book.
3. See "Creating Value Through Sustainable Fashion," Coca-Cola Journey, posted January 1, 2012, <http://www.thecoca-colacompany.com/citizenship/products_case_studies.html> accessed August 25, 2012.
4. See Ecoist/TCCC Press Release, posted June 5, 2007, <http://www.ecoist.com/coke/press_release.html>.
5. See "Recycled Candy-Wrapper Handbags," Ecoist, <http://www.ecoist.com/NewCollection.asp?collectionname=Coca-Cola&collectionvalue=3> accessed August 25, 2012.
6. The United Nations Global Compact, announced in 1999 and launched in 2000, is an initiative that encourages businesses to adopt sustainable and socially responsible policies in the areas of human rights, labor relations, and environmental practices.
7. Capt. Charles C. Boycott (1832–1897) was subjected to social ostracism organized by the Irish Land League in 1880 when the landlord for whom he was an agent refused the demands of tenant farmers for a further reduction in rents.
8. In his prescient book *One Market Under God,* Thomas Frank (2001: 114ff.) notes that the prophets of market populism in the 1990s exhorted their followers to buy shares in companies with familiar brand names (see also Willmott 2010: n21, 536).
9. See Coumans (2011) for a related discussion of corporate–NGO partnerships in the mining industry.
10. See <http://killercoke.org>.
11. See <http://killercoke.org/literature_posters.php>.
12. See "Economic Opportunity," Coca-Cola Journey, posted January 1, 2012, <http://www.coca-colacompany.com/stories/economic-opportunity> accessed August 1, 2013.
13. See "Renewing our Partnership. Expanding Our Impact," Coca-Cola Journey, posted January 1, 2012, <http://www.coca-colacompany.com/stories/converging-on-water-an-innovative-conservation-partnership> accessed August 1, 2013.
14. See the video clip at <http://killercoke.org/discrimination.php>.
15. See Marion Nestle, "The Latest Oxymoron: Oxfam Helps Coca-Cola Reduce Poverty," Food Politics, posted April 20, 2011, <http://www.foodpolitics.com/2011/04/the-latest-oxymoron-oxfam-helps-coca-cola-reduce-poverty/> accessed August 1, 2013.
16. See Michelle Simon, "Comment on 'More on Oxfam's Anti-Poverty Partnership with Coca-Cola' by Marion Nestle," Food Politics, posted April 21, 2011,

<http://www.foodpolitics.com/2011/04/more-on-oxfams-anti-poverty-partnership-with-coca-cola/> accessed August 1, 2013.

17. Ibid.

18. It is worth mentioning that mobile phone apps for ethical shopping are currently available. These apps offer ratings of brands and companies on their performance in respecting the environment, human rights, and animal welfare (see Dellinger 2012; Smithers 2011).

Chapter 3: Peopling the Practices of Sustainable Consumption: Eco-Chic and the Limits to the Spaces of Intention

1. For example, in relation to the movement of labor, see Sparke (2006) and Shuttleworth (2007); for more theoretically inclined work on borders and boundary-crossing/boundary-work see, for example, Mol and Law (2005), Eden et al. (2006), and Goodman and Sage (2013).

2. For more on this, see Goodman et al. (2012).

3. See <http://www.coopamerica.org/cabn/about/sealofapproval.cfm>.

4. See <http://www.rain-tree.com/rtmprod.htm>.

5. The ejido is the community land unit that provides usufruct rights (not title) to farmers. It was an outcome of the 1910 Revolution, but the ejido has been undermined, especially since 1992, as land and natural resources are effectively privatized.

6. Such consumption is not to be confused with practices linked to a radical social movement led by the Consumer Association of Penang and Sahabat Alam Malaysia. This movement has long addressed sustainable consumption but links it to a wider anticapitalist campaign (see <www.en.cap.org.my>).

7. See <http://dorischua.blogspot.com/2007/05>.

Chapter 4: Global Gold Connections

1. *Quote* is a business magazine best known for its *Quote 500,* which portrays the top segment of wealthy Dutch. After resigning as *Quote*'s editor-in-chief, Kelder continued his career as a television celebrity hosting various shows. All of these television programs have centered on the superrich and their ambitions to become even richer, their consumption practices, leisure activities, and so on. Kelder also appears in advertisements for banking, figuring as the guy who checks whether rich people are wearing the right suits. He has developed his own distinctive clothing style by always wearing suspenders.

2. Brandjacking is a social movement campaign strategy that draws attention to alleged abusive behavior of TNCs. A company's advertisements or logos are mimicked in the public domain to point to the negative sides of the company's activities. Starbucks's advertisements for frappuccinos, for instance, have been adapted to

highlight the stark contrast between the wealth of the product's chic consumers and the poverty of many people in the global South.

3. The initiative of setting up Wereldwinkels (World shops) in the Netherlands dates back to the late 1960s and represented an attempt to provide low-income cooperatives with better access to international markets. The earliest Wereldwinkels were aimed at fighting capitalism and its inequalities, for instance in trade and marketing. Selling products was only part of a much wider scope of political campaigns, against Apartheid in South Africa or colonialism in Angola. Later on, the Wereldwinkels abandoned political campaigns, as the marketing of third-world products became their core business. They forged institutional links with the fair-trade organization Max Havelaar. Currently, the Wereldwinkels sell upmarket certified products aimed at a much wider group of consumers and conduct market research to bring their products in line with consumer wishes, reflecting recent attempts to improve the market and capitalism from within. See Wereldwinkel (n.d.).

4. FLO (Fairtrade International) develops and reviews fair-trade standards and organizes support for producers to achieve these standards. The standards also apply to the companies who market fair-trade products, such as importers, exporters, and licensees. See <http://www.fairtrade.net>.

5. Many of such consumers were active in initiatives such the Wereldwinkel.

6. While small-scale gold mining produces a smaller proportion of gold annually, it provides livelihoods for many more people around the world than large-scale mining does. Estimates are that 25 million people work in the sector, often in bad conditions.

7. See <http://www.communitymining.org/>.

8. ARM is not part of the CRJ, but the two organizations did sign a Memorandum of Understanding in November 2011. See <http://www.fairjewelry.org/alliance-for-responsible-mining-arm-and-responsible-jewelry-council-rjc-sign-an-mou-whats-next> accessed March 21, 2013.

9. A campaign of Earthworks, a U.S.-based NGO "dedicated to protecting communities and the environment from the impacts of irresponsible mineral and energy development while seeking sustainable solutions." See <http://www.nodirtygold.org> accessed March 21, 2013.

10. "Als je je geliefde een gouden ring om de vinger schuift, denk je liever niet aan cyanide en kwik."

11. All quotes in this section are taken from <http://www.ecochicmagazine.co.uk/eco-fashion-expo/ethical-style-guide/the-essence-of-fair-trade-jewellery-ebook>.

12. See <http://www.ecochicmagazine.co.uk/eco-fashion-expo/fairtrade-matters/ecochics-ethical-jewellery-range-for-brides-to-be>.

13. CRED is a fair-trade, fair-mined jeweler. See <http://www.credjewellery.com/>.

14. See <http://www.ecochicmagazine.co.uk/ecochiccollection/ecochic-designers/ecochic-product-of-the-week-cred-jewellery>.

15. From <http://www.solidaridad.nl/nieuws/2010/11/02/bibi-der-velden-steunt-op-weg-goed-goud-campagne-met-speciale-armband> and personal communication with Solidaridad.

16. See <http://www.greengold-oroverde.org/loved_gold>.
17. See <http://www.solidaridad.nl/pers/2011/04/26/bibi-der-velden-vindt-goed-goud-colombia>. Authors' translation.
18. See <http://www.fifibijoux.com>.
19. See <http://www.youtube.com/watch?v = h-nJwl8RWXw>.
20. Compare this to 35 kilograms from a certified hard-rock mine in Peru (personal communication, Maaike Schouten, Solidaridad, May 25, 2012).

Chapter 5: Marketing the Mountain

1. Interview by Meredith Welch-Devine, 2007.
2. Interview by Seth Murray, 2004.
3. "Site of Community importance means a site which, in the biogeographical region or regions to which it belongs, contributes significantly to the maintenance or restoration at a favourable conservation status of a natural habitat type in Annex I or of a species in Annex II and may also contribute significantly to the coherence of Natura 2000 referred to in Article 3, and/or contributes significantly to the maintenance of biological diversity within the biogeographic region or regions concerned. For animal species ranging over wide areas, sites of Community importance shall correspond to the places within the natural range of such species which present the physical or biological factors essential to their life and reproduction" (Council of the European Communities 1992: 5).
4. The two major policy instruments of the European Union are directives and regulations. Directives give broad descriptions of the policy outcomes that must be achieved but do not specify the exact actions a member state must take to achieve them. They are meant to provide flexibility and to respect the differences in cultures and regulatory and market structures among the member states. Directives must be transposed into national law before they can take effect, and member states are responsible for their implementation.
5. Interview by Welch-Devine, 2007.
6. Ibid.
7. Ibid.

Chapter 6: Green Is the New Green: Eco-Aesthetics in Singapore

1. Lee Kuan Yew was Singapore's first Singapore Prime Minister. He ruled from self-government in 1959, through independence from Britain in 1965 until his retirement in 1990.
2. The Garden City Movement emerged from the urban planning philosophy of English planner Sir Ebenezer Howard (1850–1928) in nineteenth-century Britain to alleviate the problems caused by large-scale population movements from rural to urban areas. His vision was for well-planned communities to be surrounded by greenbelts. These extensive parklands would encompass the community and combine country with city living, while still encouraging commerce and trade.

Chapter 7: The Caring, Committed Eco-Mom: Consumption Ideals and Lived Realities of Toronto Mothers

1. Our analysis draws from twelve focus groups that each included four to six participants. Although groups involved both women and men, in this chapter we direct our attention to the narratives of the thirty mothers who participated in these groups. These women had children of various ages and were either single or partnered with men, although not all identified as heterosexual. Of the thirty mothers, ten identified as women of color, while the remaining twenty were white. Our analysis here deliberately brackets the issue of race, which is an important element to understand the stratified (and whitestream) characteristics of ethical eating (e.g., Slocum 2007), but not fundamental to the argument we are making in this particular chapter. Nineteen of the mothers were middle class, and eleven were working class or poor. We determined participants' class status on the basis of household income, education, and occupational prestige (Gilbert 2008).

2. While Hays does not claim that intensive mothering is limited to a North American context, the empirical evidence used to support her argument is exclusively American. Moreover, both popular journalistic writing (Druckerman's [2012] *Bringing Up Bébé: One American Mother Discovers the Wisdom of French Parenting,* among others) and empirical research (Kahneman et al. 2010) indicate that the time and intensity that mothers invest in their children is a North American cultural phenomenon.

3. The larger environmental implications of eco-consumption ideologies are up for debate, especially around the ability to address systemic environmental problems (see Szasz 2009).

Chapter 8: Afro-chic: Beauty, Ethics, and "Locks without Dread" in Ghana

1. See <http://www.afrochiconline.com> accessed January 12, 2013.

2. Shea butter is an extract from the nut of the indigenous African shea tree. See <http://www.ghanaweb.com/GhanaHomePage/health/artikel.php?ID=174597> accessed April 10, 2013.

3. The chapter is based on field research by the two authors. Anna-Riikka Kauppinen conducted fieldwork in both high-end and low-end beauty salons in Accra in spring 2010, with a follow-up in spring 2011. The research entailed extensive participant observation and informal conversations with clients in a number of salons, including natural hair salons, as well as recorded interviews with beauty professionals. Rachel Spronk conducted fieldwork for the study on the development of middle classes from an intergenerational perspective from May 2011 to May 2012.

4. *Kente* is a silk and cotton fabric made of brightly patterned interwoven strips and geometric shapes that has become iconic of African cultural heritage in Ghana and beyond.

5. All names are pseudonyms.

6. W.E.B. du Bois (1868–1963) was an American sociologist, historian, civil rights activist, pan-Africanist, and author. Racism (in the United States) was the main target of his writings and projects. He championed people of color everywhere,

particularly Africans and Asians in their struggles against colonialism and imperialism.

7. Framing the physical body as a site of black emancipation has a long and central history in Africa as well as in the Americas. It goes beyond the scope of this article to engage in more depth with the rich body of literature and popular culture on the politics of black beauty and pan-Africanism, recently addressed by Chris Rock's documentary on African American beauty salons, *Good Hair* (2009). Although Caribbean and African-American popular cultural exports as well as Rastafarianism have a presence in Ghana, this presence, in our experience, represents only a small urban minority. We, therefore, chose not to embark on a thorough analysis of Rastafarianism in Ghana, but remain attentive to its influence when we came across it in our fieldwork.

8. Anthropologists have been particularly attentive to these negotiations, namely how foreign commercial imports are popularly harnessed for negotiations on the nature of modernity (on Africa, see Burke 1996; Newell 2012).

9. General Rawlings ousted the democratic chosen leaders with a military coup in 1979. In January 1992, the military government gave way to presidential and parliamentary elections, and in late 1992, he was elected president. In 1996, he won the elections again.

10. Twi is a national lingua franca that is widely understood by people from various ethnic backgrounds, although it is principally spoken by the demographically dominant Ashanti.

11. There are several small and medium-scale companies that specialize in natural beauty products in Ghana at the moment, in both hair care and skin care: Salifu's, Jeba Natural Products, All Pure Nature, The Body Butter Company, MGL Naturals, Nasaakle Ltd, AgroHerb Inc., and Madame Yasmeen. It is noteworthy that the biggest Ghanaian manufacturer of beauty products, Forever Clair, which operates as a family business led by Grace Amey-Obeng, has also been marketing their products' natural base of locally sourced ingredients over many years. Forever Clair's effect on the Ghanaian beauty industry would merit another entire paper, because its influence extends a long way; the company also operates Forever Clair Beauty College, which attracts students from other West African countries. Forever Clair owns a factory where products are made and exported to other African countries, the United States, and Europe, and it runs a popular beauty clinic. The owners regularly appear in the media, educating the public on hair and skin care. However, for most Ghanaians we spoke to, Forever Clair's choice of natural products was not known; for them Forever Clair is simply a chic and well-established brand. Socially mobile women start using Forever Clair products when they are financially able to do so.

12. A locktician is someone who specializes in dreadlock care, maintenance, and style.

13. In black hair glossary, perm commonly refers to chemically straightened hair, while jerri curls refer to a milder treatment where the natural curly hair is softened and made more wavy.

14. However, it is noteworthy that hairstyles in West Africa have traditionally been expressive artworks adorned with different decorations (Sieber and Herreman 2000: 133–35).

15. A collection of symbols that communicate proverbs and wisdom and are frequently sewn onto cotton clothes and printed on fabrics.

16. Although most of his employees were male during our study, Mikesh also gave regular classes on dreadlocks that were attended by young female beauticians. By 2012, he had at least one woman as a full-time apprentice.

17. In the Rastafarian socioreligious movement, naturalness is close to a theological ideal, which Jaffe (this volume) describes as the "commitment to use things in their natural or organic states." In Ghana, a very small minority calls itself Rastafari, made up from artists, intellectuals, and a significant group of African Americans who have migrated to Ghana. There is also a small group of (street) youth who live from the tourist industry and are mainly responsible for giving Rastafari a bad name as being dirty, irresponsible, and smoking marijuana, which is considered a sin.

Chapter 9: Ital Chic: Rastafari, Resistance, and the Politics of Consumption in Jamaica

This chapter is a slightly revised version of the journal article, which first appeared in 2010 as "Ital Chic: Rastafari, Resistance, and the Politics of Consumption in Jamaica" in *Small Axe: A Caribbean Journal of Criticism,* 14/1: 30–45. The piece is republished by permission of the publisher, Duke University Press. I am grateful to Petrina Dacres, Anouk de Koning, Wayne Modest, and Maarten Onneweer for their critical comments on earlier versions of this article.

1. See also Robotham (2000), Bogues (2002), and Gray (2003).

2. Interestingly, some of my sources maintained that Sisterlocks is especially popular among both gay men and lesbians.

3. Sisterlocks can be taken to symbolize the domestication of the "terrible beauty," "fearful otherness," and "transformative potential" that Frank (2007: 52–53, 56, 58) locates in dreadlocks.

4. Interview, February 27, 2009.

5. See <http://www.italblends.com> accessed November 1, 2009.

6. These fashion brands, both with Jamaican roots, although CY Clothing is now based in Florida, reflect a broader international commercial appropriation of Rastafari symbols, as evidenced by the successful Rasta-inspired clothing lines produced by sportswear company Puma and haute couture company Christian Dior. See also Moody (2006).

7. See <http://cyevolution.com/aboutus.html> accessed November 23, 2009.

8. See <http://www.plumanegra.com/splash.swf> accessed November 1, 2009.

9. *Souljah* is a pun on soldier and the words *soul* and *Jah* (the Rastafari God); *Nuff okra roun' mi* translates literally as *A lot of okra around me,* but when pronounced quickly sounds like *Nuh fuck around mi,* which translates as *Do not fuck with me*; *Ganjahmekya* is a pun on ganja (marijuana) and Jamaica spelled as Jah-Mek-Ya— God made here.

10. Following some of the conventions of "dread talk," the name *yatties* for vegetarian patties stems from I-atties, a Rastafied way of saying "patties"; soup is referred to as *sip*. See Pollard (2000).

11. Yvonne Hope, interview with author, July 2, 2008.

12. See Modest (2008) and Thomas (2005). Another example of the way in which state processes intersect with ital chic consumer trends could be seen in the Jamaican government's 2008 call for increasing the cultivation and consumption of locally grown, healthy cassava over increasingly expensive imported foodstuffs.

Chapter 10: Tropical Spa Culture and the Face of New Asian Beauty

This chapter is a somewhat revised version of a book chapter "Tropical Spa Cultures, Eco-chic and the Complexities of New Asianism" that first appeared in *Cleanliness and Culture,* edited by Kees van Dijk and Jean Gelman Taylor (2011). The author wishes to express his gratitude for earlier comments that both the editors provided on that chapter. The piece is republished here with permission of the publisher, KITLV Press.

1. These books included William Turner's *A Book of the Natures and Properties of the Baths of England* (1562) and two Venetian publications: Andrea Bacci's *De Thermis* (1571) and Thomasso Guinta's *De Balneis* (1553), which listed over 200 springs in Europe (Crebbin-Bailey, Harcup, and Harrington 2005). Mackaman (1998) refers to nineteenth-century French directories and novels as a profitable industry serving both to promote and earn from spa tourism. For an early twentieth-century example, see *Pleasures of the Spa* (Duguid 1968), a pan-American guide "to the great health resorts of the world."

2. The development of the modern Asian spa market as a tourist phenomenon is hence relatively young and starts with the opening of three major spas (including the Oriental and Chiva-Som) in Thailand in 1993 (Crebbin-Bailey, Harcup, and Harrington 2005: 30). These Asian spas focused especially on the art of massage, with limited use of mechanical equipment to distinguish itself from ordinary beauty salons. Spreading to major tourist resorts such as Phuket, Samui, and Bali, spas would soon become popular in the Southeast Asian hotel scene, but also as day spas in malls or shopping centers.

3. In South India, the states of Tamil Nadu, Karnataka, and Kerala have since the late 1990s promoted themselves as health tourism destinations for both Westerners and visitors from well-off Asian economies (Hudson 2003: 283). In Malaysia, the promotion of spa resorts has similarly targeted the well-to-do in neighboring countries.

4. In a 2012 poll on most popular spa resorts among the readers of the UK-based magazine *Traveller,* five out of the ten most popular spas worldwide were located in Asia. See <http://www.cntraveller.com/awards/the-readers-spa-awards/readers-spa-awards-2012> accessed March 2013.

5. See <http://www.dewisrispa.com> accessed March 2013.

6. In our introduction to this book, we show how the term *eco-chic* in the mid-1990s gained currency especially in the world of fashion. Tanqueray (2000) was one of the first to describe the new eco-friendly lifestyle and how it has become chic. The dust jacket of her book *Eco-chic: Organic Living* (2000) states that "not so long ago, environmental awareness was left almost exclusively to the experts or the eccentrics. However, now a more environmental friendly approach to life is something more and more people aspire to....No longer the domain of the 'brown rice and sandals' brigade, eco-consciousness means knowing that you don't have to sacrifice taste or style to look after your body and the environment."

7. A mythological mountain of Balinese Hinduism from which flow the waters of eternal youth.

8. Combining the wellness industry with religion is very much in line with the desecularization of other domains of public culture (Forbes 2000). Illustrative of this phenomenon is a wide range of Christian health centers that today offer their services to a devout public, as well as publications such as *Simply Relevant HeartSpa*, in which the introduction reads "Ok, so what's a Bible series got to do with a spa, you ask? Well this series is all about how we find refreshment in Jesus—how much he wants to renew and bless us. And what better metaphor for that than a spa?" (Simply Relevant 2007: 5).

9. Hua Hin, "Chiva-Som Luxury Health Resort: Great Stay at Chiva-Som" [online customer review from a TripAdvisor member, Seattle], posted September 10, 2005, <http://www.tripadvisor.com>.

10. Ken Dedes was the queen of Singosari and famed for her beauty. Legend has it that her bathing place was situated in Singosari, just outside of Malang. The local population believes that taking a bath at this spot will make one look young, charismatic, and shiny (Suwardono 2007).

11. A good example is a CD that I bought some ago in the Central Javanese town of Yogyakarta. This CD, which offers traditional *gendhing* music, was nothing new. Rather, it was a traditional recording that is now sold under the title *Java Relaxation and Spa*. Another strategy is to record old tunes in a new-age style, complete with bird song and other natural sounds, and sell it as "Synbotanic Aromatherapy Spa music," as I found on a Chinese CD.

12. Sophie Benge was formerly the deputy director of *Elle Decoration* magazine in Hong Kong. At present, she lives in London where she works as a journalist and is a consultant in an integrated health center for women. Periplus is also responsible for other wellness and do-it-yourself eco-chic books like *Jamu: The Ancient Art of Herbal Healing* (2001) and *A Handbook of Chinese Healing Herbs* (2001). Turtle and Archipelago Press similarly have published spa books like the *Thai Spa Book: Natural Asian Way to Health and Beauty* (2003) and *Spa Style Asia* (2003).

13. While *AsiaSpa* just celebrated its tenth anniversary, the materials used in this chapter were especially taken from issues that were published in the first two years (2004–2006).

14. Tettoni is considered to be one of the best spa photographers in Asia. He also did the photography for books such as *Bali Modern* (Periplus 2000), *Tropical Asian Style*

(Periplus 1997) and the *Ultimate Spa Book* (Periplus 2006), as well as many spa portfolios for hotels and resorts throughout Asia.

15. This is proven by the recent attention spa culture has received, for example, in Indonesian newspapers and locally oriented and Indonesian-language magazines such as *Seri HomeSpa.*

16. See <http://www.asiaspa.com> accessed July 17, 2013, and an all-Indian version, <http://www.asiaspaindia.com> accessed July 17, 2013.

17. Seemingly proud of this glorious past, the staff of the hotel and spa prefers the old time spelling of *Tjampuhan* rather than its modern-day equivalent *Campuhan* to refer to the river valley at which it is located.

18. Pita Maha (literally "Grand Ancestors" and referring to the deity Brahma) was an art society founded in 1936 by local aristocrats and international artists. Pita Maha was successful in getting works by local artists into international art exhibitions (Clark 1993: 23).

19. In one case, in a Balinese spa, I found out that the management prided itself in a weekly extermination of all insects and bugs by spraying the whole area covered by the resort.

20. Quoted from Amazon.com reviews of *The Tropical Spa;* see <http://www.amazon.ca/Tropical-Spa-Secrets-Health-Rejuvenation/dp/9625932658> accessed March 2013.

21. From <http://www.tripadvisor.com>, offering online reviews of Chiva-Som Luxury Health Resort (among others), accessed September 2006.

22. The term *ethnic chic* is traced to the 1990s, when Euro-American populations started to desire clothing and items that were ethnically inspired. The term is now used to refer to the cultural production of formerly ethnic clothes that have moved into the mainstream fashion arenas internationally. Niessen, Leshkowich, and Jones (2003), for example, signal the emergence of Indo chic—haute couture interpretations of Vietnamese peasant and elite clothing. From the world of fashion, the terminology has spilled over into interior design. Here ethnic chic (or *etnik chic*) comes to stand for "the use of carvings that are ethnically inspired and applied in the context of modern living houses" (Susilowati and Zi 2003: 1).

23. Nowhere near the Tajampuhan spa did we ever, during our two-week visit in 2006, run into the bathing girls. The image clearly seems to be derived from colonial fantasies of an island of bare breasts. This image dates at least to the twentieth-century photo albums that emphasized the physical beauty of Balinese bodies, especially nude Balinese women taking their baths (Picard 1996: 28), and it illustrates how the breasts of Balinese women no doubt constituted a major attraction of the island during that time.

24. Presumably, this refers to beautifying one's appearance *(sariro)* and dress *(busono)* (Robson and Wibisono 2002: 25).

25. See <http://www.mustika-ratu.co.id/> accessed September 2006.

26. The Javanese words here presumably refer to Old Javanese that for long was the language of literature and learning in Bali. *Léha-léha* means to do at one's leisure, or *dolce far niente* (Stevens and Schmidgall Tellings 2004: 569).

27. Ayurveda is an ancient Indian system of holistic health care that according to some dates back to 5000 B.C.E. and provides "the foundation for a lot of therapies practiced in spas today" (Crebbin-Bailey, Harcup, and Harrington 2005: xv).

28. It is obvious that in reality this not always seems to work. During our own holidays in a Balinese spa resort, for example, my wife was struck by the careful attention constantly being paid by employees to a clock that was centrally positioned in the main treatment room. The clock somehow constantly seemed to remind her of common time that was ticking on outside and that eventually would signal the end of the treatment.

29. Although not yet part of spa advertising, there is indeed a long tradition of praising beauty, seeing it as a quality with which heavenly beings are endowed, and attributing king and rulers with a similar beautiful appearance. Malay *hikayat* proved the king to be a worthwhile and legitimate ruler due to his strength and extraordinary beauty (Rahmat 2001: 83). The protagonist of another classical tale, Prapanca's king in the *Desawarnana*, is described by Taylor (2004: 94) as very attractive to women. When he passed by in royal procession, the narrator says, "some village women rushed so fast to see the king that their breast-cloths fell off. Ugliness and sicknesses on the other hand were often symptomatic of a disturbed relation between the ruler and his realm" (Jordaan and de Josselin de Jong 1985: 260).

30. Asian values these days are usually associated with the leaders of East and Southeast Asian nations, the most prominent advocates being the former prime minister of Malaysia, Mahathir, and Senior Minister Lee Kuan Yew of Singapore. Asia has a unique set of values that sets it apart from the West. These values include a stress on the community rather than the individual, the privileging of order and harmony over personal freedom, refusal to separate religion from other spheres of life, an insistence on hard work, respect for political leadership, and an emphasis on family loyalty (Milner 2000).

31. See, for example, Iwabuchi (1999) on Sony's media regionalism and other forms of Asianism, and Wee (1996) on Singapore pop star Dick Lee's Asian music. At the same time, the new pan-Asian culture of manga, Pokémon, and J-Pop (Japanese pop culture) is predominantly East Asian in character, leading to assertions of neocolonialism (Thomas 2004: 178).

32. The models resemble a neutral, unmarked race of Southeast Asians. To the Asian audience, moreover, the models are attractive as they resemble Western Hollywood stars but are also a bit like the Asians themselves. As for the Malaysian ideal, obviously much has changed since the demise of the New Economic policy. With the emergence of more orthodox Islamic powers, especially in the Malaysian states of Kelantan, new beauty ideals are promoted publicly and in outdoor advertisements women are now suitably covered up with a veil (Ismail 2004; Wong 2007). Strikingly many of these Muslim advertisements continue to depict very "white" women.

Bibliography

Chapter 1: The Paradoxes of Eco-Chic

Abdul-Matin, Ibrahim (2010), *Green Deen: What Islam Teaches about Protecting the Planet*, San Francisco: Berrett-Koehler.

Bair, Jennifer (2009), *Frontiers of Commodity Chain Research,* Stanford, CA: Stanford University Press.

Banerjee, Subhabrata Bobby (2002), "Managerial Perceptions of Corporate Environmentalism: Interpretations from Industry and Strategic Implications for Organizations," *Journal of Management Studies,* 38/4: 489–513.

Barendregt, B. (2012), "Diverse Digital Worlds," in H. Horst and D. Miller (eds.), *Digital Anthropology,* London: Berg.

Barnett, C., Cloke, P., Clarke, N., and Malpass, A. (2005), "Consuming Ethics: Articulating the Subjects and Spaces of Ethical Consumption," *Antipode,* 37/1: 23–45.

Barnett, Clive, Cloke, Paul, Clarke, Nick, and Malpass, Alice (2011), *Globalizing Responsibility: The Political Rationalities of Ethical Consumption,* Malden, MA: Wiley-Blackwell.

Beard, N. (2008), "The Branding of Ethical Fashion and the Consumer: A Luxury Niche or Mass-market Reality?" *Fashion Theory: The Journal of Dress, Body & Culture,* 12/4, 447–67.

Black, Sandy (2008), *Eco-chic: The Fashion Paradox,* London: Black Dog.

Blowfield, M. (2005), "Corporate Social Responsibility: Reinventing the Meaning of Development?" *International Affairs,* 81: 515–24.

Bordi, Ivonne Viscara (2006), "The 'Authentic' Taco and Peasant Women: Nostalgic Consumption in the Era of Globalization," *Culture and Agriculture,* 28/2: 97–107.

Bryant, Raymond L., and Goodman, Michael K. (2004), "Consuming Narratives: The Political Ecology of 'Alternative' Consumption," *Transactions of the Institute of British Geographers,* 29/3: 344–66.

Cloke, P., Barnett, C., Clarke, N., and Malpass, A. (2010), *Governing Ethical Consumption,* London: Berg.

Duara, Prasenjit (2011), Sustainability and the Crisis of Transcendence: The Long View from Asia, Keynote address, Asian Modernities and Traditions conference, Amsterdam, September 9, 2011.

DuPuis, M., Goodman, D., and Harrison, J. (2006), "Just Values or Just Value? Remaking the Local in Agro-food Studies," in T. Marsden and J. Murdoch (eds.), *Between the*

Local and the Global: Confronting Complexity in the Contemporary Agri-food Sector, Oxford: Elsevier.

Eriksen, Thomas Hylland (2001), *Tyranny of the Moment: Fast and Slow Time in the Information Age,* London: Pluto Press.

Fine, B. (2002), "Economics Imperialism and the New Development Economics as Kuhnian Paradigm Shift?" *World Development,* 30/12: 2057–70.

Finnis, Elizabeth (ed.) (2012), *Reimagining Marginalized Foods: Global Processes, Local Places,* Tucson: University of Arizona Press.

Fletcher, Kate (2008), *Sustainable Fashion and Textiles: Design Journeys,* London: Earthscan.

Foster, Robert J. (2008), *Coca-globalization: Following Soft Drinks from New York to New Guinea,* New York: Palgrave Macmillan.

Gibson, Chris, and Stanes, Elyse (2011), "Is Green the New Black? Exploring Ethical Fashion Consumption," in Tania Lewis and Emily Potter (eds.), *Ethical Consumption: A Critical Introduction,* Oxford: Routledge.

Goodman, Michael K., Maye, Damian, and Holloway, Lewis (2010), "Ethical Foodscapes? Premises, Promises, and Possibilities," *Environment and Planning,* 42/8: 1782–96.

Goodman, Michael K., and Barnes, Christine (2011), "Star/Poverty Space: The Making of the 'Development Celebrity,'" *Celebrity Studies,* 2/1: 69–85.

Guthman, Julie (2002), "Commodified Meanings, Meaningful Commodities: Rethinking Production–Consumption Links through the Organic System of Provision," *Sociologia Ruralis,* 42/4: 295–311.

Guthman, Julie (2009), "Unveiling the Unveiling: Commodity Chains, Commodity Fetishism, and the 'Value' of Voluntary, Ethical Food Labels," in Jennifer Bair (ed.), *Frontiers of Commodity Chain Research,* Stanford, CA: Stanford University Press.

Hollows, Joanne, and Jones, Steve (2010), "'At Least He's Doing Something': Moral Entrepreneurship and Individual Responsibility in Jamie's Ministry of Food," *European Journal of Cultural Studies,* 13: 307–22.

Honoré, Carl (2004), *In Praise of Slowness: How a Worldwide Movement Is Challenging the Cult of Speed,* San Francisco: HarperCollins.

Johnston, Josée (2008), "The Citizen-consumer Hybrid: Ideological Tensions and the Case of Whole Foods Market," *Theory and Society,* 37/3, 229–70.

Johnston, Josée, and Baumann, Shyon (2009), *Foodies: Democracy and Distinction in the Gourmet Foodscape,* New York: Routledge.

Lewis, Tanya, and Potter, Emily (eds.) (2010), *Ethical Consumption: A Critical Introduction,* London: Routledge.

Lindenfeld, Laura (2003), "Can Documentary Food Films Like *Food Inc.* Achieve Their Promise?" *Environmental Communication,* 4/3: 378–86.

Lowenthal, D. (1992), "The Death of the Future," in S. Wallman (ed.), *Contemporary Futures: Perspectives from Social Anthropology,* London: Routledge.

Melo, Cristian J. (2010), "Left Behind: A Farmer's Fate in the Age of Sustainable Development," FIU Electronic Theses and Dissertations [online database], Paper 331, <http://digitalcommons.fiu.edu/etd/331>

Micheletti, Michele (2003), *Political Virtue and Shopping: Individuals, Consumerism, and Collective Action,* New York: Palgrave Macmillan.

Mihaljevich, P. (2007), "Case History: Duchy Originals," in Simon Wright and Diane McCrea (eds.), *The Handbook of Organic and Fair Trade Food Marketing,* Oxford: Blackwell.

Mowforth, Martin, and Munt, Ian (2008), *Tourism and Sustainability: Development, Globalization and New Tourism in the Third World,* London: Routledge.

Parkins, Wendy, and Craig, Geoffrey (2006), *Slow Living,* Oxford: Berg.

Petrini, Carlo (2001), *Slow Food: The Case for Taste,* New York: Columbia University Press.

Pilzer, P. Z. (2002), *The Wellness Revolution: How to Make a Fortune in the Next Trillion Dollar Industry,* New York: Wiley & Sons.

Pretor-Pinney, G. (2006), *Cloudspotter's Guide,* New York: Berkeley.

Prudham, Scott (2009), "Pimping Climate Change: Richard Branson, Global Warming, and the Performance of Green Capitalism," *Environment and Planning,* 41/7: 1594–1613.

Richey, Lisa Ann, and Ponte, Stefan (2011), *Brand Aid: Shopping Well to Save the World,* Minneapolis: University of Minnesota Press.

Sheller, M. (2011), "Bleeding Humanity and Gendered Embodiments: From Antislavery Sugar Boycotts to Ethical Consumers," *Humanity: An International Journal of Human Rights, Humanitarianism, and Development,* 2/2, 171–92.

Shove, E. (2005), "Changing Human Behaviour and Lifestyle: A Challenge for Sustainable Consumption?" in I. Ropke and L. Reisch (eds.), *Consumption: Perspectives from Ecological Economics,* Cheltenham, UK: Elgar.

Solier, Isabelle de (2005), "TV Dinners: Culinary Television, Education, and Distinction," *Continuum: Journal of Media & Cultural Studies,* 19/4: 465–81.

Spaargaren, G. (2003), "Sustainable Consumption: A Theoretical and Environmental Policy Perspective," *Society & Natural Resources,* 16/8: 687–701.

Spaargaren, Gert, and Mol, Arthur P. J. (2008), "Greening Global Consumption: Redefining Politics and Authority," *Global Environmental Change,* 18/3: 350–59.

Stone, M. Priscilla, Haugerud, Angelique, and Little, Peter D. (2000), "Commodities and Globalization: Anthropological Perspectives" in A. Haugerud, M. P. Stone, P. D. Little, and Society for Economic Anthropology (eds.), *Commodities and Globalization: Anthropological Perspectives,* Lanham, MD: Rowman & Littlefield.

Turner, F. (2006), *From Counterculture to Cyberculture: Stewart Brand, the Whole Earth Network, and the Rise of Digital Utopianism,* Chicago: University of Chicago Press.

Wilk, Richard (2006), *Home Cooking in the Global Village: Caribbean Food from Buccaneers to Ecotourists,* London: Berg.

Wilk, Richard (2010), "Consumption Embedded in Culture and Language: Implications for Finding Sustainability," *Sustainability: Science, Practice, & Policy,* 6/2, 38–48.

Willis, M. M., and Schor, J. B. (2012), "Does Changing a Light Bulb Lead to Changing the World? Political Action and the Conscious Consumer," *The Annals of the American Academy of Political and Social Science,* 644/1, 160–90.

Winge, T. M. (2008), "'Green Is the New Black': Celebrity Chic and the 'Green' Commodity Fetish," *Fashion Theory: The Journal of Dress, Body and Culture,* 12/4:
511–23.

Zukin, Sharon (2009), *Naked City: The Death and Life of Authentic Urban Places,*
Oxford: Oxford University Press.

Chapter 2: Adversaries into Partners? Brand Coca-Cola and the Politics of Consumer-Citizenship

Arvidsson, Adam (2009), "The Ethical Economy: Towards a Post-capitalist Theory of
Value," *Capital and Class,* 97: 14–29.

Banet-Weiser, Sarah, and Lapsansky, Charlotte (2008), "RED Is the New Black: Brand
Culture, Consumer Citizenship and Political Possibility," *International Journal of
Communication,* 2: 1248–68.

Bashkow, Ira (forthcoming), *An Anthropological Theory of the Corporation,* Chicago:
University of Chicago Press.

Benson, Peter, and Kirsch, Stuart (2010a), "Corporate Oxymorons," *Dialectical Anthropology,* 34: 45–48.

Benson, Peter, and Kirsch, Stuart (2010b), "Capitalism and the Politics of Resignation,"
Current Anthropology, 51/4: 459–86.

Bisoux, Tricia (2010), "The Connected Capitalists," *BizEd,* May/June, 24–33.

Blanding, Michael (2005), "Coke: The New Nike," *The Nation* [online journal], (March
24), <http://www.thenation.com/article/coke-new-nike#axzz2aeM5Albe> accessed
July 31, 2013.

Bobenreith, Maria E., and Stibbe, Darian (2010), *Changing Trends in Business-NGO
Partnerships: A Netherlands Perspective.* Amsterdam: The Partnering Initiative and
SOS Kinderdorpen.

Coumans, Catherine (2011), "Occupying Spaces Created by Conflict: Anthropologists,
Development NGOs, Responsible Investment, and Mining," *Current Anthropology,*
52/S3: S29–S43.

Dellinger, A. J. (2012), "8 Apps for Fair Trade and Ethical Shopping," Mac|Life, <http://
www.maclife.com/article/gallery/8_apps_fair_trade_and_ethical_shopping>accessed
February 1, 2013.

Deri, Chris (2003), "Make Alliances, Not War, With Crusading External Stakeholders."
Strategy & Leadership, 31/5: 26–33.

Deutsch, Claudia H. (2007), "For Fiji Water, a Big List of Green Goals," *New York
Times,* (November 7).

Economist Intelligence Unit (2010), *Dangerous Liaisons: How Businesses Are Learning to Work with Their New Stakeholders,* New York: Economist Intelligence Unit
Limited.

Edelman, Richard (2001), *Protect Your Global Reputation: Work With NGOS—the New
Super Brands,* 29/2: 34–36.

Esterl, Mike (2011), "Bottle Recycling Plan Is Left at the Curb," *Wall Street Journal,*
(August 19).

Ferguson, James, and Gupta, Akhil (2002), "Spatializing States: Toward an Ethnography of Neoliberal Governmentality," *American Ethnologist,* 29/4: 981–1002.

Foster, Robert J. (2008a), *Coca-globalization: Following Soft Drinks from New York to New Guinea,* New York: Palgrave Macmillan.

Foster, Robert J. (2008b), "Commodities, Brands, Love and *Kula*: Comparative Notes on Value Creation," *Anthropological Theory,* 8/1: 9–25.

Foster, Robert J. (2011), "The Uses of Use Value," in Detlev Zwick and Julien Cayla (eds.), *Inside Marketing: Practices, Ideologies, Devices,* Oxford: Oxford University Press, 42–57.

Foster, Robert J. (2013), "Things to Do with Brands: Creating and Calculating Value," *HAU: Journal of Ethnographic Theory,* 3/1: 44–63.

Frank, Thomas ([2000] 2001), *One Market Under God: Extreme Capitalism, Market Populism, and the End of Economic Democracy*, New York: Anchor Books.

Garsten, Christina, and Jacobsson, Kerstin (2007), "Corporate Globalisation, Civil Society and Post-political Regulation—Whither Democracy?" *Development Dialogue,* 49: 143–57.

Gill, Lesley (2005), "Labor and Human Rights: 'The Real Thing' in Colombia," *Transforming Anthropology,* 13/2: 110–15.

Goldsberry, Clare (2011), "Were Coke's Recycling Efforts a Victim of its Own Anti-deposit Lobbying?" *Plastics Today* [online journal] (September 1), <http://www.plasticstoday.com/articles/coke-recycling-efforts-victim-its-own-anti-deposit-lobbying-090120116> accessed September 24, 2012.

Isdell, Neville (2007), "Things Go Better with Social Justice," *Wall Street Journal,* (February 3): 10-A.10.

Isdell, Neville with David Beasley (2011), *Inside Coca-Cola: A CEO's Life Story of Building the World's Most Popular Brand,* New York: St. Martin's Press.

Lawrence, Felicity (2010), "McDonald's and PepsiCo to Help Write UK Health Policy," *The Guardian* [online journal], (November 12), <http://www.guardian.co.uk/politics/2010/nov/12/mcdonalds-pepsico-help-health-policy> accessed February 1, 2013.

Leith, Scott, and Kempner, Matt (2004), "Coca-Cola Co.: Scuffles, Catcalls Spice Meeting," *Atlanta Journal-Constitution* (April 22): 1F.

Micheletti, Michele ([2003] 2010), *Political Virtue and Shopping: Individuals, Consumerism, and Collective Action,* New York: Palgrave Macmillan.

Miller, Daniel (1987), *Material Culture and Mass Consumption,* New York: Basil Blackwell.

Miller, Daniel (1988), "Appropriating the State on the Council Estate," *Man,* 23: 353–72.

Mukherjee, Roopali, and Banet-Weiser, Sarah (eds.) (2012), *Commodity Activism: Cultural Resistance in Neoliberal Times,* New York: New York University Press.

Power, Michael (2007), *Organized Uncertainty: Designing a World of Risk Management,* New York: Oxford University Press.

Prahalad, C. K., and Ramaswamy, Venkat (2004), *The Future of Competition: Co-creating Unique Value with Customers,* Boston: Harvard Business School Press.

Rajak, Dinah (2011), "Theatres of Virtue: Collaboration, Consensus, and the Social Life of Corporate Responsibility," *Focaal—Journal of Global and Historical Anthropology,* 60: 9–20.

Reich, Robert B. (2008), *Supercapitalism: The Transformation of Business, Democracy and Everyday Life,* New York: Knopf.

Ritzer, George, and Jurgenson, Nathan (2010), "Production, Consumption, Prosumption: The Nature of Capitalism in the Age of the Digital 'Prosumer,'" *Journal of Consumer Culture,* 10/1: 13–36.

Schudson, Michael (1984), *Advertising, the Uneasy Persuasion: Its Dubious Impact on American Society,* New York: Basic Books.

Secklow, Steve (2005), "Virtual Battle: How a Global Web of Activists Gives Coke Problems in India," *Wall Street Journal,* (June 7): A1.

Smithers, Rebecca (2011), "New App Launches for Ethical Shoppers," *The Guardian* [online journal], (February 4), <http://www.guardian.co.uk/environment/2011/feb/04/app-ethical-shopping> accessed February 1, 2013.

van Dijk, Kees and Taylor, Jean Gelman (eds.) (2011), *Cleanliness and Culture: Indonesian Histories,* Leiden: KITLV Press.

Ward, Andrew (2006), "Coke Joins Battle for the Brand," *Financial Times,* (November 21): 10.

Willmott, Hugh (2010), "Creating 'Value' Beyond the Point of Production: Branding, Financialization and Market Capitalization," *Organisation,* 17/5: 517–42.

Zara, Tom (2009), *The New Age of Corporate Citizenship: Doing Strategic Good that Builds Brand Value. Interbrand 2009 Best Global Brands and IB/HP 2009 CC Study,* New York: Interbrand.

Chapter 3: Peopling the Practices of Sustainable Consumption: Eco-Chic and the Limits to the Spaces of Intention

Anderson, B. (1991), *Imagined Communities,* London: Verso.

Bacon, C. (2005), "Confronting the Coffee Crisis: Can Fair Trade, Organic and Specialty Coffees Reduce Small-scale Farmer Vulnerability in Northern Nicaragua?" *World Development,* 33/3: 497–511.

Banister, J. (2007), "Stating Space in Modern Mexico," *Political Geography,* 26: 455–73.

Barnett, C., Cloke, P., Clarke, N., and Malpass, A. (2005), "Consuming Ethics: Articulating the Subjects and Spaces of Ethical Consumption," *Antipode,* 37: 23–45.

Bauman, Z. (2000), *Liquid Modernity,* London: John Wiley and Sons.

Bourdieu P. (1984), *Distinction: A Social Critique of the Judgement of Taste,* Cambridge, MA: Harvard University Press.

Bryant, R. (2005), *Nongovernmental Organizations in Environmental Struggles: Politics and the Making of Moral Capital in the Philippines,* New Haven, CT: Yale University Press.

Bryant, R., and Goodman, M. (2004), "Consuming Narratives: The Political Ecology of 'Alternative' Consumption," *Transactions of the Institute of British Geographers,* 29: 344–66.

Chua, B. H. (ed.) (2001), *Consumption in Asia,* London: Routledge.

Clarke, N., Barnett, C., Cloke, P., and Malpass, A. (2007), "Globalising the Consumer: Doing Politics in an Ethical Register," *Political Geography,* 26: 231–49.

Doolittle, A. (2005), *Property and Politics in Sabah, Malaysia: Native Struggles over Land Rights,* Seattle: University of Washington Press.

Eccleston, B. (1996), "Does North–South Collaboration Enhance NGO Influence on Deforestation Policies in Malaysia and Indonesia?" *Journal of Commonwealth and Comparative Politics,* 34: 66–89.

Eden, S., Donaldson, A., and Walker, G. (2006), "Green Groups and Grey Areas: Scientific Boundary-work, Nongovernmental Organisations and Environmental Knowledge," *Environment and Planning A,* 38: 1061–76.

Fedick, S. (2003), "In Search of the Maya Forest," in C. Slater (ed.), *In Search of the Rain Forest,* Durham, NC: Duke University Press.

Flint, C., and Taylor, P. (2007), *Political Geography: World-economy, Nation-state and Locality.* Harlow, UK: Pearson.

Freidberg, S. (2003), "Cleaning up Down South: Supermarkets, Ethical Trade and African Horticulture," *Social and Cultural Geography,* 4/1: 27–43.

Gibson-Graham, J. K. (2006), *A Post-capitalist Politics,* Minneapolis: University of Minnesota Press.

Goodman, D., DuPuis, E. M., and Goodman, M. (2012), *Alternative Food Networks: Knowledge, Practice and Politics,* London: Routledge.

Goodman, M. (2004), "Reading Fair Trade: Political Ecological Imaginary and the Moral Economy of Fair Trade Foods," *Political Geography,* 23/7: 891–915.

Goodman, M., Maye, D., and Holloway, L. (2010), "Ethical Foodscapes? Premises, Promises and Possibilities," *Environment and Planning A,* 42: 1782–96.

Goodman, M., and Sage, C. (2013), "Food Transgressions: Ethics, Governance and Geographies," in M. Goodman and C. Sage (eds.), *Food Transgressions: Making Sense of Contemporary Food Politics,* Farnham, UK: Ashgate.

Guardian, The (2012), "Ethical Goods Sales Increase Despite Recession," [online journal], <http://www.guardian.co.uk/environment/2012/dec/29/ethical-goods-sales-increase> accessed July 14, 2013.

Guthman, J. (2007), "The Polanyian Way? Voluntary Food Labels and Neoliberal Governance," *Antipode,* 39: 456–78.

Haas, E. (1991), *When Knowledge Is Power: Three Models of Change in International Organizations,* Berkeley: University of California Press.

Haron, S., Paim, L., and Yahaya, N. (2005), "Towards Sustainable Consumption: An Examination of Environmental Knowledge among Malaysians," *International Journal of Consumer Studies,* 29: 426–36.

Held, V. (2006), *The Ethics of Care: Personal, Political and Global,* Oxford: Oxford University Press.

Hobson, K. (2004), "Researching 'Sustainable Consumption' in Asia-Pacific Cities," *Asia Pacific Viewpoint,* 45: 279–88.

Hong, E. (1987), *Natives of Sarawak: Survival in Borneo's Vanishing Forest,* Penang: Institut Masyarakat.

Jomo, K., Chang, Y., and Khoo, K. (2004), *Deforesting Malaysia: The Political Economy and Social Ecology of Agricultural Expansion and Commercial Logging,* London: Zed Books.

Koay, A. (2005), "The Fun in Recycling," *The Star [Malaysia]* (July 12).

Lawson, V. (2005), "Hopeful Geographies: Imagining Ethical Alternatives. A Commentary on J. K. Gibson-Graham's 'Surplus Possibilities: Postdevelopment and Community Economies," *Singapore Journal of Tropical Geography,* 26/1, 36–38.

Loh, A. (2005), "Pearl Lost in the Garbage and Jerebu," *Aliran Monthly,* 25/8: 25–28.

Lyon, S., and Moberg, M. (eds.) (2010), *Fair Trade and Social Justice: Global Ethnographies,* New York: New York University Press.

McEwan, C., and Goodman, M. (2010), "Place Geography and the Ethics of Care: Introductory Remarks on the Geographies of Ethics, Responsibility and Care," *Ethics, Place and Environment,* 13/2: 103–12.

Moberg, M. (2005), "Fair Trade and Eastern Caribbean Banana Farmers: Rhetoric and Reality in the Anti-globalization Movement," *Human Organization,* 64/1: 4–15.

Mol, A., and Law, J. (2005), "Boundary Variations: An Introduction," *Environment and Planning D: Society and Space,* 23: 637–42.

Mutersbaugh, T. (2002), "The Number Is the Beast: A Political Economy of Organic-coffee Certification and Producer Unionism," *Environment and Planning A,* 34: 1165–84.

Newman, D., and Paasi, A. (1998), "Fences and Neighbours in the Postmodern World: Boundary Narratives in Political Geography," *Progress in Human Geography,* 22: 186–207.

Ooi, D. (2005), "Don't Panic: Haze Enveloping Parts of Penang No Cause for Concern," *New Sunday Times [Malaysia]* (June 26).

Pile, S. (2010), "Emotions and Affect in Recent Human Geography," *Transactions of the Institute of British Geographers,* 35: 5–20.

Ramli, J. (2005), "Growing Demand for Organic Food," *New Straits Times* (March 5).

Redclift, M. (2004), *Chewing Gum: The Fortunes of Taste,* London: Routledge.

Renard, M. (2005), "Quality Certification, Regulation and Power in Fair Trade," *Journal of Rural Studies,* 21: 419–31.

Sabaratnam, S. (2005), "Pa, What's a Durian?" *New Sunday Times [Malaysia]* (June 26).

Scott, J. (1990), *Domination and the Arts of Resistance,* New Haven, CT: Yale University Press.

Seyfang, G. (2005), "Shopping for Sustainability: Can Sustainable Consumption Promote Ecological Citizenship?" *Environmental Politics,* 14/2: 290–306.

Sheller, M. (2001), *Democracy after Slavery: Black Publics and Peasant Radicalism in Haiti and Jamaica,* Gainesville: University of Florida Press.

Shuttleworth, I. (2007), "Reconceptualising Local Labour Markets in the Context of Cross-border and Transnational Labour Flows: The Irish Example," *Political Geography,* 26: 968–81.

Sirieix, L., Kledal, P., and Sulitang, T. (2011), "Organic Food Consumers' Trade-offs between Local or Imported, Conventional or Organic Products: A Qualitative Study in Shanghai," *International Journal of Consumer Studies,* 35: 670–78.

Smith, D. (2000), *Moral Geographies: Ethics in a World of Difference,* Edinburgh: Edinburgh University Press.

Sparke, M. (2006), "A Neoliberal Nexus: Economy, Security and the Biopolitics of Citizenship on the Border," *Political Geography,* 25: 151–80.

Storey, D. (2001), *Territory: The Claiming of Space,* London: Prentice Hall.

Talib, R. (2001), "Malaysia: Power Shifts and the Matrix of Consumption," in B. Chua (ed.), *Consumption in Asia,* London: Routledge.

Taylor, P. (1994), "The State as Container: Territoriality in the Modern World System," *Progress in Human Geography,* 18: 151–62.

Walker, R.B.J. (1990), *Inside/Outside,* Cambridge: Cambridge University Press.

Wilson, B. (2010), "Indebted to Fair Trade? Coffee and Crisis in Nicaragua," *Geoforum,* 41, 84–92.

Chapter 4: Global Gold Connections: Ethical Consumption and the Beauty of Bonding Artisans

Comaroff, J., and Comaroff, J. (2000), "Millennial Capitalism: First Thoughts on a Second Coming," *Public Culture,* 12/2: 291–343.

Dolan, C. (2010), "Virtual Moralities: The Mainstreaming of Fairtrade in Kenyan Tea Fields," *Geoforum,* 41/1: 33–43.

Douglas, M. (1966), *Purity and Danger: An Analysis of Concepts of Pollution and Taboo,* London: Routledge.

Foster, R. (2008), *Coca-globalization: Following Soft Drinks from New York to New Guinea,* London: Palgrave Macmillan.

Fridell, G. (2006), "Fair Trade and Neoliberalism: Assessing Emerging Perspectives," *Latin American Perspectives,* 33/6: 8–28.

Goodman, M. (2010), "The Mirror of Consumption: Celebritization, Developmental Consumption and the Shifting Cultural Politics of Fair Trade, *Geoforum,* 41/1: 104–116.

Green, T. (1981), *The New World of Gold: The Inside Story of the Mines, the Markets, the Politics, the Investors,* New York: Walker.

Mauss, M. (1923), *Essai sur le don. Forme et raison de l'échange dans les sociétés archaïques,* Paris: PUF.

Miller, D. (1995), "Consumption as the Vanguard of History," in D. Miller (ed.), *Acknowledging Consumption,* London: Routledge.

Rajak, D. (2011), *In Good Company. An Anatomy Of Corporate Social Responsibility,* Stanford, CA: Stanford University Press.

Roozen, N., and Van der Hoff, F. (2001), *Fair Trade: Het verhaal achter Max Havelaar-koffie, Oké-bananen en Kuyichi-jeans,* Amsterdam: Van Gennep.

Roseberry, W. (1996), "The Rise of Yuppie Coffees and the Reimagination of Class in the United States," *American Anthropologist,* 98/4: 762–75.

Scott, J. (1998), *Seeing Like a State: How Certain Schemes to Improve the Human Condition Have Failed,* London: Yale University Press.

Walsh, A. (2010), "The Commoditization of Fetishes: Telling the Difference between Natural and Synthetic Sapphires," *American Ethnologist,* 37/1: 97–113.

Wereldwinkel (n.d.), *Van rietsuiker tot cadeauwinkel: De geschiedenis van de Wereld-winkels, 1967–2003,* <http://www.goereeoverflakkee.cpu.nl/db/upload/documents/ontstaansgeschiedenis.pdf> accessed March 20, 2013.

Chapter 5: Marketing the Mountain: The Emergence and Consequences of Eco-Chic Practices in the Basque Region

Alphandéry, P., and Fortier, A. (2001), "Can a Territorial Policy Be Based on Science Alone? The System for Creating the Natura 2000 Network in France," *Sociologia Ruralis,* 41: 311–28.

AND International (2007), "Mieux Appréhender la Réalité et le Potentiel de Développement de l'agroalimentaire en Pays Basque," [technical report] Bayonne, France: Lurraldea.

Barham, E. (2003), "Translating Terroir: The Global Challenge of French AOC Labeling," *Journal of Rural Studies,* 19: 127–38.

Bérard, L., and Marchenay, P. (2004), *Les Produits de Terroir: Entre Culture et Règlements,* Paris: CNRS Éditions.

Berthoud, G. (1992), "Market," in W. Sachs (ed.), *The Development Dictionary. A Guide to Knowledge as Power,* New York: Zed Books.

Bidart, P. (1980), *Nouvelle Société Basque,* Paris: Harmattan.

Bowen, S. (2010), "Embedding Local Places in Global Spaces: Geographical Indications as a Territorial Development Strategy," *Rural Sociology,* 75/2: 209–43.

Braudel, F. (1988), *The Identity of France. Vol. II—People and Production,* New York: Harper and Row.

Carrier, J. (2010), "Protecting the Environment the Natural Way: Ethical Consumption and Commodity Fetishism," *Antipode,* 42/3: 672–89.

Council of the European Communities (1992), *Council Directive 92/43/EEC of 21 May 1992 on the Conservation of Natural Habitats and of Wild Fauna and Flora,* Brussels.

Demossier, M. (2011), "Anthropologists and the Challenges of Modernity: Global Concerns, Local Responses in EU Agriculture," *Anthropological Journal of European Cultures,* 20/1: 111–31.

Douglass, W., and J. Zulaika (2007), *Basque Culture: Anthropological Perspectives,* Reno: University of Nevada Press.

Foster, R. (2008), *Coca-Globalization: Following Soft Drinks from New York to New Guinea,* New York: St. Martin's Press.

Galop, D. (2005), "Jalons pour l'Histoire d'une Forêt Mythique," *Jakintza,* 2005/32: 13–16.

Hudson, I., and Hudson, M. (2003), "Removing the Veil: Commodity Fetishism, Fair Trade, and the Environment," *Organization and Environment,* 16/4: 413–30.

Idoki (1992), "Agriculture Paysanne, sincere et citoyenne. Charte Générale," <http://www.idoki.org/site_magsys/File/nouvelle charte.PDF> accessed October 1, 2012.

Institute for European Environmental Policy (IIEP) (2002), Promoting the Socio-economic Benefits of Natura 2000, Conference Proceedings of the European Conference on "Promoting the Socio-Economic Benefits of Natura 2000," Brussels, November 2002.

Kosoy, N., and Corbera, E. (2010), "Payments for Ecosystem Services as Commodity Fetishism," *Ecological Economics,* 69/6: 1228–36.

Marx, K. ([1867] 1990), *Capital,* New York: Penguin Books.

Ministère de l'Ecologie du Développement et de l'Aménagement Durables (2007), *Projet de Loi de Finances pour 2008: Ecologie, Développement et Aménagement Durables,* <http://www.senat.fr/rap/a07-092-4/a07-092-4.html > accessed October 10, 2012.

Murray, S. (2003), "L'évolution des Frontières de l'état Français et de l'identité Culturelle Basque: Perspectives Anthropologiques," *Lapurdum: Revue d'Études Basques,* 8: 375–88.

Murray, S. (2009), "Enduring Conflicts and Cooperation: The Contested Spaces of the Basque Countryside, *Nevada Historical Society Quarterly,* 52/4: 269–79.

Pitte, J. R. (1999), "A Propos du Terroir," *Annales de Géographie,* 605: 86–89.

Szarka, J. (2002), *The Shaping of Environmental Policy in France,* New York: Berghahn Books.

Teil, G. (2012), "No Such Thing as Terroir? Objectivities and the Regimes of Existences of Objects," *Science, Technology, Human Values,* 37/5: 478–505.

Trubek, A. (2008), *The Taste of Place: A Culinary Journey into Terroir,* Berkeley: University of California Press.

Trubek, A., Guy, K., and Bowen, S. (2010), "Terroir: A French Conversation with a Transnational Future," *Contemporary French and Francophone Studies,* 14/2: 139–48.

Watson, C. (2003), *Modern Basque History: Eighteenth Century to the Present,* Reno: University of Nevada Press.

Welch-Devine, M., and Murray, S. (2011), " 'We're European Farmers Now': Transitions and Transformations in Basque Agricultural and Pastoral Practices," *Anthropological Journal of European Cultures,* 20/1: 69–88.

West, P. (2012), *From Modern Production to Imagined Primitive: The Social World of Coffee from Papua New Guinea,* Durham, NC: Duke University Press.

Chapter 6: Green Is the New Green: Eco-aesthetics in Singapore

Aitken, L. (2008), "From Eco-Geek to Green Chic," *Media: Asia's Newspaper for Media, Marketing and Advertising* [online journal], (April 3), <http://connection. ebscohost.com/c/articles/32734279/from-eco-geek-green-chic> accessed December 10, 2012.

Black, G. (2007), "Life in the Fast Lane," *OnEarth,* <http://www.onearth.org/article/life-in-the-fast-lane> accessed December 12, 2012.

Boden, S., and Williams, S. J. (2002), "Consumption and Emotion: The Romantic Ethic Revisited," *Sociology,* 36/3, 493–512.

Campbell, C. (1987), *The Romantic Ethic and the Spirit of Modern Consumerism,* Oxford: Basil Blackwell.

Centre for Urban Greenery and Ecology (2011), "Introduction to CUGE," <https://www. cuge.com.sg/Introduction-to-CUGE> accessed March 10, 2013.

Ching T. Y., and Ng, B. (2008), "Realising the Marina Bay Vision," *The Business Times* [online journal], (March 22–23) <http://www.marina-bay.sg/BT_22-23Mar08(pg7)_Realising%20the%20Marina%20Bay%20vision.pdf> accessed December 4, 2012.

Chua, B. H. (2003), *Life Is Not Complete without Shopping. Consumption Culture in Singapore,* Singapore: Singapore University Press.

Chung, C. J., Inaba, J., Koolhaas, R., and Sze, T. L. (2002), *The Harvard Design School Guide to Shopping,* Cambridge, MA: Harvard Design School.

Dezeen Magazine (2012), "We Wanted Real Drama in a Flat Landscape—Paul Baker on Gardens by the Bay," <http://www.dezeen.com/2012/11/04/we-wanted-to-create-real-drama-in-a-very-flat-landscape-paul-baker-on-gardens-by-the-bay> accessed February 3, 2013.

Esty, D. C., and Winston, A. S. (2009), *Green to Gold: How Smart Companies Use Environmental Strategy to Innovate, Create Value and Build Competitive Advantage,* Hoboken, NJ: John Wiley and Sons.

Featherstone, M. (2007), *Consumer Culture and Postmodernism,* 2nd ed., Los Angeles: Sage.

George, C. (2000), *Singapore. The Air-Conditioned Nation. Essays on the Politics of Comfort and Control, 1990–2000,* Singapore: Landmark Books.

Giddens, A. (1991), *Modernity and Self-Identity,* Stanford, CA: Stanford University Press.

Han, F. K, Fernandez, W, and Tan, S. (1998), *Lee Kuan Yew. The Man and His Ideas,* Singapore: Straits Times Press.

HotelClub (2013), "PARKROYAL on Pickering Singapore Hotel," <http://www.hotelclub.com/PARKROYAL-On-Pickering-Singapore-Hotel> accessed January 5, 2013.

Jones, V. (2008), *The Green Collar Economy: How One Solution Can Fix Our Two Biggest Problems,* New York: HarperCollins.

Lash, S., and Urry, J. (1994), *Economies of Signs and Space,* London: Sage.

Lee, K. Y. (2000), *From Third World to First. The Singapore Story: 1965–2000,* New York: HarperCollins.

Lee, S. H. (2011), "High 5 for LKY: Singapore's Chief Gardener," *Straits Times* [online journal], <http://global.factiva.com/ha/default.aspx> accessed January 12, 2013.

Liptrot, M. (2012), "Singapore: A City in a Garden," *The New Zealand Herald* [online journal], <http://www.nzherald.co.nz/travel/news/article.cfm?c_id=7&objectid=10818595> accessed March 11, 2013.

McCabe, Christine (2012), "Green Peace in Singapore," *The Australian (Travel and Indulgence),* (March 10).

Ministry of National Development, Singapore (2009), "Singapore: City in a Garden. Celebrating a Century and a Half of Botanical Success," *MND Link,* <http://www.mndlink.sg/2009/2009_May/NParks_article.htm> accessed January 14, 2013.

Ministry of National Development (n.d.), *From Garden City to City in a Garden,* <http://www.mnd.gov.sg/MNDAPPImages/About%20Us/From%20Garden%20City%20to%20City%20in%20a%20Garden.pdf> accessed February 27, 2012.

National Parks (2011), *Our City in a Garden,* <http://www.nparks.gov.sg/ciag/index.php?option= com_content&view=article&id=49&lang=en> accessed March 8, 2013.

Parkroyal on Pickering Singapore (2013), "Weekend Wind-Down," <http://www.parkroyalhotels.com/en/hotels/singapore/pickering_street/parkroyal_on_pickering/specials/opening_special.html?utm_source=google_tig&utm_medium=cpc&utm_campaign=google_brand_english_2012_prpickering&utm_content=openingspecial> accessed July 14, 2013.

Postrel, V. (2003), *The Substance of Style: How the Rise of Aesthetic Value Is Remaking Commerce, Culture and Consciousness,* New York: HarperCollins.

Ritzer, G. (2010), *Enchanting a Disenchanted World. Continuity and Change in the Cathedrals of Consumption,* London: Sage.

Siemens AG (2011), *Megacity Singapore Is Asia's Greenest City. Asian Green City Index Study Analyzes the Environmental Sustainability of 22 Major Cities in Asia,* <http://www.siemens.com/press/en/pressrelease/?press=/en/pressrelease/2011/corporate_communication/axx20110240.htm> accessed July 14, 2013.

Solomon, C. (2005), "Where the High Life Comes Naturally," *The New York Times Travel* [online journal], <http://travel.nytimes.com/2005/05/01/travel/01eco.html> accessed July 14, 2013.

Tanqueray, R. (2000), *Eco Chic: Organic Living,* London: Carlton Books.

Thomas, S. (2008), "From 'Green Blur' to Ecofashion: Fashioning an Eco-lexicon," *Fashion Theory,* 12/4: 525–40.

Thrift, N. (2004), "Intensities of Feeling: Towards a Spatial Politics of Affect," *Geografiska Annaler Series,* 86: 57–78.

Thrift, N. (2010), "Understanding the Material Practices of Glamour," in M. Gregg and G. J. Seigworth (eds.), *The Affect Theory Reader,* Durham, NC: Duke University Press.

Urry, J. (1990), *The Tourist Gaze,* London: Sage.

Urry, J. (1992), "The Tourist Gaze and the 'Environment,'" *Theory, Culture and Society,* 9: 1–26.

Wee, C.J.W.-L. (2007), *The Asian Modern. Culture, Capitalist Development, Singapore.* Singapore: National University of Singapore Press.

Winge, T. (2008), "'Green is the New Black': Celebrity Chic and the 'Green' Commodity Fetish," *Fashion Theory,* 12/4: 511–524.

Wong, T. (2011), "Mr. Lee Takes in Blooms at Gardens by the Bay," *Straits Times,* (November 15).

Yuen, B, Kong, L., and Briffett, C. (1999), "Nature and the Singapore Resident," *GeoJournal,* 49: 323–31.

Zukin, S. (1991), *Landscapes of Power: From Detroit to Disneyworld,* Berkeley: University of California Press.

Chapter 7: The Caring, Committed Eco-Mom: Consumption Ideals and Lived Realities of Toronto Mothers

Barnett, C., Clarke, N., and Cloke, P. (2005), "The Political Ethics of Consumerism," *Consumer Policy Review,* 15/2: 45–51.

Beagan, B., Chapman, G., D'Sylva, A., and Raewyn Bassett, B. (2008), "'It's Just Easier for Me To Do It': Rationalizing the Family Division of Food Work," *Sociology,* 42: 653–71.

Bellows, A. C., Alcaraz, G., and Hallman, W. K. (2010), "Gender and Food: A Study of Attitudes in the USA Towards Organic, Local, U.S.-grown and GM-free Foods," *Appetite,* 55/3: 540–50.

Blair-Loy, M. (2001), "Cultural Constructions of Family Schemas: The Case of Women Finance Executives," *Gender & Society,* 15: 687–709.

Blair-Loy, M. (2003), *Competing Devotions: Career and Family among Women Executives,* Cambridge, MA: Harvard University Press.

Bordo, S. (1994), *Unbearable Weight: Feminism, Western Culture, and the Body,* Los Angeles: University of California Press.

Bugge, A., and Almas, R. (2006), "Domestic Dinner: Representations and Practices of a Proper Meal among Young Suburban Mothers," *Journal of Consumer Culture,* 6/2: 203–28.

Cairns, K., Johnston, J., and MacKendrick, N. (2013), "Feeding the 'Organic Child': Mothering through Ethical Consumption," *Journal of Consumer Culture,* 13/2: 96–117.

Caplan, P. (1997), "Approaches to the Study of Food, Health and Identity," in Pat Caplan (ed.), *Food, Health and Identity,* New York: Routledge.

Chabon, M. (2010). *Manhood for Amateurs,* New York: Harper Perennial Canada.

DeVault, M. (1991), *Feeding the Family,* Chicago: University of Chicago Press.

Doucet, Andrea (2006), *Do Men Mother?* Toronto: University of Toronto Press.

Douglas, S. J., and Michaels, M. (2004), *The Mommy Myth: The Idealization of Motherhood and How It Has Undermined Women,* New York: Free Press.

Druckerman, P. (2012), *Bringing Up Bébé: One American Mother Discovers the Wisdom of French Parenting,* New York: Penguin Press.

Gilbert, D. (2008), *The American Class Structure in an Age of Growing Inequality,* London: Sage.

Goodman, D., Dupuis, M., and Goodman, M. (2012), *Alternative Food Networks: Knowledge, Practice and Politics,* New York: Routledge.

Goodman, M. (2010), "The Mirror of Consumption: Celebritization, Developmental Consumption and the Shifting Cultural Politics of Fair Trade," *Geoforum,* 41/1: 104–116.

Guthman, J. (2003), "Fast Food/Organic Food: Reflexive Tastes and the Making of 'Yuppie Chow,'" *Social and Cultural Geography,* 4/1: 45–58.

Hawkins, R. (2012), "Shopping to Save Lives: Gender and Environment Theories Meet Ethical Consumption," *Geoforum,* 43/4: 750–59.

Hays, S. (1996), *The Cultural Contradictions of Motherhood,* New Haven, CT: Yale University Press.

Hill, H., and Lynchehaun, F. (2002), "Organic Milk: Attitudes and Consumption Patterns," *British Food Journal,* 104/7: 526–42.

Hochschild, A. (1989), *The Second Shift: Working Parents and the Revolution at Home,* New York: Viking.

Johnston, J. (2008), "The Citizen-consumer Hybrid: Ideological Tensions and the Case of Whole Foods Market," *Theory and Society,* 37: 229–70.

Johnston, J., and Baumann, S. (2010), *Foodies: Democracy and Distinction in the Gourmet Foodscape,* New York: Routledge.

Johnston, J., Biro, A., and MacKendrick, N. (2009). "Lost in the Supermarket: The Corporate Organic Foodscape and the Struggle for Food Democracy," *Antipode: A Radical Journal of Geography,* 41/3: 509–32.

Johnston, J., and Cairns. K. (2012), "Eating for Change," in S. Banet-Weiser and R. Muhkerjee (eds.), *Commodity Activism: Cultural Resistance in Neoliberal Times,* New York: New York University Press.

Johnston, J., and Cappeliez, S. (2012), "You Are What You Eat: Enjoying (and Transforming) Food Culture," in M. Koc, J. Sumner, and T. Winson (eds.), *Critical Perspectives in Food Studies,* Toronto: Oxford University Press.

Johnston, J., Rodney, A., and Szabo, M. (2012), "Place, Ethical Eating and Everyday Food Practices: A Tale of Two Neighbourhoods," *Sociology,* 46/6: 1091–108.

Johnston, J., and Szabo, M. (2011), "Reflexivity and the Whole Food Market Shopper: Shopping for Change, or Cruising for Pleasure?" *Agriculture and Human Values,* 28: 303–19.

Johnston, J., Szabo, M., and Rodney, A. (2011), "Good Food, Good People: Understanding the Cultural Repertoire of Ethical Eating," *Journal of Consumer Culture,* 11/3: 293–318.

Kahneman, D., Schkade, D., Fischler, C., Krueger, A., and Krilla, A. (2010), "The Structure of Well-being in Two Cities: Life Satisfaction and Experienced Happiness in Columbus, Ohio, and Rennes, France," in E. Diener, J. Helliwell, and D. Kahneman (eds.), *International Differences in Well-Being,* New York: Oxford University Press.

Keller, K. (1994), *Mothers and Work in Popular American Magazines,* Westport, CT: Greenwood Press.

Lachance-Grzela, M., and Bouchard, G. (2010), "Why Do Women Do the Lion's Share of Housework? A Decade of Research," *Sex Roles,* 63: 767–80.

MacGregor, S. (2006), *Beyond Mothering Earth: Ecological Citizenship and the Politics of Care,* Vancouver: University of British Columbia Press.

Miller, D. (1998), *A Theory of Shopping,* Ithaca, NY: Cornell University Press.

Murphy, A. J. (2011). "Farmers' Markets as Retail Spaces," *International Journal of Retail and Distribution Management,* 39/8: 582–97.

Okopny, C. (2012), *Burden of Care: Women's Environmental Responsibility in Popular U.S. Media,* Unpublished doctoral dissertation, Baltimore: University of Maryland.

Organic Trade Association (2010, June), "Food Facts: Organic Food Facts," <http://www.ota.com/organic/mt/food.html> accessed February 10, 2013.

Sandilands, C. (1993), "On 'Green' Consumerism: Environmental Privatization and 'Family Values,'" *Canadian Woman Studies,* 13/3: 45–47.

Slocum, R. (2007). "Whiteness, Space and Alternative Food Practice," *Geoforum,* 38/3: 520–33.

Smith, A. N. (2010), "The Ecofetish: Green Consumerism in Women's Magazines," *Women's Studies Quarterly,* 38/3–4: 68–83.

Starr, M. A. (2009), "The Social Economics of Ethical Consumption: Theoretical Considerations and Empirical Evidence," *The Journal of Socio-Economics,* 38/6: 916–25.

Stolle, D., and Micheletti, M. (2006), "The Gender Gap Reversed: Political Consumerism as a Women-Friendly Form of Political Engagement," in B. O'Neill and E. Gidgengil (eds.), *Gender and Social Capital,* London: Routledge.

Szasz, A. (2009), *Shopping Our Way to Safety,* Minneapolis: University of Minneapolis Press.

Thompson, C. J. (1996), "Caring Consumers: Gendered Consumption Meanings and the Juggling Lifestyle," *Journal of Consumer Research,* 22/4: 388–407.

Zelezny, L., Poh-Phung, C., and Aldrich, C. (2000), "Elaborating on Gender Differences in Environmentalism," *Journal of Social Issues,* 56/3: 443–57.

Chapter 8: Afro-chic: Beauty, Ethics, and "Locks without Dread" in Ghana

Akyeampong, Emmanuel (2000), "Wo pe tam won pe ba (You like cloth but you don't want children), Urbanization, Individualism and Gender Relations in Colonial Ghana c. 1900–39," in D. M. Anderson and R. Rathbone (eds.), *Africa's Urban Past,* Oxford: James Currey.

Barth, Fredrik (1963), *The Role of the Entrepreneur in Social Change in Norway,* Bergen: Universitetsförlaget.

Berlan, Amanda, and Dolan, Catherine (2013), "Of Red Herrings and Immutabilities: Rethinking Fair Trade's Ethic of Relationality among Cocoa Producers," in M. Goodman and C. Sage (eds.), *Food Transgressions: Making Sense of Contemporary Food Politics,* Aldershot, UK: Ashgate.

Blay, Yaba A. (2009), "Ahoofe kasa!: Skin Bleaching and the Function of Beauty among Ghanaian Women," *JENdA: A Journal of Culture and African Women Studies,* 14: 51–85.

Burke, Timothy (1996), *Lifebuoy Men, Lux Women. Commodification, Consumption & Cleanliness in Modern Zimbabwe,* London: Leicester University Press.

Chalfin, Brenda (2004), *Shea Butter Republic. State Power, Global Markets, and the Making of an Indigenous Commodity,* New York: Routledge.

Coe, Cati (2005), *Dilemmas of Culture in African Schools: Youth, Nationalism and the Transformation of Knowledge,* Chicago: The University of Chicago Press.

Cohen, A. P., and Comaroff, J. L. (1976), "The Management of Meaning: On the Phenomenology of Political Transactions," in B. Kapferer (ed.), *Transactions and Meaning: Directions in the Anthropology of Exchange and Symbolic Behavior,* Philadelphia: Institute for the Study of Human Issues.

Comaroff, Jean (1996), "The Empire's Old Clothes: Refashioning the Colonial Subject," in D. Howes (ed.), *Commodities and Cultural Borders,* London: Routledge.

Comaroff, John, and Comaroff, Jean (2009), *Ethnicity, Inc.,* Chicago: University of Chicago Press.

de Witte, Marleen (2001), *Long Live the Dead! Changing Funeral Celebrations in Asante, Ghana,* Amsterdam: Aksant Academic.

de Witte, Marleen (2004), "Afrikania's Dilemma: Reframing African Authenticity in a Christian Public Sphere," *Etnofoor,* 17/1–2: 133–55.

de Witte, Marleen, and Meyer, Birgit (2012), "African Heritage Design. Entertainment Media and Visual Aesthetics in Ghana," *Civilizations,* 61/1: 43–64.

Dolan, Catherine (2009), "Market Affections: Moral Encounters with Kenyan Fairtrade Flowers," *Ethnos: Journal of Anthropology,* 72/2: 239–61.

Essah, Doris (2008), *Fashioning the Nation: Hairdressing, Professionalisation and Performance of Gender in Ghana 1900–2006,* Unpublished PhD Dissertation, University of Michigan, Department of History, Ann Arbor.

Gifford, Paul (2004), *Ghana's New Christianity: Pentecostalism in a Globalising African Economy,* Bloomington: Indiana University Press.

Gott, Suzanne (2009), "Asante *Hightimers* and the Fashionable Display of Women's Wealth in Contemporary Ghana," *Fashion Theory,* 13/2: 141–76.

Graeber, David (2001), *Toward an Anthropological Theory of Value. The False Coin of Our Own Dreams,* New York: Palgrave.

Haynes, Naomi (2012), "Pentecostalism and the Morality of Money: Prosperity, Inequality, and Religious Sociality on the Zambian Copperbelt," *Journal of the Royal Anthropological Institute,* 18: 123–39.

Hickel, Jason, and Khan, Arsalan (2012), "The Culture of Capitalism and the Crisis of Critique," *Anthropological Quarterly,* 85/1: 203–27.

James, Deborah (2011), "The Return of the Broker: Consensus, Hierarchy and Choice in South African Land Reform," *Journal of the Royal Anthropological Institute,* 17/2: 318–38.

Lambek, Michael (2008), "Value and Virtue," *Anthropological Theory,* 8/2: 133–57.

Leissle, Kristy (2012), "Cosmopolitan Cocoa Farmers: Refashioning Africa in Divine Chocolate Advertisements," *Journal of African Cultural Studies,* 24/2: 121–39.

Mbembe, Achille (2001), "African Modes of Self-writing," *Public Culture,* 14/1: 239–73.

Meyer, Birgit (1998), "Make a Complete Break with the Past. Memory and Postcolonial Modernity in Ghanaian Pentecostal Discourse," *Journal of Religion in Africa,* 27/3: 316–49.

Newell, Sasha (2012), *Modernity Bluff. Crime, Consumption and Citizenship in Côte d'Ivoire,* Chicago: University of Chicago Press.

Nkrumah, Kwame (1963), *Africa Must Unite,* London: Panaf.

Pierre, Jemima (2013), *The Predicament of Blackness. Postcolonial Ghana and the Politics of Race,* Chicago: University of Chicago Press.

Ross, Doran H. (1998), *Wrapped in Pride: Ghanaian Kente and African American Identity,* Los Angeles: UCLA Fowler Museum of Cultural History.

Ross, Mariama (2000), "Rasta Hair, U.S and Ghana: A Personal Note," in Roy Sieber and Frank Herreman (eds.), *Hair in African Art and Culture,* Munich: Prestel.

Schneider, Jane (2006), "Cloth and Clothing," in Christopher Tilley et al. (eds.), *Handbook of Material Culture,* London: Sage.

Shipley, Jesse Weaver (2009), "Aesthetic of the Entrepreneur: Afro-Cosmopolitan Rap and Moral Circulation in Accra, Ghana," *Anthropological Quarterly,* 82/3: 631–68.

Sieber, Roy and Herreman, Frank (eds.), (2000), *Hair in African Art and Culture,* Munich: Prestel.

Spronk, Rachel (2012), *Ambiguous Pleasures. Sexuality and Middle Class Self-Perceptions in Nairobi,* New York: Berghahn.

Spronk, Rachel (forthcoming), "From Modes of Production to Modes of Sophistication: Exploring Middle Class in Nairobi," *African Studies Review.*

Szasz, Margaret C. (ed.) (2001), *Between Indian and White Worlds. The Cultural Broker,* Norman: University of Oklahoma Press.

Thalén, Oliver (2011), "Ghanaian Entertainment Brokers: Urban change, and *Afro-cosmopolitanism,* with Neoliberal Reform," *Journal of African Media Studies,* 3/2: 227–40.

Žižek, Slavoj (2009), *First as Tragedy, Then as Farce,* London: Verso.

Chapter 9: Ital Chic: Rastafari, Resistance, and the Politics of Consumption in Jamaica

Bell, Monica (2007), "The Braiding Cases, Cultural Deference, and the Inadequate Protection of Black Women Consumers," *Yale Journal of Law and Feminism,* 19/1: 125–53.

Bogues, Anthony (2002), "Politics, Nation and PostColony: Caribbean Inflections," *Small Axe,* 6/1: 1–30.

Chevannes, Barry (1998), "Rastafari and the Exorcism of the Ideology of Racism and Classism in Jamaica," in N. S. Murrell, W. D. Spencer, and A. A. McFarlane (eds.), *Chanting Down Babylon: The Rastafari Reader,* Philadelphia: Temple University Press.

de Koning, Anouk (2009), "Gender, Public Space and Social Segregation in Cairo: Of Taxi Drivers, Prostitutes and Professional Women," *Antipode,* 41/3: 533–56.

Edmonds, Ennis B. (2003), *Rastafari: From Outcasts to Culture Bearers,* Oxford: Oxford University Press.

Edwards, Nadi (1998), "States of Emergency: Reggae Representations of the Jamaican Nation State," *Social and Economic Studies,* 47/1: 21–32.

Frank, Kevin (2007), "'Whether Beast or Human': The Cultural Legacies of Dread, Locks, and Dystopia," *Small Axe,* 11/2: 46–62.

Gray, Obika (2003), "Predation Politics and the Political Impasse in Jamaica," *Small Axe,* 7/1: 72–94.

Meeks, Brian (2002), "Reasoning with Caliban's Reason," *Small Axe,* 6/1: 158–68.

Micheletti, Michele (2004), "Introduction," in Michele Micheletti, Andreas Follesdal, and Dietlind Stolle (eds.), *Politics, Products and Markets: Exploring Political Consumerism Past and Present,* New Brunswick, NJ: Transaction.

Ministry of Education, Youth, and Culture (2003), *Towards Jamaica the Cultural Superstate: The National Cultural Policy of Jamaica,* Kingston: Culture Division, MEYC.

Modest, Wayne (2008), Rethinking the Political Present in Jamaica, Paper presented at M. G. Smith and the Emergence of Social Anthropology and Social Theory in the Caribbean and Beyond, University of the West Indies, Mona Campus, June 11–13.

Moody, Shelah (2006), "Dread Threads: From Rags to Designer Riches, Reggae Infuses Fashion with Rhythm," *San Francisco Chronicle,* (June 18): D1.

Parkinson, Rosemary (2003), "Ashanti: Food Fit for the Gods," *Jamaica Gleaner* (April 10).

Pollard, Velma (2000), *Dread Talk: The Language of Rastafari,* Kingston: Canoe.

Robotham, Don (2000), "Blackening the Jamaican Nation: The Travails of a Black Bourgeoisie in a Globalized World," *Identities,* 7/1: 1–38.

Rydin, Yvonne (1999), "Can We Talk Ourselves into Sustainability? The Role of Discourse in the Environmental Policy Process," *Environmental Values,* 8/4: 467–84.

Spaargaren, Gert, and Mol, Arthur P. J. (2008), "Greening Global Consumption: Redefining Politics and Authority," *Global Environmental Change,* 18/3: 350–59.

Stolzoff, Norman (2000), *Wake the Town and Tell the People: Dancehall Culture in Jamaica,* Durham, NC: Duke University Press.

Thomas, Deborah A. (2004), *Modern Blackness: Nationalism, Globalization and the Politics of Culture in Jamaica,* Durham, NC: Duke University Press.

Thomas, Deborah A. (2005), "Development, 'Culture,' and the Promise of Modern Progress," *Social and Economic Studies,* 54/3: 97–125.

van Dijk, Frank Jan (1988), "The Twelve Tribes of Israel: Rasta and the Middle Class," *New West Indian Guide,* 62/1–2: 1–26.

vom Bruck, Gabriele (2005), "The Imagined 'Consumer Democracy' and Elite (Re)Production in Yemen," *Journal of the Royal Anthropological Institute,* 11/2: 255–75.

Williams, Colin C., and Millington, Andrew C. (2004), "The Diverse and Contested Meanings of Sustainable Development," *Geographical Journal,* 170/2: 99–104.

World Commission on Environment and Development (1987), *Our Common Future,* Oxford: Oxford University Press.

Chapter 10: Tropical Spa Culture and the Face of New Asian Beauty

Amazon.com (1999), "Bali Is Becoming the Asian Spa Mecca," [customer reviews of *The Tropical Spa: Asian Secrets of Health, Beauty and Relaxation*], (October 30, 1999), <http://www.amazon.com/The-Tropical-Spa-Secrets-Relaxation/product-reviews/0794602622> accessed February 1, 2013.

Amazon.com (2005), "A lovely book filled with photos and ideas," [customer reviews of *Spa*], (May 2, 2005), <http://www.amazon.com/Spa-Allison-Arieff/product-reviews/3822858900> accessed February 1, 2013.

AsiaSpa (2005), "Born to Spa," (January/February): 10.

Benge, S. (2003), *The Tropical Spa: Asian Secrets of Health, Beauty and Relaxation,* Singapore: Periplus.

Ching, L. (2000), "Globalizing the Regional, Regionalizing the Global: Mass Culture and Asianism in the Age of Late Capital," *Public Culture,* 12/1: 233–57.

Chua, B. H. (2003), *Life Is not Complete without Shopping: Consumption Culture in Singapore,* Singapore: Singapore University Press.

Clark, J. (1993), *Modernity in Asian Art.* Broadway, NSW: Wild Peony.

Corbett, T. (2001), *The Making of American Resorts: Saratoga Springs, Ballston Spa, Lake George,* New Brunswick, NJ: Rutgers University Press.

Crebbin-Bailey, J., Harcup, J. W., and Harrington, J. (2005), *The Spa Book: The Official Guide to Spa Therapy,* London: Thomson.

Crismer, L. M. (1989), *The Original Spa Waters of Belgium,* Spa, Belgium: Spa Monopole.

Duguid, J. (1968), *Pleasures of the Spa: Pan Am's Guide to the Great Health Resorts of the World,* New York: Macmillan.

Eriksen, T. H. (2001), *Tyranny of the Moment: Fast and Slow Time in the Information Age,* London: Pluto Press.

Forbes, B. D. (2000), *Religion and Popular Culture in America,* Berkeley: University of California Press.

Rahmat, H. (2001), *In Search of Modernity: A Study of the Concepts of Literature, Authorship, and Notions of Self in "Traditional" Malay Literature,* Kuala Lumpur: Akademi Pengajian Melayu, Universiti Malaya.

Hendry, J. (2000), *The Orient Strikes Back: A Global View of Cultural Display,* Oxford: Berg.

Heryanto, A. (1999), "The Years of Living Luxuriously," in M. Pinches (ed.), *Culture and Privilege in Capitalist Asia,* London: Routledge.

Hudson, S. (2003), *Sport and Adventure Tourism,* New York: Haworth Hospitality Press.

Ismail, R. (2004), "Women and Islam in Malaysia," *Kyoto Review of Southeast Asia* [online journal] 4, <http://kyotoreview.cseas.kyoto-u.ac.jp/issue/issue4> accessed July 17, 2013.

Iwabuchi, K. (1999), "Return to Asia: Japan in Asian Audiovisual Markets," in Kosaku Yoshino (ed.), *Consuming Ethnicity and Nationalism: Asian experiences,* Honolulu: University of Hawaii Press.

Jordaan, R. E., and de Josselin de Jong, P. E. (1985), "Sickness as a Metaphor in Indonesian Political Myths," *Bijdragen tot de Taal-, Land- en Volkenkunde,* 141: 253–74.

Jurriëns, E., and De Kloet, J. (2007), *Cosmopatriots: On Distant Belongings and Close Encounters,* Amsterdam: Rodopi.

Kemper, S. (2001), *Buying and Believing: Sri Lankan Advertising and Consumers in a Transnational World,* Chicago: University of Chicago Press.

Lee, G., and Lim, C. Z. (2003), *Spa Style Asia: Therapies, Cuisines, Spas,* London: Thames & Hudson.

MacCannell, D. (1989), *The Tourist,* New York: Schocken Books.

Mackaman, D. P. (1998), *Leisure Settings: Bourgeois Culture, Medicine, and the Spa in Modern France,* Chicago: University of Chicago Press.

Milner, A. (2000), "What's Happened to 'Asian Values'?" in G. Segal and D.S.G. Goodman (eds.), *Towards Recovery in Pacific Asia,* London: Routledge.

Nicol, Catherine (2005), "Born to Spa," *AsiaSpa,* (January/February): 10.

Niessen, S., Leshkowich, A., and Jones, C. (eds.) (2003), *Re-Orienting Fashion: The Globalization of Asian Dress,* Oxford: Berg.

Ottino, A. (2000), *The Universe Within: A Balinese Village through Its Ritual Practices,* Paris: Karthala.

Panlilio, E. E., and Sta. María, F. (2005), *Slow Food: Philippine Culinary Traditions,* Pasig City, Philippines: Anvil.

Parkins, W., and Craig, G. (2006), *Slow Living,* Oxford: Berg.

Picard, M. (1996), *Bali: Cultural Tourism and Touristic Culture,* Singapore: Archipelago.

Puntowati, S. W. (1992), "The Dukun Pengantin: Mediator at the Javanese Wedding Ceremony," in S. Bemmelen (ed.), *Women and Mediation in Indonesia,* Leiden: KITLV Press. [Verhandelingen 152.]

Rafael, V. L. (1995), "Taglish, or the Phantom Power of the Lingua Franca," *Public Culture,* 8: 101–26.

Robson, S., and Wibisono, S. (2002), *Javanese English Dictionary,* Hong Kong: Periplus Editions (HK).

Simply Relevant (2007), *Simply Relevant HeartSpa: Relational Bible Series for Women,* Loveland, CO: Group.

Stevens, A. M., and Schmidgall Tellings, A. E. (2004), *A Comprehensive Indonesian-English Dictionary* (rev. ed.), Athens: Ohio University Press, in association with the American Indonesian Chamber of Commerce.

Susilowati, and Zi, A. (2003), *Sentuhan etnik. Seri rumah gaya,* Jakarta: Gramedia Pustaka Utama.

Suwardono (2007), "Identifikasi Ken Dêdês dalam arca perwujudan sebagai Dewi Prajñaparamita: Tinjauan Filsafat Religi dan Ikonografi," *Berkala Arkeologi,* 27/1: 127–54.

Tanqueray, R. (2000), *Eco-chic: Organic Living,* London: Carlton Books.

Taylor, J. G. (2004), *Indonesia: Peoples and Histories,* New Haven, CT: Yale University Press.

Thomas, M. (2004), "East Asian Cultural Traces in Post-socialist Vietnam," in K. Iwabuchi, S. Muecke, and M. Thomas (eds.), *Rogue Flows: Trans-Asian Cultural Traffic,* Hong Kong: Hong Kong University Press.

Wee, C.J.W.-L. (1996), "Staging the New Asia: Singapore's Dick Lee, Pop Music, and a Counter-modernity," *Public Culture,* 8/3: 489–511.

Wong, L. (2007), "Market Cultures, the Middle Classes and Islam: Consuming the Market?" *Consumption, Markets and Culture,* 10/4: 451–80.

Yon, Melinda (2005), "Ex-Spa-tations," *AsiaSpa* (January/February): 14.

Afterword: From Eco-Chic to Eco-Smart

Gomez, Eduardo (2013), "Brazil, China, and India Are Fat, and Getting Fatter," *The Atlantic* [online journal], <http://www.theatlantic.com> accessed April 8, 2013.

Kowitt, Beth (2013a), "H. Alshaya: The Mystery Company Importing Americana to the Mideast," *Fortune* [online journal], <http://management.fortune.cnn.com> accessed February 12, 2013.

Kowitt, Beth (2013b), "Cheesecake Factory Inches Closer to World Domination," *Fortune* [online journal], <http://management.fortune.cnn.com> accessed February 22, 2013.

Sonne, Paul, Maylie, Devon, and Hinshaw, Drew (2013), "With West Flat, Big Brewers Peddle Cheap Beer in Africa," *Wall Street Journal* [online journal], <http://online.wsj.com> accessed March 19, 2013.

Wilson, Eric (2013), "Front Row: Designers Take a Walk on the Green Side," *New York Times*, (April 18).

Index